THROUGH THICK AND THIN

THROUGH THICK AND THIN

My story so far

Rosemary Conley

Published in Great Britain in 2022

Society for Promoting Christian Knowledge
36 Causton Street
London SW1P 4ST
www.spck.org.uk

Cover photo credit © Elisabeth Hoff. Hair and make-up by Jane Tyler.

British Library Cataloguing-in-Publication Data
A catalogue record for this book is available from the British Library

Hardback ISBN 978–0–281–08761–7
Paperback ISBN 978–0–281–08762–4
eBook ISBN 978–0–281–08763–1
Audiobook ISBN 978–0–281–08764–8

Typeset by Fakenham Prepress Solutions, Fakenham, Norfolk, NR21 8NL
Printed & bound in Great Britain by Clays Ltd, Elcograf S.p.A.
eBook by Fakenham Prepress Solutions, Fakenham, Norfolk, NR21 8NL

Produced on paper from sustainable forests

Contents

Contents

1

Surviving against the odds
1946–61

The name 'El Alamein' will for ever haunt the British imagination. This was the site of the great battle in the North African desert that many consider to be a turning point in the Second World War. There were 13,500 Allied casualties, of whom 4,500 were killed, but among the fortunate survivors was a young man from Leicester, Oswald Neil Weston.

Oswald Weston escaped death by seconds – and you could say that this was when the word 'survivor' was etched deeply into my family history. Oswald Weston was my father. He joined the Tank Regiment of the legendary Eighth Army in North Africa in 1942 and was sent on a wireless (radio) course in Cairo. He wrote to my mother: 'I am pleased I am going to do this course but being in a wireless car is more dangerous than being in a tank!'

At the time of El Alamein, he was sent to take over a radio car. A few moments before he arrived, the vehicle was blown up and all the occupants were killed. My father spent the night in a hole in the ground before he was rescued and taken back to base.

If it were not for that very lucky escape, I would not be here to write this book, because I was born on 19 December 1946: Rosemary Jean Neil Weston. I arrived in the world completely innocent and unaware of the terrible upheaval that had just shaken the globe – one of many babies of the post-war era who were born, almost miraculously, against the odds.

And I still feel lucky today, despite many ups and downs in my life ever since.

My father left for Africa when my brother Robert was only six weeks old and returned to Leicester just in time for Robert's fifth birthday. It's hard to imagine such things – the high price that was paid even by those who didn't lose their lives. Of course, like most veterans of the war, he never really spoke about it, but that period of hardship influenced us all very deeply. Along with the painful memories and the bleakness of those years, I had my own challenges – my own 'battleground' if you like – from a very young age indeed.

Within months of birth, I was diagnosed with severe eczema. My mother, Celia, wrote in her personal family memoir:

Two months after Rosemary was born she developed eczema and her little face was covered with running matter. Fortunately, I was able to breastfeed her for nine months. She would have nothing else. I really felt it saved her life. Every time I fed her it took an hour to put on the plastic ointment and then the other healing ointment. Her little arms had to be in splints so she couldn't scratch. Needless to say, looking after her was a day and night job, but she was so good, never crying. I loved her very much and the constant attention didn't worry me, and she was peaceful in herself. When she was seven months, she was well enough to be christened and that was a real celebration.

I remember as a toddler having to wear pyjamas with socks sewn into the ends of the arms so that I couldn't scratch. Later, as I was generally unwell, the doctor presumed I had measles, but she couldn't properly tell as I had virtually no top skin. It must have been a nightmare for my mother.

By the time I was two I had also developed severe asthma. There was no doubt that my health was a major issue, so at age eight it was suggested that I spend three months in a children's hospital in Market Bosworth in Leicestershire. This was due to happen in the autumn of 1955.

In an attempt to save me from going into hospital my grandmother (whom I loved dearly) paid for me and my mother to travel to South Africa to visit my mother's cousin. My gran believed that fresh air and foreign travel to warmer climes would be the best cure for my ailments. She had grown up in an era when people with tuberculosis (TB) and respiratory diseases were sent off to recuperate in the mountain air of Switzerland – and what could be better than two weeks on a Union-Castle liner sailing the ocean and arriving in glorious Cape Town?

Interestingly, while I was on the ocean, I was free of asthma, although once on dry land the problem returned.

The idea of going on a special holiday was exciting, but I was very sad to be leaving my beloved dog Sue behind. Sue was a Sheltie crossbreed with a tan and white coat. She and I were so close and I really worried how she would feel when I was away, though I don't think I fully appreciated the extent of the time we would be absent from home. While we were gone, I kept sending Sue postcards addressed to Sue Weston, The Pink Chair, and our address!

One memorable event on the voyage was being taken on to the bridge, then known as 'the Captain's deck' – the ultimate privilege – and being allowed to steer the ship. My mother watched proudly, but she was hiding her deepest fears. To this day, I wonder if I had been granted this special favour because the Captain had been told that I was a frail child and might not survive for very long.

I have always remembered that boat trip in the early spring of 1955 as a particularly exciting experience in my young life. It was a great adventure and, as it happened, it was also the occasion of my first ever business transaction, at the age of eight.

During the voyage, we stopped off at the island of Madeira. While there, I was utterly captivated by a magnificent walkie-talkie doll. I spent the whole of my £2 spending money on this beautiful, beyond-my-wildest-dreams doll! I played with her on the ship and was so proud of her with her golden locks and pretty dress and the fact that she said 'Mummy' in a somewhat plaintive tone.

After we had settled into our relatives' home in Cape Town, some three or four weeks into our eight-week stay, a distant cousin came to visit with her own little daughter. The girl was also utterly captivated with my doll and really, really wanted her, so I sold the toy to her for £2 10s (two pounds and 10 shillings in pre-decimal British currency; £2.50 in today's money)! She was very happy and, considering I had had my pleasure over the previous five weeks, I was happy to get a return on my investment. The other factor was that I needed to replenish my holiday money, which I had blown by impulse buying!

Looking back, it's curious how unsentimental I was over that doll. I suppose I could have kept her for years and years, perhaps way into adulthood – and the crumbling old doll might be feebly murmuring 'Mummy' from a box in my loft. But somehow I knew it was the right thing to do, and I was very excited at making a profit on the deal.

Altogether, my mother and I spent eight weeks with our relatives in their beautiful house, in glorious warm weather, in the shadow of Table Mountain. If any place on earth could have brought healing, surely this was it. This period of my life was like a brief taste of paradise. Of course, I was completely unaware of the terrible injustices of the world of apartheid South Africa and the cruel repression that was going on all around me. I was merely a very young and innocent guest in a comfortable white enclave of privilege.

Sadly, there was no lasting improvement to my health and, after the three-month trip away, I was forced to spend several months in hospital.

It came as something of a shock to me when, many years later, my parents told me that when I was very young the doctors had warned them that I was unlikely to reach my 10th birthday.

My mother could not have done more to help save my life. She took me to faith healers and physiotherapists. It seemed to be a journey of trial and error.

Memories of my long stay in hospital are vivid – as if that strange interruption to my life had only happened yesterday. Naturally, I was distraught when I was first dropped off by my parents, finding myself among a group of children aged from five to 15 who were all strangers. But at least I had the love and care of my parents not far away, and I knew they were extremely worried for me.

I remember staying in a very large ward for children with 'chest problems'. Each morning, a nurse would come into the classroom and give every one of us what looked like an orange Smartie. On my first day I took mine and started to chew it, but to my horror it wasn't a Smartie but a multivitamin tablet! It tasted more horrible than anything I had ever tasted in my life.

As well as having our temperatures taken morning and night, we also had to lie down over a type of 'A'-shaped board to encourage the mucus in our lungs to be expelled – with the help of gravity, I presume. We each had a sputum pot to spit into – if we could manage to cough up anything at all. It was all rather grim, but we had to do it. It was one of life's very British lessons: 'Just get on with it.' And we did.

One night, I woke up to go to the loo and was utterly shocked at seeing a male night-nurse on duty. I had never in my life seen a male nurse and I was completely freaked out! Looking back, perhaps it was silly to be so scared but, as an eight-year-old, anything different from the norm can unsettle your whole world. I didn't even know that men could be nurses.

I longed for the weekends, when my parents would come and visit me, and sometimes they brought my beloved dog Sue with them. That was the high spot of my week. We would go for a walk and they always had a few treats with them and gave me two shillings (10p) in pocket money, which I could use to buy sweets.

After the horrible early weeks, I settled in and made friends, including with one of the nurses. She was so kind to me. And there were a few other good memories too. Every weekday, a teacher came and we were all schooled together, irrespective of our age. This made education an experience full of surprises – which it should be. For instance, we learned nursery rhymes in French, which was fun.

After three months and numerous medical tests I was sent home to join the family again. I was grateful to be back – although, strangely, I had completely settled in to life at Market Bosworth hospital and had really felt at home there. It just shows how adaptable children can be.

I went home for Christmas and soon adapted to normal life with my family, and particularly my closest companion, Sue the dog. It is hard to convey the importance of such a special friendship; in many ways, Sue was the centre of my world. It had been agonising to leave her behind when I travelled to South Africa and, soon after that, I had to leave her again when I went into hospital. Sue and I were soulmates and we had so many adventures together. I would dress her up and wheel her around in my doll's pram. I also created a special doggy show-jumping course for her and she would faithfully jump over the hurdles – with a little encouragement! I will never forget the day when she saw her 'Romeo' pass by in the street; eager to get to him, she did a death-defying leap through an open upstairs sash window! She survived the ordeal and lived to the ripe old age of 15 years. Dogs have been so important in my life and Sue was one of the best. She was named after the Queen's first corgi – 'Susan' – given to the young princess on her 18th birthday.

Because of my frailty I was sent to a private school from the age of four to eight, initially for mornings only. Then, after coming out of hospital, I went to the village school in Countesthorpe, where we lived. In my school report when I was nine, for 'PE and Games' my teacher wrote: 'Interested but physical disability impedes her'.

I have lived with asthma all my life, and in recent years I have had regular appointments with a respiratory specialist, Professor Ian Pavord. I had been suffering with too many chest infections and my doctor suggested I see him. At this point I was in my early 70s and Professor Pavord explained that part of my problem was due to the fact that my lungs were underdeveloped, even before I went to school. Not only that; I had since suffered some significant damage to my lungs through bouts of whooping cough and pneumonia. He added that if I hadn't followed the career path and lifestyle that I had, my health and my life would be a very different story today.

Looking back at my life, it seems ironic that such a poorly child, who had such trouble breathing, was transformed into a successful fitness teacher who would go on to appear on television and encourage members of the British public to get off their sofas and exercise. To me, this is evidence of a divine sense of humour!

***

My family had moved to the countryside when I was only a year old and I loved growing up in Countesthorpe in Leicestershire. Our house was quite a large detached house with almost an acre (about half a hectare) of garden and a big old cowshed at the top. Having moved to my new junior school, I soon palled up with Lizzie Sterland, who became my best friend. We would spend many a happy hour tending our pets in the 'Pet House', as we called it, situated in the big old cowshed. We would sometimes climb up on to its roof and wave to the drivers of the steam trains as they passed by many feet below on the Great Central Line to London. I also loved dancing and 'skating', which I did in my socks on a wooden floor in our sun lounge for hour after hour after school. Little did I know that I would be in my 60s before I ever skated on real ice!

Despite my physical restrictions and frail health, I enjoyed my childhood and gradually seemed to get stronger, which must have been a huge relief to my parents. They gave me enormous freedom. I joined the Brownies and Guides and I loved my many pets; in fact, I had a passion for animals, particularly dogs and horses. I also loved organising things with Lizzie, such as a treasure hunt around the village, followed by a fish and chip supper with our pals.

Few people had a television in the early 1950s, but there was a sudden surge in sales in 1953 – in time for the coronation of Queen Elizabeth II. I was thrilled when my parents bought a TV set. The crowning of a new monarch was such an exciting occasion, and it was wonderful that lots of our neighbours came in to watch too. What an extraordinary spectacle! And the Queen looked so beautiful. I adored all the pomp and ceremony and the glittering diamonds on her crown. The gold coach being drawn by the horses was like a fairy-tale carriage, with everyone looking so grand. I was captivated by it and was given a pop-up book of the event which I pored over for hours and hours for months afterwards.

Before the era of television we could only see news at a cinema, when there would be a newsreel before the main film. To be able to see the news in our own home, instead of just hearing it on the radio, was quite sensational.

When I was 11, Lizzie and I organised a pet show in our garden to raise money for the RSPCA. My parents were very accommodating of our exploits and didn't mind that we were going to invite the general public into our garden – together with all their pets! Looking back, they must have been saints.

My mother suggested that we should write to a few pet food companies and ask them for prizes. Lizzie and I typed letters on an old typewriter and waited to see what would happen. Suddenly, cartons of dog food, boxes of rabbit food, certificates and general paraphernalia started arriving. It was so exciting! So we then wrote to more companies, and when the day of the pet show arrived we had everything we needed: posters, certificates for first, second and third places, right down to 'Highly Commended', and prizes for everyone.

The event itself was well attended and the proceeds were given to the RSPCA. The Secretary of the Leicester branch and an RSPCA Inspector were the judges. Everyone had fun and all the animals survived, despite the close mingling of such a wide array of pets, from cats and dogs to guinea pigs and white mice. At the time, my mother wasn't enjoying the best of health, so I was doubly grateful that she and my father had let Lizzie and me go ahead with our venture.

As I have mentioned, my brother, Robert, was born six weeks before my father was conscripted to serve in the Second World War, and my dad returned just in time for his son's fifth birthday. Robert became a very talented golfer, playing off a 'handicap of 2' in his early 20s. I can remember my parents taking him to play at St Andrews Golf Club in Scotland when he was 14. He later went to Birmingham University and achieved a Bachelor of Science degree in Economics. He then joined a major British chemicals company, ICI, in Cheshire. It wasn't long before he met his lovely future wife, Jane, and later they were blessed with two beautiful daughters, Nicola and Suzannah. They have all lived in Cheshire ever since.

My parents were very proud of Robert's golfing prowess. In my 20s, I called in at the Christian bookshop where my father had been a manager – his last job before retiring – and introduced myself. The assistant said, 'Oh! I didn't know Mr Weston had a daughter. He only ever talked about his son.'

I remember walking out and thinking, *My goodness!* It was a bit of a shock. And the irony was that 20 years later, when I was in my 40s, my book was a No.1 bestseller and my father couldn't stop bragging about me – which I hated because it was so embarrassing!

One of the most distressing memories of my childhood was my father's ill health. He developed epilepsy, caused, we think, by the stress of running his own business, and often had 'petit mal' or minor seizures. Very occasionally he had a 'grand mal', which was a major fit that caused him to collapse on the floor, kicking his legs wildly and foaming at the mouth. It was immensely upsetting for everyone, particularly my mother and me, and exhausting for my father once the seizure had passed. For a 10-year-old child it was devastating. I was so embarrassed by my father's fits that every time we went to church, I would pray very hard that he wouldn't have a petit mal, particularly as we always sat in the front row.

One summer, when I was about 11, we were on holiday at a Christian Endeavour holiday home in Overstrand in Norfolk. We used to love going there because there were lots of great people to meet and a variety of activities to do. One day, in the residents' lounge area, Father had a grand mal. I was horrified and tried to hide him from everyone's view by standing over him and covering him with my body. The other guests realised what was going on and pulled me back and took care of my father. They were very kind to me and somehow empathised with my distress. Their kindness and understanding was so helpful to me that somehow, from that day on, I coped better with my father's epilepsy, while of course still being very concerned for him. On one occasion, when he was walking along the cliffs of Overstrand with my mother, he had a petit mal and nearly walked off the edge! I don't know how my mother dealt with it all. It must have been a huge strain to live with someone with such a condition. The medication available then was nothing like as effective as it is today.

My mother was quite entrepreneurial and, to help boost the family finances, she invented a 'beauty cap'. In the 1950s and 1960s, if you wanted to have curls in your hair you slept in curlers. Heaven knows how you managed to sleep! It was also not the most flattering look. Mother had quite a designing talent and was able to create knitting patterns from scratch and was also an accomplished artist, both in oils and watercolours. She realised that if you could find some pretty netting, use a sewing machine to put rows of sheer elastic through it, and attach a ribbon at each end (so that you could draw it around your head), you would have a 'beauty cap'! You could stretch it and tie the ribbons on top of your head, so concealing the curlers in a more elegant way. Consequently, the wearer would look more attractive in bed and the curlers would stay in place.

Mother enlisted some of the women from her local Women's Institute group who were happy to earn some extra cash producing these items. Then, with her range of samples, she went down to London and sold them to Harrods! Lizzie and I were paid 3d ('threepence' in old currency; about 1p in today's money) per dozen for packing them in cellophane bags with a sticker to seal them. It was quite an enterprise and caused a fair bit of excitement among the farmers' wives and others who turned their talent to becoming beauty-cap machinists. I don't think any fortunes were made, and after a while the sales dwindled and the enterprise came to an end, but I have fond memories of that time and I certainly learned from my mother's courage and confidence and her entrepreneurial spirit.

***

My school experience was rather up and down, but eventually I went to Bushloe High School and loved it. The morale of the staff was understandably high because this was a brand-new school and there were very good facilities. The students were happy to learn and I had some excellent teachers. In those two years I learned more than in the rest of my school life, particularly English, biology and art, and I especially loved PE. I wasn't interested in history or geography, I tolerated maths and physics and chemistry, and I certainly didn't enjoy Latin. But I loved PE and was sometimes asked to dance in front of the class when we did 'movement to music'. I guess that my hours of 'skating in my socks' at home and my very early ballet lessons had given me some confidence, so I was happy to dance. Despite being quite shy in many ways, strangely I didn't mind performing in front of others.

When I had to move on from Bushloe High School to Guthlaxton Grammar, it was a different story. As we had recently moved house, I had to take three bus journeys to get to school and, to be honest, I felt lost in this vast and somewhat impersonal environment. School became exhausting and demoralising, and soon it was decided that I should leave. It was a week before my 15th birthday.

My mother had been a secretary, so she thought I would make a good secretary too! I started at secretarial college just when my father's business had to close and I remember this as a very sad time.

My father was a gentle man and people liked him. He could also be really frustrating, and he had some very peculiar views about life and was prone to exaggeration. I used to get quite exasperated with him, as did my mother, but despite that, I really loved him. He was so kind to me when I was little and very poorly with my asthma. He would spend hours rubbing my back to help me breathe more easily and gave me lots of piggyback rides, which I loved. Thankfully, over time, my health improved. In my teens my eczema was minimal and my asthma was not as bad as it had been when I was younger.

Father was kind in his business dealings too, and he would always give the shop owners whom he supplied with knitwear and hosiery extra credit if they were struggling to pay. As the larger retailers began establishing themselves, the small local traders found it harder to keep their head above water. Sadly, their businesses often failed, and time after time my father was left with people owing him money, which in the end caused his own business to go down. Maybe he realised that this outcome was partly of his own making; so, after his business went into liquidation, he paid his suppliers with a loan from the bank which he paid off over time.

It was January 1961 when I enrolled at Goddard's Secretarial College. I loved it. My health continued to improve and for the first time in my life I felt 'normal'. The girls were really friendly and the teachers were delightful. It was the early 1960s and growing up in that era was so much fun. Soon it became apparent how good my education had been compared with that of my fellow students. English was one of my strengths because I enjoyed words and the intricacies of language. However, it turned out that I was only mediocre at typing, and sadly I was one of just two students who failed the shorthand exam! Strangely, I didn't mind too much as I just loved secretarial work.

Life was exciting as a teenager and I was ready for the adventure that lay ahead. As far as I was concerned, the future was full of hope – and more than half a century later, I still believe that.

2

Gaining weight

1962–9

During my time at secretarial college there was a TV series called *Compact*. This drama was set in the offices of a women's magazine publisher. I was utterly fascinated by what the actors did, the characters they portrayed and the exciting storyline. In fact, all my fellow students were fixated on this programme. But it rang a bigger bell with me and left a real yearning that one day, maybe, I could work in a magazine office.

At the same time, my mother went down with double pneumonia and was dangerously ill. I did most of the cooking and housekeeping with my father. My brother was at university so of course he wasn't around to help. Mother recovered, but it wasn't long before poor health hit her again.

I started my first job as a junior secretary with a stationery firm at age 16, earning £5 a week. The company supplied office furniture and had a stationery shop. I loved having a proper job. I enjoyed the experience of learning different skills and working with adults who were really kind to me. It was also rewarding to earn my own money. From my £5 wages, I had to give £2 to my mother for my board and lodging, and I lived and clothed myself with the rest.

By 1962 the 'swinging sixties' pop scene was exploding and life was exciting. The music was new and energetic, and everyone seemed happy. Elvis Presley, Cliff Richard and The Shadows, The Beatles, Gerry and The Pacemakers – they were all sensational. It was a celebration of youth and freedom, and such a fabulous time to be a teenager.

After a year or so, I moved on to work in an architect's office: Bryan, Harding & Bordoli. I enjoyed working as a secretary and receptionist for Mr Harding, an elderly gentleman, and Mr Bordoli who was younger. In 2002, I was the guest on the British TV show *This Is Your Life*, which recaps the life story of a chosen celebrity, and Roy Bordoli was there. It was wonderful to see him again after 40 years!

***

I started dating when I was 15, which added even greater excitement to my life. After several boyfriends, there was one young man who particularly caught my eye. His name was Phil Conley.

We met at the church youth club. He was very handsome, superfit and a really lovely guy. All the girls fancied Phil. He also played the drums in a pop group, and I can remember falling in love with him the moment he played a perfect drum solo from the chart-topping tune 'Diamonds' by Jet Harris and Tony Meehan (previously of The Shadows). Our relationship blossomed, and my life revolved around Phil and his lovely mum and dad, Evelyn and Henry. They also had wonderful next-door neighbours who were like family to them – Stan and Mabel. I was totally in love with Phil and I adored his family.

It was when we were at the youth club one night that we heard the news of President Kennedy's assassination. With no mobile phones or internet, the communication of breaking news relied on radio and television, but this was a world-shattering event and word spread like wildfire. It was the first 'shock' news I think any of us had ever heard, and it was certainly my first experience of one of those 'I can remember where I was when . . .' moments. I have never forgotten that day.

We had a really great group of friends from the youth club. One of them, Dave Jenkins, had known Phil since they first attended infant school together aged four. Dave had an old Post Office van into which we would all pile if we were going out. No way would that vehicle pass its MOT test these days, but back then there was no such requirement by the Government. As for us, we took no thought at all for issues of safety or roadworthiness. One day, the accelerator had broken, so Dave attached a piece of string to the part of the engine that the pedal normally operated. The windscreen wound open outwards, thus allowing the string to be passed inside the car and into Dave's hand – and off we went!

Phil was an ace cricketer at school and was a good scholar. He worked hard and passed his A-level exams with flying colours. He then decided to become an articled clerk with the aim of qualifying as a chartered accountant, and he studied incredibly hard most evenings.

While Phil studied after work, I would sew or draw. I have always enjoyed drawing and painting and had won the art prize at Bushloe High School. Phil and I saw each other most evenings and were very much in love. At 18 we became engaged.

As I was now employed, for some reason I decided to take out a life insurance policy into which I would pay a very modest sum each month; but to do so I needed to have a medical exam. Little did I know that this medical would change my life.

When I attended the doctor's surgery, he did various tests and asked a lot of questions. Then he disappeared from the room for about 20 minutes. I became so bored I decided to look at what he had written about me. He described me as 'well covered'! It just goes to show how sensitive young women can be because I read those two words as '*fat*'! I had been a skinny child and now I was being described as '*fat*'! I had never worried about my weight, but from that moment I became aware of my body size.

It was around this time that I enrolled on a 'Good Grooming' course at night school run by an ex-model, Kathy Parker, who also ran her own modelling agency. I was interested in making the most of myself and loved learning about make-up and deportment – how to stand, sit and walk elegantly. The course finished with a fashion show where we all modelled clothes on a catwalk. I loved it. I wore a purple dress and jacket that I had made, and Kathy lent me a beautiful pink hat to finish off the ensemble. It was very exciting, and another defining moment in my life.

From then on, I transformed the way I looked with hairstyling and make-up and as a result my confidence began to grow. Later, this led to a professional photographic session which resulted in some modelling jobs. I was too short and not slim enough to do it professionally, but I enjoyed the experience.

***

For Phil and me, money was incredibly tight, but we seemed to cope. Phil learned to drive and passed his test while he was still 17 and then he bought his first car, a 1937 Hillman (registration number: FAT 512!) for just £10. Phil's dad, Henry, was furious. Henry was a very quiet, almost timid man, so this reaction was completely out of character. In fact, I never saw Henry angry again in the whole of his life. But he thought it was totally irresponsible for Phil to buy a car, as both of us were earning so little. Thankfully, Evelyn and Henry's next-door neighbours, Stan and Mabel, asked if we would drive them to their relative's house about 30 miles (48 km) away each Friday evening and collect them again on the Sunday. Stan was very generous and the money he gave to Phil for petrol was enough to run the car on a day-to-day basis. We worked on trying to improve the look of the car, and a few months later we sold it for £18. We were so thrilled to have made a profit that we decided to do the same again. In fact, buying cars that we could 'do up' and sell for a profit became a bit of a hobby.

Phil would recondition the engines, I would sand down the bodywork so that Phil could plug any holes with fibreglass and then paint it, and between us we developed a skill for successfully moving up the car-status ladder. Evelyn and Henry lived in a terraced house so the only parking was on the street, which made car renovation difficult. Fortunately, my parents, who really liked Phil, were extremely tolerant of our using their front drive as a 'car improvement' area. Over time, our car-trading skills progressed until by the time we were married in 1968 we had a very smart blue Jaguar.

Looking back, it is extraordinary how tolerant both sets of parents were of our various exploits. Phil had his drum kit set up in his mum and dad's front room and all our friends would pile into this small space for a band practice. Guitars, drums, singing – the works! Fortunately, their neighbours in the street were also tolerant!

One very vivid memory of the mid-1960s was going to see *The Sound of Music* at the cinema. To this day, I still think it is the best film ever made, and Julie Andrews is so perfect as Maria. I cried all the way through because it was such a beautiful and emotional love story set against the most enchanting and exquisite backdrop of Austria. Little did I know that this would start my love affair with that beautiful country.

Phil and I had lots of fun growing up in the 1960s but, as the decade wore on, our relationship ran into difficulties and after four years we split up. I can't remember anything in particular that started going wrong.

I think it was simply because we had settled into a relationship when we were very young, Phil was studying every evening and money was continually tight. After all, we had met when I was 16 and Phil was 17, and we were growing up in a very exciting time for teenagers. We were both changing, and I decided to break off the engagement.

It wasn't long before I realised what a mistake I had made and how much I still loved Phil. Fortunately, we got back together and soon set the date for our wedding. As my brother Robert and his fiancée Jane were also getting married in 1968, we decided to follow rather than precede their wedding in May. Phil and I married on 3 August 1968. It was a wonderful day and everyone was very happy for us.

Earlier that year, I had started working for a firm of chartered accountants called Mark J Rees. Mark Rees was probably the cleverest man I have ever known. He was an inspiration. He was not only a chartered accountant; he also had a law degree and a degree in engineering. One day, I was struggling to read my shorthand for a letter he had dictated to me, so he asked to look at my notepad. He read it immediately. Yes, he could do shorthand too!

I wanted to work in an accountancy office as I felt I would be able to better understand my husband's career. Mr Rees was a man of few words, and working with him really sharpened my brain and my reflexes. He didn't believe in small talk. He gave instructions and directions very concisely and expected you to do the same and to understand his requirements instantly.

We worked in quite a quaint old office over a shop. The 'general office' where I had my desk was right next to Mr Rees's office and had a frosted glass panel in the door, so I could see Mr Rees approaching as I sat directly opposite the doorway. The door was on a power spring, allowing it to close automatically. Mr Rees would burst in, utter six or seven words of instruction and hand me papers and I would hand him my papers with one-word explanations and, like a whirlwind, he would be out of the door before it automatically closed again behind him. It didn't take long to learn his style, and our relationship was very good. I liked him and I respected him. He was scrupulously honest and exceptionally knowledgeable.

***

The first marital home for Phil and me was an 11th-floor rent-controlled council flat. We furnished our flat very frugally and, to save money, we built our own sofa. I made the cushions and Phil assembled the frame. We also installed a wall unit with a folding-down table – the idea of an architect friend, Tony Rodgers, whom we met outside a pub one day when he and his wife Margaret were admiring our car, an old Morris 8 Tourer. They invited us round for a drink at their flat and we became friends.

Despite being located in a tower block, our flat was delightful and quite unusually furnished and everyone who visited us thought it was beautiful. I was really proud of our first home, and to have built our own furniture was no small achievement. I think it was my mother who suggested that I should write to the publishers of a women's magazine as they might be interested, and that's what I did. *Woman's Realm* sent a photographer and did a three-page feature because the furnishing was so original!

It was while we were living in the flat that a neighbour who was a keen cook introduced me to a Cordon Bleu part-work that had just been published. I was anxious to improve my culinary skills, so I ordered my weekly editions at the newsagents – all 72 of them, costing 4/6d (four shillings and sixpence, or about 23p) a week. There was, however, one drawback. As I became a more accomplished cook, producing utterly delicious food that I couldn't stop eating, the pounds began to pile on.

Some nine months later, Phil qualified as a chartered accountant with flying colours, which meant that his salary increased significantly and we were able to buy our first house – a well-proportioned three-bedroomed semi with a long garden – in Thurnby in Leicestershire.

As I continued to create (and overeat) delicious Cordon Bleu meals, so my weight increased. In addition, unfortunately, our pre-marriage break-up had left its scars and somehow our relationship was never quite the same again, with the result that I turned to food for comfort. It wasn't long before I developed a really bad relationship with food: bingeing and starving as I struggled to keep my weight under control. But I was losing the battle.

I can remember sitting at my desk at work with a packet of fig roll biscuits and half a pound of butter in my desk drawer. I would take a fig roll and scrape it along the length of the block of butter and eat it. By the end of the day the biscuits were gone, along with most of the butter!

Another day, I had already eaten my packed lunch and then went to the Chinese restaurant next door to our office and sat down to a full three-course lunch! My eating habits became almost uncontrollable.

It didn't take long before my weight problems escalated. Not only was the Cordon Bleu food delicious, but also, the more weight I put on, the harder it became to stop binge eating. The bigger I became, the unhappier I was – and the more I 'comfort-ate'. It was a vicious cycle of self-destruction. I will never forget how unhappy and desperate I felt; such memories have never left me. That is why I am so empathetic with people who struggle to lose weight.

Then I decided to join Weight Watchers. At that time, I weighed 9 st. (126 lb or about 57 kg) and I needed to lose a whole stone.

I found it helpful having the discipline of being weighed each week and being with other women who were just like me. Over several weeks I lost 13 lb (5.89 kg) and was only a pound off my goal weight when Easter arrived. Somehow, with Easter eggs and hot cross buns and all kinds of goodies, my willpower just collapsed and I couldn't stop eating. I weighed myself daily and, by the time I was due back at Weight Watchers, I had gained 5 lb (2.26 kg)! I was so scared to go back to the class that I decided never to return. Because the total weight losses of all the dieters in the class were calculated each week and the average weight loss announced, I was scared of ruining the average and being a disappointment to everyone.

Sadly, I then regained all the weight I had lost, plus more. I became even more obsessed by food and totally panicked about my weight, with the result that I became increasingly depressed. I would eat and eat and then eat some more: ice cream, cooking chocolate, anything I could lay my hands on. I remember standing in front of the mirror and saying to myself, 'You big fat pig!' and then promising myself that I would stop. Before I knew it, I was downstairs eating my third slice of heavily buttered toast with marmalade! Heaven knows how I could eat that much.

This battle went on for a couple of years and I gained 2½ st. (15.87 kg) to reach 10 st. 7 lb (66.67 kg). Not a huge weight by today's standards, but I was barely 5 ft 2 in. (1.57 m) tall with small bones (I take size 3 shoes). I looked really big for my height and I loathed myself. I was a size 14 and I couldn't see my toes because of my big stomach. It seemed that the more I tried to lose weight, the more I gained. My eating problem was like a runaway train and I was getting desperate. It was having such a negative effect on my life and my self-confidence.

I wasn't used to being overweight. I had been a sickly child who was underweight, and I remember my father asking a friend, whom I visited for tea when I was about seven, 'What can we do to fatten her up?' Well, it was a very different story now.

Then one day an ex-boyfriend, John Blackburn, called round with his very beautiful – and slim – new girlfriend. I had been crying because I was so distressed about my weight problem and she, Annette, was wonderfully caring and positive.

She said, 'You would look so lovely if you lost your weight.'

And somehow those kind words triggered something in my brain that would turn my life around.

3
Tupperware, tribulations and triumphs
1969–71

It is difficult for me to find the words to adequately describe how much I hated being overweight. I loathed the way I looked and how my clothes didn't fit, but most of all I was disgusted with myself for being so out of control with my eating. In fact, I hated *myself*.

Life at home was suffering and I found myself becoming more and more depressed and not wanting to socialise. When we did go to join friends for dinner, I became so anxious that I would gorge myself beforehand – and make myself feel even worse. Inevitably, by the time we arrived at their home, I felt like a beached whale. I felt isolated and very lonely on my path of self-destruction. But Annette's kind comment made me realise that I *had* to do *something*.

In desperation I joined another slimming club called Silhouette, run by a delightful woman, Ann Gorrod. The class was held in the Edward Wood Hall in Leicester, the same room where some 16 years previously my mother had entered me into a piano competition. I was about six and must have appeared diminutive on its vast stage. On my assessment sheet the examiner had written: 'A brave effort from such a tiny competitor'. I felt anything but tiny these days.

Ann Gorrod was a very elegant and charismatic woman. She was always patient and encouraging as I continued to struggle with my weight.

After a few weeks of yo-yoing on the scales, I exclaimed: 'I think I'm just *meant* to be fat!'

Immediately, Ann responded with, 'Oh no you're not! It just takes time and perseverance. You *can* do this.'

Like all weight-loss diets in the 1960s, the Silhouette diet was based on a daily allowance of 1,000 calories, but that was just too little for me – by 6 pm I had eaten all my calories and was hungry, and I fell off the wagon and binged.

I tried to think how I could resolve this unrelenting battle. I found sticking to 1,000 calories a day impossible. Then, in a moment of revelation, I decided to create my own diet – based on a more generous daily allowance of 1,400 calories. I found I could stick to this, and amazingly, and gradually, the weight began to drop. I stopped all snacking between meals, ate three meals a day, and rarely drank alcohol as we hardly ever dined out. For Phil and me, a special night out would be chicken-in-the-basket and a glass of Babycham in a pub. Babycham was a popular drink back in the 60s – I guess it has been replaced in taste and texture by Prosecco in the 21st century. On a special anniversary or birthday, a major treat was going to a popular restaurant where our favourite menu choice was prawn cocktail; steak, onion rings, mushrooms and chips; and Black Forest gateau. Such occasions occurred probably two or three times a year – it was that rare!

Thankfully, pound by pound my weight came off. Allowing myself more food was proving to be the answer. I continued to attend Ann's class, but I didn't tell her my secret – that I was eating 40% more calories than she prescribed. I continued to enjoy Ann's support and the encouragement of Ann and my weight-battling comrades, particularly because – at last – I was one of the successful ones. As my trimmer body began to emerge, so did my confidence and sense of self-worth.

***

Now that Phil and I were living in a house with a garden, I wondered whether we could possibly have a dog. I had grown up with dogs and cats and I missed the companionship and love they so freely gave. Phil and I didn't even consider having a dog when we were living in a flat in a tower block, but now we had our own outdoor space. Thankfully, and after much persuasion, Phil agreed that we could have one.

I knew having a dog would be really good for me, mentally and physically. I have always loved Pyrenean Mountain dogs because they are so beautiful. They are a gentle giant of a breed, resembling a St Bernard but with coats that are mostly white.

We heard about a young Pyrenean who had been part of a household but was now unwanted. Sadly, when the family's new baby arrived, the poor young dog was shut in the coalhouse for hours on end. Not surprisingly, this had caused significant stress to her and, in the end, the owners decided to give her away. Now Sheba was to be ours.

Sheba was amazing. Almost pure white and about 11 months old, she loved all the attention and the brushing, combing and affection that I showered upon her. I instantly fell in love with her and she gave me immense love and pleasure in return. Having a dog not only cheered me up but also became a wonderful distraction from food, and walking Sheba every day provided valuable exercise.

Initially, Sheba wasn't keen on walking. On one occasion, we had gone just 100 yds (90 m) down the road when she sat down and refused to move. I had to physically carry her home and she was *so* heavy! Thankfully, she eventually learned to enjoy her outings and we used to walk for miles – which, of course, was good for both of us.

Despite taking Sheba for a good walk before I went to work, I soon realised that she hated being left alone. Our home was beginning to suffer from her antics. One day, she broke a window in the door from the kitchen to the conservatory and pulled a goatskin rug through the broken window. As I walked in, to my horror, there in front of me was this white hairy mass, covered in blood! I immediately thought the worst, but in fact it was the rug that was blood-marked and Sheba was relatively unscathed, with only a small cut to her paw and a few superficial cuts to her face. On another day she ate all my birth control pills, and on yet another day was seen by our neighbour bouncing on our bed as if it were a trampoline. (The birth control pills did her no harm; she just came into 'season' early.)

One evening, I was scanning the 'Situations Vacant' column in our local newspaper for a job where I could take my dog along, and I came across an advertisement for Tupperware dealers. I had been a Tupperware dealer for a short while when I was 18, so I knew what was involved and I thought this might work well – I could take Sheba with me in the car when I did a Tupperware party, and I would be at home with her for most of the day.

It was with a heavy heart that I decided to leave my job with Mark J Rees. When I told Mr Rees what I was going to do, he generously commented, 'I think you'll be good at that.' Over my time working for Mr Rees, I had become friends with him and his family, so I knew we would stay in touch and indeed we did. I was even invited to his younger daughter's wedding.

I enjoyed selling Tupperware in all its shapes and sizes to groups of housewives and their friends in the comfort of their own home. Fortunately, I enjoyed some success partly because I filled my display Tupperware with Cordon Bleu creations such as almond and apricot flan (which looked very impressive) and apple and hazelnut galette, among others. The food seemed to bring these plastic containers to life and made everything look very attractive.

Within six weeks I was promoted to 'Manager' status, as I had successfully recruited some additional dealers like me to sell a lot of Tupperware. My reward was a company car, a bright new Avenger! The only thing I had to do was to insure it and fill it with fuel. It was all very exciting and provided such an amazing incentive to do well, and I really went for it. Sheba accompanied me in the car and we pottered around happily together during the day, making deliveries as necessary. Sheba was more settled and I loved my new job – though I found it very tempting when I was faced with the delicious refreshments provided by the 'Hostesses' holding the parties.

While the commission we received from selling Tupperware items was adequate, the real reward came from participating in the company's seasonal promotions when we were incentivised with the promise of some significant prizes. The more successful you were, the bigger the prizes. This was when I learned the importance of having a goal. My reasoning was that if I aimed for the top prize, even if I didn't achieve it, I would probably win a bigger prize than I would have won if I had not bothered to aim high. And it worked. I earned myself a dishwasher, an automatic washing machine and lots more. These incentive promotions were based on our being rewarded with 'tokens' calculated on the basis of sales of goods, but we could also earn 10 times the number of tokens for each new dealer we recruited. I seemed to manage to attract recruits relatively easily and the 'prizes' flowed. I loved running my 'mini business' as I enjoyed meeting people and found it easy to sell a product that I believed in.

I continued as a Tupperware Manager for about 18 months when, unfortunately, Sheba decided she had had enough. One evening I returned to the car after completing my Tupperware party, only to find her encased in the entire headlining! She had torn it down, piece by piece. My pristine Avenger had to be completely relined.

Again, I realised I had to make some changes, so I enrolled in an employment agency for a secretarial job but stipulated that I needed to be able to take my dog with me.

It was something of a surprise when I received a phone call telling me that the recruitment agency had found a company that didn't mind my taking a dog. Crimpfil Ltd was a yarn merchant situated on Highcross Street in the centre of Leicester. At my interview with the boss, Mr Jackson, he enquired as to what type of dog I would be bringing to work. When I explained that she was quite a large dog, Mr Jackson, a kindly, fatherly gentleman, suggested that she and I should go for a trial day. I really wanted this job because it was paying £900 per annum (a good salary in 1970). In addition, Mr Jackson explained that there wasn't a lot of work to do and he didn't mind what I did to occupy myself in between answering the occasional phone call and typing the odd letter. I liked Mr Jackson and I really wanted the job so, to ensure that Sheba stayed quiet on our trial day, I gave her half a sedative tablet. Needless to say, she was as good as gold, sleeping for most of the time. We got the job and we all worked happily thereafter.

The staff there were a delight. Mr Jackson was the manager, plus his son Kit (sales), John Williams (technical) and Peter Duus (admin/accounts). While I was working there, Kit Jackson had a son, Ben, who today is a well-respected presenter on BBC Radio Leicester.

Peter fell in love with Sheba and would often take her into the next-door graveyard where a famous 18th-century Leicester dignitary was buried – Alderman Newton. Peter spoke with a rather posh accent and he also had a penchant for alcohol. When Peter was inebriated, his posh accent became even more pronounced. 'I think I'll just take dear Sheba to see Alderman Newton for a pee and I'll have a quick ciggy!' he would say in his aristocratic voice. It always amused me.

It wasn't unusual for Peter to run short of money by the end of the month and then he would come to me for an advance out of petty cash:

'I wonder, dear Rosemary, do you think you could lend me a fiver out of petty cash? Just a bit short, you know. I promise I'll pay you back on Friday.'

Initially I gave in, but as it became a regular request and he was drinking much too much for the good of his health, I decided to say no.

'Ooh, you're a hard woman,' he would respond, chuntering in disappointment as he drifted away.

Peter and I got along really well, despite my being 'a hard woman'. When he lost his flat because the friend he shared it with died, he moved into a bedsit at my grandmother's house and I would drive him in to work. We remained good friends long after I left Crimpfil, right up until his death some years later. It was one of the saddest funerals as only his ex-wife, her husband and sister, and a carer and I attended. Peter was a lovely man and I remember him very fondly.

I was still enjoying my Cordon Bleu cookery skills and sometimes cooked for Mr Jackson when the directors of Crimpfil visited our office from their head office in Wales. They were pleasantly surprised that they were served a cooked lunch rather than sandwiches.

During my time at Crimpfil, and whenever there wasn't a great deal to do, I studied nutrition and weight loss, and learned about calories and exercise. I discovered that I had a real fascination for the subject. This helped me to further understand the principles of weight loss and how to eat healthily for my own benefit. Before long, I had managed to lose more weight and was down to a very respectable 8½ st. (54 kg) by following my own 1,400-calories-a-day diet.

Sheba and I would walk around Leicester in our lunch hour, but sadly this was where we came across a serious problem. We would be walking along and suddenly Sheba would leap aggressively towards a passer-by. It was so upsetting and inexplicable. The passer-by hadn't tried to stroke her or do anything that might provoke a reaction, yet this behaviour persisted. Then, on one particular day, there was an awful moment when Sheba leapt aggressively towards a child for no reason. I felt enough was enough, so I called the vet in desperation. He explained that, with a dog that had been mistreated in its early life, such behaviour was not uncommon, and he suggested that the safest course of action, without a doubt, was to have Sheba put to sleep. I took her to the surgery straight away and it was heartbreaking. I loved that dog and I knew she loved me, and I felt I had lost a best friend, but I knew the vet was right. There was no alternative.

I called my friend, Lorna Ireland, who was a breeder of Pyrenean Mountain dogs and was the person who had found Sheba for us in the first instance. Understandably, she was as upset as we were at the loss of Sheba and swiftly offered us one of her own dogs, Beauty. This magnificent, gentle giant had been bred for breeding but unfortunately didn't like sex. Lorna, a highly respected breeder of Pyrenean champions, offered Beauty to us because she felt she would probably have a better life as a sole dog in the household rather than as one of the dozen or so that she owned. Of course, Beauty was delighted to discover that she had finally become 'top dog'!

Beauty settled in with us very easily and also enjoyed going to work at Crimpfil. All the guys were kind towards her, and Mr Jackson particularly took to her. In fact, he and Beauty struck up a special relationship. Beauty would wait until I went out of my office to make the tea for everyone; then she would take the opportunity to slink along the corridor to Mr Jackson. She would sit next to him at his desk, pushing her nose towards his top right-hand drawer where she knew he kept his biscuits. He would tease her and say, 'There aren't any,' but Beauty kept nosing the drawer until he gave her one. Then she would creep back to my office looking sheepish! Peter Duus, who had been very sad to say goodbye to Sheba, totally fell in love with Beauty. She truly was a lovable gentle giant.

***

Having lost most of my weight, I now felt liberated. With renewed confidence and a burning desire to help others escape the misery that I had suffered, at the end of 1971 I decided to start a slimming class of my own and invited a few friends and neighbours around to our house on Monday evenings for a weigh-in. I offered them a 1,400-calorie diet and the opportunity to learn some of the things I had learned from my Good Grooming course some years before. They were very excited and, much to my delight, in just six weeks my class of six had each lost about a stone (14 lb; 6.35 kg) and were putting into practice some of the good grooming tips. It was wonderful to see their transformation and how they too were increasing in self-confidence.

Inspired by their success, I thought it would be fun if we carried the concept into the village hall to see if anyone would like to join us. It was early in 1972 that I had 30 posters printed at a cost of £8 (that's about £110 in today's money) and placed them around our village of Thurnby. On Tuesday 6 February I opened my first public class, supported by my team of neighbours. When 29 members joined on the first night, we were all so excited. They willingly queued up to be weighed, happily took the 1,400-calorie diet plan, which had been approved by my doctor, and lapped up the good grooming tips. They loved it. The following week they all returned with more new members, and my first Slimmer of the Week had lost no less than 11 lb (5 kg)! The place was buzzing, and soon more and more people joined. We charged a joining fee of £1 and a weekly fee of 25p. (In the same month, the UK's currency went decimel and hundreds of years of everyday currency was turned into history overnight.)

As I ran my classes each week, I was getting an enormous buzz from seeing people losing weight and transforming themselves. It was then that I realised I had found my vocation. I was happy standing up and speaking to the class and they enjoyed listening; most importantly, they were losing weight. It was wonderful and I loved it. My experience of facing up to my own weight issues had taught me so much. In addition, my experience of selling plastic containers to people who didn't really want them made it a great deal easier to sell the concept of weight loss and making the most of yourself – two things that people very definitely *did* want!

Running the class was proving so fulfilling and rewarding that I decided to leave Crimpfil to work on what was to become my full-time career. Phil was in a good job with a significant salary as a chartered accountant, so we could afford to lose my regular income as a secretary. As I handed in my notice to Mr Jackson, he offered to buy shares in my new business. I declined because I didn't need an investor – all I needed was to find more venues around Leicestershire and advertise the classes – but I was very touched by his confidence in me.

Tony Rodgers, our architect friend, suggested that I needed a snappier name than 'Slimming and Good Grooming Club' and suggested we take the initials of the title to rename it 'SAGG'! What an unlikely name for a slimming club! But, amazingly, it worked. Tony designed the logo and, with that, my new career was launched.

4

Expanding!
1972–80

One day, I was walking around town when I saw a young woman in a white trouser suit and a big burgundy floppy hat. She looked amazing and was obviously a 'promotional girl' dressed to impress customers at some exhibition that must have been happening in town. It suddenly occurred to me that I should do a similar thing to promote our new classes: hand out leaflets for my new SAGG clubs while standing in the city centre.

I told my members in Thurnby about my plans for expansion and promotional enterprise, and very kindly a seamstress in my class offered to make our outfits. I thought we would have even greater impact if we were accompanied by a Pyrenean Mountain dog. I had my own, of course – Beauty; and my friend, Lorna Ireland, who bred Pyrenean Mountain dogs, brought one along too. We wore white trousers, a purple jacket and a white floppy hat and, accompanied by our huge, white, magnificent, show-stopping mountain dogs, we were certainly noticed as we handed out our flyers! I also contacted BBC Radio Leicester, the first local BBC radio station to launch in the UK, to see if it was interested in SAGG. I was interviewed by Joan Stephens, one of its presenters, and Joan and I became close friends from that day on.

The following week, my classes in four different venues were launched, some better attended than others, but overall they were a great success.

Not only did I expand my own classes but also I soon decided to extend my network across Leicestershire. I took on other class leaders whom I called 'consultants', and in a short while SAGG became a delightful little business that was popular with our members because we did so much more than the other slimming clubs whose leaders just weighed members and talked about food in their sessions. I organised all kinds of activities, from trips to London, to visiting TV shows, to running our own fashion shows where club members were the models. Every year, we raised a lot of money for charity and this gave us added purpose. One year, we organised a sponsored slim in aid of three charities and raised £3,000 just in Leicestershire (that's around £20,000 in today's money). We all loved fundraising as it gave us a goal and we had fun organising our various activities. Needless to say, the charities – Guide Dogs for the Blind, the new Leicestershire hospice 'LOROS', which was yet to be built, and the Handicapped Children's Pilgrimage Trust – were delighted.

Because the business was going so well, I thought it would make sense to open my own premises. Next door to where I worked at Crimpfil there was a converted three-storey cottage available to rent. It had a large room at the back and several rooms suitable as offices over three floors. I took a lease on the property and found myself in a building that desperately needed decorating – and we were due to open in five days' time! There was no way I could have redecorated it myself in the time available, so one of my class consultants recommended a friend who was a decorator. Thankfully, Martin, who became a lifelong friend from that day on, managed to do the job and transform the downstairs into a smart-looking office and exercise room. I opened 'The SAGG Centre' in Highcross Street, in Leicester, and we were soon running over 20 classes a week from the premises. The business positively flourished. I was in my element.

What was rewarding then, and is still exactly the same today, is that our members, who come from all walks of life and in all shapes and sizes, find themselves happily getting together and sharing a common goal – to lose weight and make the most of themselves. I cannot think of anywhere else in society where this happens. The only difference is that in the 1970s it was 'ladies only', whereas now men and women mix in together very happily.

It wasn't long before we decided to include exercise in our classes. We were aware of Eileen Fowler doing exercises on television and thought we would try too. As there was no formal training available back then, we just made up our own exercise routines to the music we chose, and all my consultants took to teaching exercise like ducks to water. We loved leading aerobic exercise to popular music by the likes of Neil Diamond, The Bee Gees and Donna Summer. I also led a yoga class so, between us, we covered all tastes. This activity brought a new dimension to our classes and with it lots of new members. I enjoyed going to the SAGG Centre every day as my office base, and Beauty happily came with me.

***

Early in 1975 I couldn't understand why I felt so tired and sick. My doctor suggested a pregnancy test, but I was absolutely sure I wasn't pregnant. I had lost a fallopian tube some years earlier and been tested for infertility when Phil and I had tried for a family some years before. We had sadly come to terms with the fact that we would never be able to have children.

When I rang the doctor for the result, the receptionist said 'Yes, it's positive,' to which I responded, 'What does that mean?'

'It means you're going to have a baby!'

I immediately called Phil at his office and he came straight round to the SAGG Centre. We were both in a state of delightful shock.

Then, when I went for my first check-up, I was told that not only was I having a baby but I was also four months into the pregnancy!

I adored being pregnant. Our families were thrilled at their much-anticipated grandchild, and all my class members were so excited that they knitted bootees, matinee coats and cardigans by the dozen.

My pregnancy was trouble-free and I continued to work and teach my classes right up until the baby was due. Because I was asthmatic the doctors decided to induce me on my due date, to avoid any unnecessary stress. I was admitted to the Leicester General Hospital and I remember feeling so happy. Phil and I were on cloud nine, floating joyfully together!

It was decided that I would be given an epidural. This seemed like a really good idea, but when they started to induce me nothing happened. I had to be turned every 15 minutes, which must have been a real nuisance for the nursing staff. I was getting quite frustrated because after a while it seemed that other women were coming on to the ward and going into labour, and babies were being born in a wonderful maternal production line, but nothing was happening with my baby.

I had a heart monitor attached to my abdomen to record my baby's heartbeat and every now and again it missed a number of beats. I was really worried and called the nurse.

'Oh, don't worry,' she said, very casually. 'That monitor's faulty!'

Not surprisingly, I was getting more and more stressed.

By midnight, some 16 hours after the first dose of the epidural drug, still nothing was happening, so I pleaded with the doctor to do something to get my baby out. I had reached a stage where I really didn't care how they did it. So, into surgery I went for a caesarean section. Apparently, as soon as they cut me open, out climbed Dawn as if to say, 'This is much easier, isn't it?'! She was born at 2.30 am weighing 5 lb 14 oz (2.66 kg).

Our beautiful baby girl was perfectly healthy, had a shock of black hair just like her dad and was a most adorable baby who was never any trouble. In fact, Dawn was the most precious gift in the world, and her arrival brought renewed love and happiness into our marriage. Phil's mum and dad were thrilled to be grandparents and were always ready to babysit whenever we asked. By now, my parents had moved to Norfolk because of my mother's ailing health, so they were more distant grandparents. To us all, Dawn was a truly wonderful blessing.

I was completely consumed with the joy of motherhood. Dawn was such a good baby and, once I had recovered from the caesarean, she came to work with me and Beauty – at the SAGG Centre – which was perfect. I continued to breastfeed her for a year. I have no doubt that breastfeeding not only created a very powerful bond between us but also worked wonders in helping me to shed any baby weight, not that I had gained much. Within a few months I was down to 8 st. (about 51 kg).

Dawn played perfectly happily while I carried on the business. Since I worked on my own, I was able to potty-train her at an early age, and by the time she was nine months old she was out of nappies during the day and amazingly was dry at night at 10 months.

She was the happiest child and was very content to play on her own while I worked. By the time she was a year old she was walking and talking well, and by 18 months was chattering away in sentences. Phil's mum and dad, Evelyn and Henry, adored looking after her and Dawn loved being with them. I am sure her speaking so well so early was greatly due to their constant interaction with her.

***

As time went on, my own mother, Celia, had become increasingly weak and later spent some time in hospital as she was so ill. Very sadly, at the age of just 67 she passed away. It was so sad but, at the same time, it was also a blessing because she had been unhappy and quite poorly for a long period, spending most of her time in bed. My brother Robert and I would visit our parents in Norfolk when we could and it was really upsetting to see my mother in such poor health. My father, Oswald, had been devoted to her and cared for her with great love for many years.

Somewhat surprisingly, Oswald got over the passing of his wife of over 40 years quite quickly, and within a year or so he was looking for some company. Then one morning, as Oswald was reading his Bible and praying as he did every day, he felt God say to him: 'You should marry Mabel.' This might seem a rather unlikely kind of divine instruction, but my father was convinced! He knew Mabel, as she was part of his Bible study group at the local church and they would meet weekly in the different homes of the various members of the group.

Mabel Pegg was a spinster in the truest sense of the word. She was in her early 50s (by now Oswald was approaching 70) and she lived on her own, having nursed her mother and her father until their deaths some years earlier. Mabel had never had a boyfriend in the whole of her life but, on this day, her life was going to change for ever.

After hearing what he believed was God's calling, Oswald rushed round to Mabel's house five doors away.

'You will never guess what the Lord has just said to me!' he told Mabel.

As he appeared in a bit of a flap, she invited him in for a cup of tea – the familiar British response to an emotionally demanding situation – and he proceeded to tell her: 'God has told me that we should get married.'

I wish I could have seen her face! Apparently, he then went on to say, 'I'll go into town and do my shopping and come back and see what you think.' Only my father could do that.

Mabel was, not surprisingly, somewhat overwhelmed but, as Oswald continued to court her over the coming weeks and months, she began to enjoy his company and attention and soon they were inseparable.

Father then rang me and my brother Robert to tell us his exciting news. He was getting engaged! We were flabbergasted and suggested that maybe he shouldn't 'rush into anything' and could perhaps come and stay with each of us for a holiday and chat things over.

First, he stayed with Phil and me in Leicester, and then he drove up to Cheshire to stay with Robert and Jane, but he soon became love-sick. He decided to go home to be back with his new love and we all wished them great happiness together. A few months later, they were married.

***

By 1980 my business was flourishing, so I persuaded Phil to let me move the SAGG Centre to a larger, more modern building just two doors away from the old one but on a main road. Vaughan Way is a major dual-carriageway in Leicester, so having a 'shop window' – and it was a big one – on such a busy road gave the business significant presence. I managed to negotiate the term of the lease, reducing it from 25 years to five years, and Phil agreed to a budget of £5,000 to refurbish this new SAGG Centre, which was 1,000 sq. ft (93 sq. m) of open space with 24 bundles of wires dangling from the ceiling, and huge bare windows looking on to Vaughan Way.

I set about buying second-hand light fittings, partitioning, furniture and essential materials by placing 'Wanted' advertisements in the local paper, the *Leicester Mercury*. Soon the phone was ringing and I drove around Leicester in my Volvo estate collecting various random items: partitioning from a garden room someone had decided not to build; spotlights from a shop that was being refurbished; strip lighting and second-hand chairs. All contributed to the creation of a very smart new SAGG Centre.

A builder friend of Phil's put up all the partitions, an electrician fitted all my random light fittings and, in no time, there was a stylish reception area, huge 'before' and 'after' photographs of our success stories displayed in each of the vast windows, a sauna, a beauty/massage room, offices and a large exercise floor. We held over 30 classes a week there, and everybody loved it.

It's an irony of life that sometimes when things are going brilliantly well in some areas – the gift of a child, a flourishing business – other things begin to fall apart. My marriage to Phil was faltering once again. Perhaps we didn't want to admit it, but our life together was now teetering on the edge. We had slowly but surely become more and more distant, with the inevitable result that Phil and I had begun to grow apart in the kind of way that is hard to reverse. Our marriage, which had begun with such love, was now in serious trouble. I was enjoying developing my business, which took up more and more of my time, and Phil was working hard too – and when he wasn't, he was often out playing badminton. We were sharing a home, but emotionally we were living at a distance.

Our one common ground, of course, was Dawn, who brought both of us, and Phil's parents, such joy. Dawn blessed us both so richly and, through this difficult period, helped me to keep strong and survive in the growing crisis.

Thankfully, for the time being, our marital differences were very much kept away from everyone.

5

Challenges and disappointments
1981–5

My professional life began to grow in all sorts of exciting ways. As well as my weekly classes, I was by now doing regular radio slots on BBC Radio Leicester and BRMB, a popular commercial radio station in Birmingham. I loved the medium of radio and I enjoyed my monthly slots talking about various aspects of health, well-being and good grooming. Now with super-successful dieters, I started submitting their stories to women's magazines. This caught the attention of IPC Magazines, which published *Woman*, *Woman & Home* and *Woman's Own* among many others. One particular magazine, *Successful Slimming*, which was an offshoot of *Woman's Own*, had published many of my success stories, and I struck up a great relationship with its Assistant Editor, Sarah Touquet. So it was an obvious choice that when I began organising a fashion show which would feature our top slimmers as models, I invited Sarah to join my panel of judges to choose my first SAGG Slimmer of the Year.

Shortly after that event, I was invited to meet the members of Sarah's management team as they were interested in my SAGG classes becoming associated with their *Successful Slimming* magazine. In fact, they wanted me to sell my business to them. They had heard from Sarah about our classes being different from those run by *Slimming* magazine – a competitor of their *Successful Slimming* publication. They liked the fact that we incorporated exercise and good grooming as it fitted well with their core message.

I was invited to London to meet Jane Reed – the Editor of *Woman's Own*. Jane Reed was awesome. Powerful. Charismatic. Inspirational. While I was in her office someone brought in two alternative options for the cover of the next issue of *Woman's Own*. She looked at them and quickly made her decision. *Wow! How exciting!* I thought. It was just like the TV show *Compact* all those years ago. And Jane wanted *me* to run a chain of classes for it! I took to Jane straight away and felt that I could work really well with her.

IPC wanted me to create a national network of classes similar to my SAGG classes in order to compete with *Slimming* magazine, which was the market-leader in its sector and which also had clubs to support it. I was hugely flattered but, while I agreed to set up a chain for them nationally, I was not prepared to sell my own classes. I was unsure as to whether I could trust this huge company, particularly since Jane Reed, shortly after our meeting, had been promoted and would not now be directly involved in this new operation. I wasn't prepared to allow my little business, or my class consultants or the members, to fall into the clutches of a big corporate public company, but I *was* prepared to test the market for them with a trial class outside of Leicester.

I suggested that I open classes in the Holiday Inn in Birmingham on Thursday evenings as a pilot. The classes launched and again they were very successful. My name wasn't known in Birmingham other than through my radio slots on BRMB, but the fact that the classes ran profitably greatly encouraged IPC.

In the end, IPC reluctantly agreed to appoint me as Managing Director of the new venture without taking over my own personal business. They paid me well and gave me a brand-new company car, and I proceeded to set up classes nationwide. With no qualifications available to teach our diet and exercise classes, recruitment was easy and training took only a couple of days, which we did at the SAGG Centre in Leicester. Our Consultants were paid a set fee for each class and earned commission on any profit from their classes once the expenses had been cleared.

The Clubs grew quickly because they were advertised in *Successful Slimming* magazine, and all went well. In fact, so well that after six months I decided to offer to sell my SAGG classes to IPC. The team I was working with at IPC were really pleasant and my main contact was a delightful guy, Frank Farmer. He was charming and witty. He made me laugh, so I called him and said, 'Do you want the good news? I'm happy to sell!'

The next week, I was invited down to London and the executives involved took me to lunch at the Savoy Hotel. I managed to negotiate a sale price of £52,000 for my little company and a five-year contract with them to run the network. Little had I realised, when I made my initial investment of £8 for those 30 posters nine years earlier, that it would turn into a very saleable business. Phil was astonished at the sale price as he hadn't really considered SAGG to be of any great value.

The IPC bosses were happy initially as we continued to grow the classes, which were opening all across the UK. To keep costs down I was working over 80 hours a week and it was tremendously challenging.

Phil's mother, Evelyn, was a wonderful help as Dawn grew older and she was more than happy to look after her whenever we asked her – and Dawn adored her 'grandma'. Dawn went to school not far from our house, and on alternate days she and her friends would either come to our house or go to her friends' house for tea, and either I or Evelyn would be there.

***

As time went by, it became obvious that Phil and I were drifting further and further apart and our marriage was disintegrating. Although we weren't falling out, the marriage was lacking love and affection, and after a while we both realised that it just seemed hopeless. Sadly, we also lost Beauty when she was quite old and became ill. It was a really difficult time.

The funds from the sale of the business made it possible for me to buy another house, so in 1982 Phil and I decided to separate. But there was one condition that Phil insisted on: he was adamant that Dawn would live with him.

I had not even considered this possibility – I had thought that Dawn would always be with me. But when we discussed what was best for Dawn, it became clear that the least disruptive home for her during the school week was in the original family home, where Phil would continue to live. This lovely house was situated only a mile away from Dawn's school, which was convenient, and then she would come and stay with me at weekends. Phil's mother and father, Evelyn and Henry, loved looking after Dawn; so, if neither of us was around for whatever reason, they would always gladly step in, and Dawn adored them.

From the proceeds of the sale of SAGG we decided that I would pay off some of the mortgage on the family home, and with the balance I bought myself a new house. I was still able to collect Dawn from school whenever needed. My new house was just a few miles away and Dawn had fun when she came to stay with me at weekends. Phil would ring me any time he needed help, day or night, and particularly if Dawn was unwell. It was a totally amicable arrangement and we never, ever fell out, even when we went for our divorce in 1984.

Phil helped me move and would sometimes come and stay at weekends. In fact, we got on better after we had separated, and it proved to be a friendship that was to last a lifetime. To be honest, looking back, I don't think we ever stopped being very fond of each other. It was just that the marriage didn't work.

***

From the time when Dawn was very young, I had started writing a book about weight loss. I used to write it while sitting in the doorway of Dawn's bedroom every night as she went to sleep. She didn't like going to sleep with no-one there. I didn't mind sitting with her and I happily put pen to paper, describing my philosophy of how to lose weight without starving yourself. I decided to call the book *Eat Yourself Slim* because I had successfully lost weight by eating 1,400 calories, over a third more calories than the 1,000 calories recommended at the time by GPs. I described my personal experience of how I had managed to slim down on a more generous calorie allowance. After running the classes and seeing my diets working well, and having spent some time studying basic nutrition while I worked at Crimpfil, I felt adequately knowledgeable to write a book on the subject as I was living proof that it worked.

One of the benefits of working with IPC was that it had a book publishing arm. Soon my book was published by Hamlyn. It was very exciting to see my work in print. It was published in 1983, was reprinted twice that year and was also sold in Australia. With a special edition also published for our members, it sold around 60,000 copies, which was far more than I ever expected.

Some months after Phil and I had separated, I was invited to a dinner party and introduced to a guy called John. He was very charming and we hit it off immediately. We dated for a few months and I grew very fond of him, but somehow I had a sixth sense that something wasn't quite right.

My life with IPC was becoming more and more challenging, and one night I was working late and alone in the office when some youths broke in and stole my purse and the office keys that were on my desk. I called the police, and officers came round and interviewed me, but obviously the youths had fled and I hardly saw what they looked like. After the police had gone, I called John to see if he could help but was given a very hushed response and no offer of assistance or comfort. I was very disappointed and became suspicious. It was only later that I found out that when we started dating, he was already in another relationship.

As I had no means of locking up, I decided to barricade myself in this four-storey office block and attempted to sleep on the sofa in my office. I felt very lonely and really scared. You have no idea how much noise a large building makes when it is entirely empty of people. It creaked all night long and, because I had just been burgled, I was highly stressed anyway. I hardly slept a wink.

Next morning the staff arrived and I went home to change and freshen up. I was in the bathroom when a light bulb fell out of a light socket. With my nerves already in shreds, plus the lack of sleep, I nearly had heart failure! I was now a nervous wreck.

That night I suddenly had a thought: I needed a guard dog. Dramatic, I know, but I often worked late in the office and I also lived alone. So the next day I found a breeder and, two weeks later, Nikki, an eight-week-old German Shepherd, took up residence with me.

John, the unhelpful two-timing boyfriend, was totally unimpressed and disapproved of my allowing Nikki on to my sofa. Needless to say, all things considered, when faced with the decision of being with him or the dog, I brought my relationship with John to a swift end.

That spring bank holiday, I went on a pony-trekking weekend with a few friends. I had loved horse riding ever since I was a child, so I leapt at the opportunity to spend a weekend on horseback. Nikki went back to the breeders for the weekend and a colleague and friend, Sue, from the office, also came along. She was single too and we thought it would be fun. There were about a dozen of us and we piled into a minibus. One of the group was a stunning guy called Mike. I noticed him early on and enjoyed chatting to him during the evening. In fact, we chatted together all evening. He was funny, charming, incredibly good-looking and delightful company, and I was strangely impressed by the fact that he could drink 12 pints (6.8 l) of beer and still appear sober. We just seemed to click.

The next day, we were all allocated our horses and off we went trekking in the Brecon Beacons in Wales. I was impressed that within 20 minutes of sitting on a horse for the first time in his life, Mike was rising to the trot. As the day progressed, we chatted and chatted and spent another lovely evening together in the pub where we were staying. I knew Mike was younger than me, but I hadn't quite realised how much younger. He was only 23 and I was 36, but neither of us seemed to care.

As we prepared to leave, I was thinking of any possible way I could manoeuvre myself to be sitting next to Mike for the journey home. I needn't have worried because, when I walked out of the hotel with my bag, he was waiting for me beside the minibus.

I felt I had found someone special. I hoped Mike felt the same. Thankfully, the next day he rang to ask me out.

We decided that, for our 'date', I would cook a meal at my house as I was now the proud owner of my new guard-dog puppy. Mike took to Nikki immediately and volunteered to house-sit and puppy-sit when I had to go away overnight the following week.

Nikki seemed to melt everyone's heart – at the office and particularly with Dawn, who totally fell in love with her. She had so much fun playing with her when she was staying with me.

It didn't take long before my relationship with Mike was flourishing. He was really kind and loving, he made me laugh and I loved being with him. On top of that, he was utterly gorgeous. After a few months the relationship had grown into something very special and it became obvious to me that Mike should move in to my house. He was single and at that time was living at home with his parents. But before he moved in, I arranged to have lunch with Phil to explain our plans. The following Friday, Mike and I called at Phil's house to collect Dawn for the weekend. Phil went out to the car to meet Mike and they got on really well, which was a great relief. Mike was also wonderful with Dawn and seemed to have a natural way with children.

As our relationship developed, it became clear that it would progress to marriage, and that's when Phil and I filed for divorce. We made our appointment to see our solicitor, but he refused to act for us as he was a friend of both of us, and instead suggested that we should do it ourselves. We did, with no disagreements other than trying to be too generous with each other. In the end, it cost us just £40 for the divorce and we stayed close friends for ever after.

Some time later, we had to go to court to formalise the custody arrangements for Dawn. It was strange as we sat on our own in the anteroom awaiting our turn, chatting away happily. All the other couples in there were with their respective solicitors and everyone was sitting in stony silence.

Phil also somewhat surprised me with a comment: 'You were just so capable. You ran the house, looked after Dawn, ran your business. I felt a bit inadequate, to be honest.'

I was shocked. This was the first compliment he had paid me in over 13 years! I can remember thinking, *I can't believe you've just said that. If only you had said that kind of thing to me before!*

When we were called before the judge, he could see we had an amicable relationship. He asked a few questions and then enquired if either of us had a new partner. I said I had, and the judge turned to Phil and asked, 'What is he like? Is he all right?' to which Phil replied, 'Yes, he's a really nice guy.'

Then the judge said, 'So, what would you like? Joint custody?' and of course we both agreed.

By the August of 1983 Mike had moved in and soon we were looking for a new home. The house I had bought when Phil and I split up was ideal for me on my own, as it had just a postage-stamp of a garden, but now we had Nikki, and we needed more space. Nikki went to work with me and loved being part of the staff. The business had grown and we now occupied another floor of the SAGG Centre, employing over a dozen members of staff. Mike was employed with a television repair company at the time and occasionally took Nikki into work. One day, he put her in the Manager's office because the boss was out all day, but was surprised when he happened to look through the frosted glass door and saw the boss sitting at his desk. Worried that the guy would be shocked at finding a fully-grown German Shepherd in his office, Mike went in to apologise. But there was no Manager, just Nikki sitting in the boss's chair!

It wasn't long before Mike and I found an elegant property for sale called 'The Old Parsonage', where the vicar of the parish had once lived. Now it was on the market and needed significant renovation. I had always loved old properties and I loved space. This was a large house positioned on the main A6 trunk road, directly opposite St Peter's Church in Mountsorrel near Loughborough. It was Grade II*-listed and an 18th-century house that had been described by the famous architectural historian Nikolaus Pevsner as 'exceptionally elegant'. A visitor once said the house was 'a rose in the wrong garden' because of the heavy traffic that passed by, but I could see that this was a property with huge potential. It was in poor condition, so we managed to buy it for just £42,000.

This was the start of an exciting challenge as we worked together to renovate and transform our new home. Little did we know that the Old Parsonage was to provide the setting for a life-changing adventure that would ultimately take us on a journey beyond our wildest dreams . . . but there were yet to be a few ups and downs that we had to endure.

Initially, we had to live in a small caravan. Phil and I had used it on many a summer holiday, but now, in November, this was where Mike, Nikki and I would stay while the woodworm treatment and other disruptive work was completed in our new home. It wasn't without its amusing moments. One morning, when I knew I would be late back, I left a slow-cooker on all day with a casserole for Mike. Returning from work that evening, he popped to the off-licence to buy a few cans of beer, only to find that Nikki had eaten the entire casserole by the time he returned! On one particular day, when it was extremely cold, Nikki gave Mike a present – a frozen dead mouse – as if to say, 'Do you realise how cold it is in here?!' Nik, as we called her, was an amazing character and she and Dawn adored each other. Nik had become very much part of the family.

After three weeks, we moved in to one bedroom that had been redecorated. Gradually, each room was painted, furnished and fitted out as we could afford it. Mike did a lot of the work as he decided to leave his job and chose to concentrate on renovating the house. In addition, to earn some extra money, he started a business selling M&S 'seconds' pottery on a market stall in a nearby shopping centre.

Having found a warehouse in Stoke-on-Trent which sold a vast variety of household items, including M&S goods, we realised this could all prove rather exciting. As I went to Birmingham every Thursday to take the new classes at the Holiday Inn, I decided to take the opportunity to drive first to the warehouse in Stoke, load up my car with goods, then drive to Birmingham to teach my classes. I would get home around 9.30 pm. Then Mike and I would unload the products, wash them and price them, ready for him to run his market stall the next day. We loved it.

In between selling pottery, Mike and his friend Jim fitted a new kitchen, and gradually the Old Parsonage emerged as a really beautiful property.

A year later, after we had become engaged while in Austria, we celebrated with a fancy-dress party, asking everyone to wear costumes of the era when the house was built, the 1820s. It was a really splendid occasion and everyone looked amazing.

Dawn, who was now nine, enjoyed coming to stay, and our weekends together were so happy. She was such a lovely child – never any trouble and always kind, like her grandma (Phil's mother, who was one of the kindest and most thoughtful and unselfish people I have ever known). Mike was brilliant with Dawn and we really enjoyed our life together. Nik loved running around the garden, and soon we decided to let her have pups, which was another great adventure. Shortly afterwards, George the cat (female!) had kittens! We had no idea she was pregnant – we just thought she was getting fat. We kept one of Nik's pups, Sheba, and she too came to work with me at the SAGG Centre, and we decided to keep two of the kittens, Oscar and Harry, who stayed at home.

***

By 1984 the classes were not proving as profitable as IPC had hoped, not helped by a national miners' strike that year and the UK economy's plunge into a recession. In short, the income from the classes was insufficient to run the business as it stood. So the accountants at IPC looked at the possibility of changing the set-up of the business and turning it into a kind of franchise. Instead of the teachers being paid a small fee plus commission, it was decided that they should pay the company a set fee of £13 per class per week, but they would be responsible for all their expenses (room hire and so on). However, their potential reward would be much greater as all the profit from each class they ran was theirs to keep. For the very popular teachers with high numbers, this was a real opportunity for them to make a significant income, but for the not-so-successful ones, it was risky. At the time, we had approximately 600 classes run by around 300 women across the UK every week but, from IPC's point of view, the company would be better off with just 130 classes paying £13. And I had the job of visiting the groups of teachers to break the news.

One group was located in the north of England. Mike drove me up to Scarborough to address around 40 women, many of them miners' wives. To expect them to take the risk of having to pay a fee to run the classes was of course overly optimistic. With their husbands on strike, these women hardly had enough money to buy food for their families. They were almost ready to lynch me at the suggestion.

With the stress of it all, things were going horribly pear-shaped at home. By now, Mike was working in the shoe trade, so at least he was financially independent. But he wasn't happy in his job and mine was falling apart and this was affecting our relationship. Towards the end of the year, we decided that Mike would buy a cottage in the next village and move out. Life was so difficult on every front except for one very special person. Only Dawn coming to stay with us at weekends brought any kind of calm or relaxation.

In an attempt to save the business, drastic measures had to be taken. Together with my management team at IPC, we graded the performance of all the classes in the network from AA for the top performers down to C, D and E. It was decided that keeping the 130 AA, A and B classes going should be a no-brainer for the teachers, and IPC's calculations were based on the fact that they would thrive under the new regime and would be happy to stay under the new arrangement.

However, at the next Board meeting, I described the reaction I had received in my regional meetings and reported that even some AA-graded classes would not be continuing because leaders didn't like the new arrangement.

My Chairman at IPC, Pat Barnes, was livid and retorted, 'Why don't *you* go and take these AA classes!'

I was being expected to be in Basildon in Essex and Newcastle-upon-Tyne – all at the same time! It was unbelievable. I was so stressed and so exhausted because I was giving every ounce of effort to making the business work, I felt this was so incredibly unfair, and I exploded. I then slammed my hands on the table, screamed at Pat in frustration and ran out in floods of tears!

Having composed myself, I returned to the room and we carried on.

After much unpleasantness, I attempted to build the number of Clubs over the next few months. I had always believed we could turn it all around and that we would reach the break-even level of 130. And in less than a year we had done it. For the first time, we were actually set to make a modest profit. I was delighted and hugely relieved.

Then, out of the blue, at the end of 1985 I received a call from Frank Farmer, one of the Directors. Frank had been a good friend throughout the whole saga of events at IPC, but now he had some startling news. The magazine *Successful Slimming,* with which the Clubs had been associated, had been sold, along with various other magazines within the group, and the new owners would not allow the classes to continue under the name 'Successful Slimming'. This meant changing 40 items of stationery for every Club, and we had three months to organise it.

However, my five-year contract still had a year to run and I had made it very clear that I would not renew it. I had had enough of boardroom politics. In addition, the lease on our offices was due to expire in April. The IPC bosses decided that there was no choice but to close the business. I can remember crying in disbelief that all the efforts of the past year were for nothing – except that they had proved that the business could be made to work. I dreaded telling my lovely staff members who had been so loyal and supportive. They were my friends. It was so disappointing that it had come to this.

Christmas 1985 was a very sad time. The Clubs were to be disbanded and given to the women who ran them, and it was my job to close down the operation.

My relationship with Mike had totally fallen apart. We broke off our engagement, and on 26 December he moved out of the Old Parsonage. What a miserable Christmas it turned out to be!

As 1986 arrived I was on my own, winding up a business, and had no job. I decided to sell the Old Parsonage and move my personal classes to the Holiday Inn in Leicester as the SAGG Centre had now closed.

I could never have guessed then that 1986 was to prove to be the most important year of my life.

6

Amazing transformations
1986–8

January arrived. A new year and a fresh start. I was physically and mentally exhausted after the stress of the previous months. With no more anguish from IPC and away from the challenges of my failing relationship with Mike, I enjoyed being on my own. It was a strange relief. I had dogs Nik and Sheba, and cats George, Oscar and Harry as company, so I never felt lonely. Also, Dawn and her friend helped me at my new classes, which I moved over to the Holiday Inn in Leicester, and Dawn stayed with me every weekend.

The corporate colours for the Holiday Inn were green and white, and the Managers were very happy for me to brand and market my new classes as 'Rosemary Conley at the Holiday Inn'. I had green and white tracksuits made for Dawn and her friend, Katherine, and they looked very smart as they cashiered for me on Monday evenings, along with my friend Gwen who helped me with my three Monday classes. On Fridays I led an aquarobics class in the hotel pool, followed by two sessions of diet and exercise.

Gwen Cherry had been a member of my classes since before Dawn was born and had become a family friend as well as a very capable cashier. My team of helpers were exceptional and my members were very happy to move over to our exciting new venue from the SAGG Centre. I saw several hotel General Managers come and go, but I continued my classes there for 25 years and only left in the end because the private car park became prohibitively expensive for my members.

Mike and I had split up on Boxing Day, but rather unexpectedly he invited me round to his cottage for his birthday in mid-January. He cooked me a lovely meal and we had a very happy evening. It was great to see him again, but I was confused. The decision to split up hadn't been taken lightly. Mike and I had gone to the effort of buying him a cottage, and furnishing it, so it was crazy to consider getting back together again after just three weeks! I felt I had to go back to the Old Parsonage to be on my own after our enjoyable evening.

Then suddenly, in late February, I fell ill. I couldn't stop vomiting and I kept passing out. I didn't know who else to turn to, so I asked Mike if he could come over and help out, and thankfully he stayed with me until I was whisked away in an ambulance. He then remained at the house to look after the cats and the dogs while I was kept in hospital for a week. I felt really poorly and I looked dreadful as my mouth was a mass of cold sores. I had no idea what was wrong with me.

After numerous tests, I was diagnosed with gallstones and the surgeon suggested I have my gallbladder removed, but when he told me I would be off sick for 10 weeks I explained that it wasn't an option as I was in the middle of winding down a business. (This was some years before keyhole surgery was commonplace; at that time, a gallbladder removal was a major operation.) Reluctantly, and rather grumpily, the surgeon explained that the only way I was likely to avoid surgery was by following a very low-fat diet, which I proceeded to do.

I rarely read women's magazines because I never had time, but now, in hospital, I had all the time in the world. I happened to notice in a copy of *Woman's Own* an advertisement for a book called *Power for Living*, promoted by Cliff Richard, Lord Tonypandy (the Speaker in the House of Commons) and Gerald Williams, a TV tennis commentator of the time. The book was offered free to anyone who would like to find power for living through a personal relationship with God. At this messed-up stage of my life, I certainly felt I needed some divine intervention, so I sent for the book.

The *Power for Living* book arrived on the day I was due to go back to hospital for a cholecystogram as an outpatient. For this procedure, the patient swallows some revolting-tasting fluid and, when the liquid reaches the gallbladder, the ultrasound machine shows up any gallstones. While waiting for the gunge to reach the appropriate spot, I started reading my copy of the book.

I was pleasantly surprised. It was a book about Christianity that seemed to speak directly to me. I had been brought up to go to church on Sundays and I attended Sunday school throughout my childhood, but somehow the Church of England's way of worship back then seemed so ritualistic and impersonal. The *Power for Living* book approached Christianity differently. I felt it was talking to me in everyday language that I could understand, and suddenly it all made sense. It was compelling reading and I was riveted. Soon I was called for my scan and, yes, I did have lots of small stones in my gallbladder.

That evening, back at home, I continued reading my new favourite book in bed, and on page 61 it gave me the opportunity to pray a prayer to invite God into my life, to ask for my sins to be forgiven, and to ask God to show me the way forward in my life, his way.

I knelt at the side of my bed and earnestly prayed the prayer. I had made a complete and utter disaster of my life – a broken marriage, a business that had closed down, a failed relationship, no job, ill health, needing to sell my home . . . In fact, my life was a total mess. Yes, I needed divine help and I was prepared to pray on my knees to ask for it.

This was the prayer I prayed:

Dear Lord, I've been living my life my own way. Now I want to live it your way. I need you and I am now willing for you to take control of my life. I receive your Son, Jesus Christ, as my personal Saviour and Lord. I believe He died for my sins and has risen from the dead. I surrender to Him as Lord. Come, Lord Jesus, and occupy the throne of my life. Make me the kind of person you want me to be.

As I knelt at the side of the bed, I said the prayer and earnestly meant every single word. As I prayed, I felt my body being 'washed through'. There were no flashing lights, no flames, no claps of thunder or puffs of smoke, just a feeling of being 'brand new'. A new beginning. A fresh start. It was as though God had taken my list of mistakes and wiped the slate clean. I felt he was saying: 'I am now the Chairman of your life. Follow me and I will show you the way forward.'

I got back into bed. I felt like a brand-new person. I felt 20 years younger, totally confident about my future and hugely relieved that someone else was now in charge of my life. I even felt he was telling me that I didn't need to move house. Little did I know what the new Chairman of my life had in store for me!

I hardly slept that Friday night as I had this amazing sense of excitement. Somehow, I just knew everything was going to be all right. I felt convinced that I didn't need to sell the Old Parsonage, and I was so glad because I loved that house. Despite my lack of sleep, next morning I got up feeling rested and energised. I cleaned the house from top to bottom and felt on top of the world.

On the Sunday afternoon, Mike called round unexpectedly on the pretext that he was missing the dogs. He was very loving towards me and admitted he was really missing me. I had to admit that I had missed him too, though I didn't tell him about my 'transformation'. He stayed for dinner, and together we decided we would rekindle the relationship. And completely out of the blue, that evening, I felt God tell me that I should marry Mike. Oh, my goodness! I couldn't help thinking of my father's moment of divine inspiration when God told him to marry Mabel! But somehow, this gentle command seemed a little less bizarre – Mike was gorgeous and I already loved him.

Unlike my father, I didn't say anything. I waited until the following Friday evening when we decided to go out for a meal to celebrate being back together. While he was in the middle of eating his rump steak, I proposed to Mike. I then told him what had happened a week earlier and what I felt God had told me on that Sunday evening. He was flabbergasted but very happy, and we went straight round to his parents, Jeanne and Philip, to tell them our good news. They were delighted.

We didn't have much income as Mike had had a difference of opinion with his boss and had walked away from his job a week earlier. Fortunately, when I negotiated the initial deal with IPC, my contract was for five years; so, when the business closed after four years, I was entitled to a year's salary, which was a life-saver. We managed on this, together with the income from my weekly classes.

Just a few months later, Mike also became a Christian after reading *Power for Living*.

One of the things Mike always drilled into me was the importance of understanding the equality of people, that we are all equal on this earth. He is very bright and knowledgeable on matters of life and the world in general, which has proved extremely helpful in my life. We also found a mutual interest in seeking justice and discovered that we enjoyed watching TV programmes based on the law. Later, Mike became a Justice of the Peace (JP).

***

During my time with IPC, I had been asked to run activity holidays in Austria in the summer, organised by the magazines *Successful Slimming* and *Woman's Own*, and I had done this during the previous three years. I had fallen in love with Austria after watching *The Sound of Music* in the mid-1960s. It was – and still is – my favourite film of all time, and the scenery in real life is just as breathtaking as it is in the movie, if not more so. We stayed in a family hotel, The Berghof, in a village in the Arlberg region called Lech. Now, in 1986, the Lech tourist office was inviting me to stay at the Berghof for a week to teach the locals about healthy eating. Of course I accepted, but this also provided the perfect honeymoon opportunity, so I asked the hotel management if I could bring my new husband with me. Thankfully, Peter and Brigitte Burger, the owners of the Hotel Berghof, were more than happy to welcome Mike along, as it was at their hotel that Mike and I had become engaged some three years previously while on one of the *Woman's Own* holidays.

We were married on 26 July 1986 at Loughborough Registry Office. Dawn was bridesmaid and her dad, Phil, and Trish, his partner, came to the wedding. We had so little money, but it didn't matter. We both wore clothes that we had in the wardrobe already, I self-catered for the reception at the Old Parsonage, one of my class members made the cake, and my sister-in-law, Jane, created the wedding bouquets and button-holes. It was a very happy occasion. The next day, we flew off to Austria for our honeymoon. We were so broke that we ate well at breakfast and had nothing to eat until evening, when we enjoyed a beautiful five-course meal. All I had to do was give a daily talk to the locals at 5 pm, which was, of course, a pleasure.

Every day, Mike and I walked through the enchanting summer landscape. The meadows were filled with wildflowers of every colour you could imagine, all surrounded by waterfalls and magnificent snow-topped mountains. Someone once said that 'when God made the world, he picked up Austria and Switzerland in his hands and kissed them'. I think that sums up the beauty of this most amazing place on earth.

Upon our return, we had our marriage blessed by Canon George Crate at St Peter's Church, the church that was literally opposite the front door of the Old Parsonage.

Soon after I had prayed the prayer of commitment, I started attending St Peter's Church regularly. Then I went along to a 'Nurture' course organised by the church. This provided the perfect environment for new believers like me to learn about the Christian faith and to be able to ask questions without feeling embarrassed. Churches now regularly run Alpha courses which do just that.

One of the things I learned about was tithing – that means giving the first 10th of your income to God. It's a strong principle in the Bible and in Christian tradition, and it's a kind of 'thank offering', a way of giving to good causes and those in need and, in this way, making it clear that God always comes first. We had very little money, but I was determined to tithe even though the kingdom of God would not be benefiting by it very much. It is something that Mike and I have done ever since.

Amazingly, soon afterwards, our finances became much easier. The modest royalties from my earlier books and my income from my classes helped us to get back on our feet, helped even more by the fact that Mike now had a full-time job back in the shoe trade.

But then another miracle happened. I had been following a strict, very low-fat diet in an attempt to avoid surgery for my gallstones. Without trying, I lost 6 lb (2.7 kg) but, extraordinarily, it seemed that all six of those pounds had gone from my previously voluptuous jodhpur thighs! Surprisingly, I had gone from being a 'Williams' pear shape to a 'conference' pear shape. Still a pear shape but a much more slender one. The women at my classes were astonished at the difference in my appearance in just a few weeks and pleaded with me to share my secret.

I set about trying to create a low-fat diet for them. It was received with great enthusiasm and, yes, it worked for them too. Within a few weeks my pear-shaped members were looking significantly more streamlined, and that's when I realised I had hit on something really special. It was then that I decided to write a book about it.

After writing *Eat Yourself Slim* in the late 1970s, followed by two more small paperbacks, *Eat and Stay Slim* and *Positive Living*, I was confident that I would be able to get this new book published, despite not now being part of IPC.

But I needed more proof that the diet worked, so I decided to run a trial. Mike helped me print the diet sheets on an old Gestetner duplicating machine which we had to operate manually (this was long before home photocopiers were available), together with questionnaires which the volunteers were to complete after four and eight weeks. To launch the trial, I went on BBC Radio Leicester and BBC Radio Nottingham to ask for volunteers.

Being able to chat on the radio about a new diet that effectively slimmed your hips and thighs was a great help towards publicity. Understandably, the programme caused a great deal of interest, and I was very enthusiastic and passionate about the diet because of my own success. I asked for anyone interested in being part of the trial to send me a stamped addressed envelope to the Old Parsonage, and soon responses began to arrive. The addresses on several of the envelopes were in themselves highly amusing, including The Old Partridge, The Old Bakerhouse and The Old Parsnip, and I was given a variety of names from Rosemary Colleridge to Rosemary Clooney! A big 'well done' to our postman who realised that all these strangely addressed envelopes were in fact meant for us.

After eight weeks of following the diet, the results from my 120 volunteers were astonishing. The trialists were thrilled with their success, and their enthusiastic letters were so exciting to read. Comments varied from 'I was never hungry on this diet and now I can walk upstairs without puffing and bend down without grunting!' to my favourite, which was from a woman who wrote, 'I have been on and off diets all my life. Nothing has worked on my figure like this one. Now, I can't stop looking in the mirror . . .' and in brackets after her name she wrote 'aged 73'!

Furnished with the results, the statistics and the positive comments and experiences of my trialists, I set about writing my new book. I included lots of recipes I had created and adapted to be low-fat, thanks to my learnings from that Cordon Bleu cookery course back in the late 1960s. I also greatly extended the diet, but there was one snag: I couldn't think of a snappy title. After racking my brains for six months I decided to call it what it was: *Rosemary Conley's Hip and Thigh Diet*. I somehow knew this book was going to be special because I realised that this diet worked like no diet I had ever tried before, and my trialists had proven it too. It was a very special moment when I went to the local post office to send my manuscript by recorded delivery to Arrow Books (previously Hamlyn) in early 1987. (Email hadn't yet been invented.)

The publishers were enthusiastic about the story behind the book and gave me a desperately needed advance of a few hundred pounds. Arrow had planned to publish in the autumn of 1987 but decided it would be better to wait till January after everyone had overeaten following the festive season.

Since my earlier books were published, I had come to understand that the best way to publicise a book was through serialisation in a national newspaper. Previous attempts by my publishers had not met with success, however, so I decided to take on the task myself.

During my time with IPC, I had worked with their holiday department, which had organised the Austrian activity holidays. On one notable occasion, the coach company that had originated the activity holiday told me that for one of our weeks we would have a journalist joining us from the *Kent Messenger* newspaper; would I try to ensure that she went back with a positive opinion of our annual summer trips? Of course I agreed.

On this occasion, Mike joined me for the holiday and we invited the journalist to sit with us at mealtimes and did everything we could to look after her throughout the week. All her travel costs were met by the coach company, her hotel accommodation was paid for by the Lech tourist office, and the hotel didn't charge her for any of her drinks. We all looked forward to reading her piece in the newspaper in a few weeks' time.

Some months later, the coach company contacted the Editors of the *Kent Messenger* to ask when the article might be appearing, only to be told that they employed no journalist by that name and that they knew nothing about it. It appeared that this woman had conned her way into getting a completely free holiday!

Once my relationship with IPC had come to an end, I continued to organise the Austrian holiday privately with the Hotel Berghof, but instead of travelling by coach we went by air. To this day, my love of Austria has continued, and our group of holidaymakers has stayed at the same hotel in Lech every summer for over 37 years – with the exception of 2020 and 2021 due to the Covid-19 pandemic. It is an extraordinary week, and many friends have been made over the years. Much fun and laughter, as well as fitness and frivolity, have been enjoyed by all who have joined us.

Because the activity holidays were advertised in *Woman's Own*, I had worked with the Head of the Holiday Department, Christine, since the beginning. One day, we happened to be speaking on the phone when she asked what I was doing now that the IPC-owned Clubs had closed. I enthused about how effective my new *Hip and Thigh Diet* was and explained that I was trying to find a newspaper to serialise the book but I didn't know where to start.

Then Christine said, 'I know the Deputy Features Editor on the *Sunday Express*. I'll give him a call and ask him to call you and just listen to what you have to say.'

I was so grateful and anxiously awaited the call. I didn't have to wait long – but didn't expect a call on a Saturday.

Ever since I was a child, I had dreamed of owning my own horse. Now, as I had more time and we lived in the countryside, and with Mike's blessing, I bought Splash, a mature white Appaloosa mare who somewhat resembled a Shire horse. I realised I needed a hobby – something where I could lose myself and get over the mental and physical exhaustion of the previous four years running a national network of slimming clubs for IPC. Relaxing around the countryside on horseback seemed like the perfect solution, and it was just what I needed. Having discovered that Mike was a natural horseman, before long we bought him April, a beautiful bay mare. Splash and April became great pals, and Dawn began to love riding too. She and I would thoroughly enjoy our weekends when we would head out together on horseback.

On one Saturday, Dawn, now 12, and I had just come back from a ride. Dawn had been riding Splash who was bomb-proof – nothing would spook her – and I had been riding April who had been playing up, so my adrenalin was really pumping. The phone rang and Dawn answered it.

'It's some guy from the *Sunday Express*,' she said as she handed me the phone.

In my adrenalin-pumped state I blurted out, 'Hi, thank you for calling me. I've written an amazing new diet book that is going to change the eating habits of the nation.' It was a somewhat overconfident statement, but it just came out.

He asked me to send him the manuscript and said he would get back to me.

A week later he called. I was expecting him to be interested, but I wondered how much he would offer for the serialisation rights.

'Thank you for the manuscript,' he said. 'Yes, we would like to run it over two weeks and we are prepared to pay you £10,000.'

Ten thousand pounds! I tried my best not to sound too impressed, but actually I just wanted to jump up and down! To anybody, £10,000 is a phenomenal amount of money (that's around £30,000 today). Most importantly, my exciting new book would be hitting the national press, which would greatly enhance its chances of selling more copies.

The *Sunday Express* commissioned a photographer who took pictures of me with Mike and our two dogs, Nik and Sheba. One of the paper's journalists, Danae Brook, came to the house to interview me, and on 10 January 1988 the serialisation appeared. We were so excited and I really hoped the book would do well.

I need not have worried. By February my *Hip and Thigh Diet* had gone straight into the *Sunday Times* non-fiction bestseller list at number one! Arrow, the publisher, was having to reprint the book every few weeks as it was flying off the shelves. Across the UK, eager dieters were queueing in bookshops to place their order, and a week later they were queueing to collect their keenly awaited copies. (This was long before online shopping had been invented.) The diet was working and everyone was talking about it.

I then started travelling around the country doing radio and press interviews, and used the time in my various hotel rooms to reply to the dozens of letters I was receiving from people asking me questions and telling me how they were shedding their inches – particularly from those hard-to-shift areas on the hips and thighs! Mike was happy to look after things at home and help in the office. He was amazingly supportive.

Within a couple of weeks, it became obvious that I needed to write a sequel. Folks were asking for more vegetarian recipes and menus, and for more ideas for packed lunches. So I approached my publishers, who were very enthusiastic. Fortunately, I had kept all the letters and cards sent by grateful dieters with their comments and success stories, and these all added to the composition of the next book, which I decided to call *Rosemary Conley's Complete Hip and Thigh Diet*.

I will always remember 1986 as the year when my life took off – spiritually, emotionally and financially. It was a golden year, a trailblazer for many exciting times to come.

7
Crazy times!
1988–90

It's not every day that you discover a whole hidden level in your own house. This is what happened to Mike and me, and I like to think that it's a picture of the incredible hidden potential in all our lives. It's important to unlock the secret doors and explore the mystery staircases in our hearts and in our lives.

It was when we moved into the Old Parsonage that we discovered a whole floor that wasn't mentioned in the sale details. Half of the staircase to the second storey had been demolished to accommodate the building of a bathroom, and the remaining stairs were hidden behind what appeared to be a cupboard door. There were three rooms up there that hadn't been inhabited for over 60 years!

This 'lost floor' was in a shocking state, but Mike and Martin, our decorator friend, went to work on it and managed to create a really useful space for offices, which became accessible with the help of a wrought-iron stepladder. We had this custom-made to help us reach the remaining wooden stairs up to our secret domain! Incredibly, without any prompting or supervision, Nik and Sheba quickly mastered the skill of leaping up these precarious steps and joined us happily as we worked in our new offices. Thankfully, they also managed to jump down safely every evening. Both dogs lived to be over 13 years old and never had any hip or joint problems, so we can only assume these acrobatics caused them no harm.

By now we had come to the conclusion that we couldn't cope on our own with all the mail and press interest, especially as I was busy writing another book quite quickly, so we decided to employ a part-time secretary. Di Stevens was a local woman who had worked in the navy and was meticulous in her office procedures. She was just what we needed, and the significantly increased advance for the new book paid for her salary. With everything getting busier, we were relieved to find another local woman, Vicky, who was happy to look after the horses in return for riding them as if they were her own. We had built stables for Splash and April at home so that we could still feel they were around us without our having to worry about their everyday care, and Vicky loved looking after them. Despite this, Splash gave us some hairy moments.

Soon after we got her, we thought it would be great to put Splash into foal, so we bought a horse-trailer and made the appointment for her to meet her stallion. We were very excited at the possibility of a foal appearing in almost a year's time.

At one point, Splash wasn't well. The vet visited and did a James Herriot-style internal examination, and said he could feel the foal. We proceeded to feed the mum-to-be with special food for pregnant mares and she positively blossomed.

Around the due date we were on tenterhooks, and when Splash appeared to find walking difficult I called the vet, a different one from last time. He examined her and then turned to me, saying, 'What makes you think she's pregnant? If she is, there's no milk there . . . No. She's just fat!'

The previous vet had been mistaken and all our efforts had been in vain.

Poor Splash. From having three meals a day and no exercise, she was now on grass only and extensive daily exercise! Her plight caused great hilarity within the village: 'Rosemary Conley's horse wasn't in foal – it was just fat!'

Some months later, Mr Paul, the barber in Mountsorrel, was giving a customer a short back and sides when something caught his eye. In fact he thought he was dreaming when he saw a huge white horse galloping up the main A6 trunk road directly outside his shop. April was out being ridden by our horse-helper, Vicky, and Splash had apparently cleared a five-bar gate out of her field, galloped up our lane and headed on to the A6 in search of her!

✳✳✳

The *Hip and Thigh Diet* topped the *Sunday Times* bestseller list for most of 1988, and in the summer of that year I was invited to go on a book tour to Australia and New Zealand. Oh, my goodness! What was happening? When God said he was now the 'Chairman of my life', I really wasn't expecting this.

The furthest I had ever flown was to Europe and I was nervous about going on a three-week tour on my own, so I asked the publishers if Mike could come too. Thankfully, they said that if I was prepared to fly 'economy' instead of 'club class', they were happy for Mike to accompany me.

By now the book was selling in hundreds of thousands, but (as is normal practice) I didn't receive any royalties until 10 months after publication. That would be in October, and now, in August, we were going to travel to the other side of the world. Not only that, but I was also expected to look like a successful bestselling author. So off I went to C&A (rather like Zara today), where I bought stylish clothes for both of us, fairly inexpensively, paying for them with my new and very flexible friend, the credit card. This was still a very unusual form of payment in 1988.

By the time we were due to go on our book tour, I had completed my manuscript for the *Complete Hip and Thigh Diet* and sent it off to Arrow. Our secretary Di and her family kindly moved into our home while we were away for the three weeks to house-sit and dog-sit. We had also engaged another member of staff, Angie Spurr, as our bookkeeper. Between them, they held the fort.

The thought of flying to Australia was very exciting, and at Heathrow we stepped on to the biggest aeroplane I had ever seen. We just weren't used to living like this. With films to watch and unlimited at-seat service, we set off on our long and rather daunting adventure.

We stopped in Singapore for a few days to do a few press interviews and adjust to the changing time zone. Mike and I marvelled at the Shangri-La Hotel where we stayed. The sheer vastness of this magnificent building took our breath away. We even had our own butler to tend to our every need, and we loved pressing the button to open and close the curtains. Remember, this was over 30 years ago and such gadgetry was unheard of.

Our publishers organised their local representative, Bruno Tan, to look after us and show us around, and we had a fabulous time. We ate in the finest restaurants and also tasted local cuisine, including 'fish-head curry'! I didn't eat the eyes, but it was the most amazing curry I have ever eaten before or since. It seemed that we were in another world and it was extraordinarily exciting.

Two days later, we boarded our plane to Australia, landing in Sydney, where we stayed for a few days to undertake numerous press, radio and TV interviews and book signings. I will never forget dining at the world-renowned seafood restaurant Doyles and eating huge garlic prawns. They were so big, so luscious and so mouth-wateringly delicious. After all the press and PR activities in Sydney, we flew to Melbourne for a couple of days to do it all again, before flying on to Adelaide.

Our last stop in Australia was Brisbane. We were met off the plane well into the evening and taken out to dinner by the local rep from the book publishers and his wife. Again, it was a seafood restaurant and we ordered, between the four of us, a seafood platter. I had never seen anything like it before and never have since. Imagine a dish as large as a turkey platter, piled high with lobster, crab, prawns, giant prawns and mega-giant-prawns-called-something-else, covered with a magnificent silver dome. It was like eating in heaven!

After this wonderful hospitality, we were dropped off, with our luggage, at the stunning Gazebo Hotel (now called the Pacific) at around 11 pm. Our host went on his way. Worryingly, when we went to check in, the staff told us that as we were so late, our room had been given to someone else. Somewhat shocked, I explained that they needed to find us a room somehow as the following day I was expecting to do 11 press and radio interviews from the room. A rather embarrassed receptionist consulted her boss, who decided to put us into the penthouse suite. Another very exciting experience and one that definitely impressed the journalists the following day!

Then it was time to fly to New Zealand. I had no idea that New Zealand was 2,500 miles (4,020 km) from Australia. I loved its pampas grass hedgerows and beautiful plants. We visited Wellington, Christchurch, Palmerston North and lastly Auckland.

Thankfully, I jotted down what we did in those three weeks:

- 4 national TV shows and 2 regional TV shows;
- 28 radio interviews;

- 14 press interviews;
- 19 book signings and 2 literary lunches.

We flew 11 times and stayed in nine different hotels.

We were given so many gifts, and we were looked after like royalty as we stayed in five-star hotels throughout our trip. Then it was time to leave, so we flew from Auckland to Melbourne and then caught another flight to Kuala Lumpur, where we had one of those horrible moments. As we waited for our luggage at Kuala Lumpur International Airport, nothing appeared except one suit-carrier containing a couple of suits and a few bits and pieces of clothing. There was no sign of our two big cases. Having had to pack and unpack them so many times, we had become somewhat cavalier about what we put in them. But our lives were in those suitcases and there was no sign of them.

As we left 'baggage claim' rather deflated, we were met by the local rep from the publishers who helped us to the hotel and then to the local shopping precinct to buy emergency clothes and toiletries, make-up and hairstyling things. I was to do a press interview the next day, so I had to look presentable.

The loss of our belongings was such a shame after our memorable tour. However, we were happy that the following day we would be heading home. Despite the luxury and sheer fantasy of our experience over the last three weeks, we were ready to sleep in our own bed, see Dawn, and stroke the dogs and cats.

Two weeks later, the cases arrived at the door of the Old Parsonage all intact – thankfully!

***

Gradually, normal life was resumed and we came back down to earth. By the end of the year, the *Hip and Thigh Diet* had sold almost half a million copies.

On 16 December 1988, *The Bookseller* magazine published its list of 'best subscribed' books for the following year. This 'top 20' is determined by how many pre-orders had been made by the book retailers. My *Complete Hip and Thigh Diet* was number one on the list! There was enormous excitement and anticipation from the publisher and retailers alike.

The Sun bought the serialisation rights and, in the new year, the *Complete Hip and Thigh Diet* went straight to number one. In fact, the new book turned out to be even more successful than the original and sold 420,000 copies in the first six weeks. By May, the two *Hip and Thigh Diet* books had sold over a million copies, and between them they had enjoyed 30 weeks at number one in the *Sunday Times* bestseller list. Arrow Books, the publisher, organised a spectacular celebration for me at the Savoy in London, and Mike and Dawn were there too to mark the occasion. Then the publishers presented me with their first ever Golden Arrow Award. To be honest, we were in a bit of a daze about its significance, but we loved every minute. It was very exciting.

Looking back, it was somewhat surprising to achieve so much success without the help of an agent, but it didn't even occur to me to have one. I had a great relationship with my publishers and seemed to be able to do all my own negotiating without any problems.

It was a strange feeling to go from local acknowledgment to suddenly becoming 'famous'. Being photographed for the front cover of Sunday magazines and appearing on television and radio was a massive leap from what I was used to. And then there were the invitations to appear at events and present awards. Perhaps the most exciting invitation was to open a brand-new shopping centre called Fosse Park in Leicestershire, situated just off junction 21 of the M1 motorway. When I was asked to cut the ribbon to signify its official opening in 1989, I felt very honoured.

Over the years, the area of the retail park has grown enormously and is Leicester's key out-of-town shopping centre. I smiled when, recently, one of my class members mentioned that she had suddenly found the commemorative plaque, which is set in the ground just outside the M&S store. She had no idea that I had been asked to perform such an honour all those years ago. I do all my shopping there, and to this day I feel a real affinity with the place.

Another unexpected invitation came from United Christian Broadcasters, known as UCB. This organisation is well respected in Christian circles for its *Word for Today* daily inspirational Bible-teaching aid, which is given away free all over the world. UCB had just built a brand-new radio studio in Stoke-on-Trent from which it would be broadcasting all across the UK and ultimately further afield, and I had been asked to officially open it. These were the lovely bonuses of suddenly becoming well known.

The *Complete Hip and Thigh Diet* went on to sell over two million copies worldwide over the next few years. I set off on a book tour again to Australia and New Zealand, but this time on my own. While it was amazing to fly club class and to sit on the upper deck of a 747 jumbo jet, I can remember being most excited on the return journey – I was longing to see Mike again as I had missed him so much and, of course, Dawn. Other book tours included two to South Africa (Mike came on the first trip), Canada and the USA. It was an extraordinary privilege and I couldn't get over the welcome I received everywhere I visited. It was a terrific experience and I was so grateful to Mike for not minding my absences as I travelled all over the world.

The books went to number one in all the countries I visited except the USA, where a different publisher was handling the book. Despite touring to New York, Dallas and other big cities, I kept being told by this new publisher that there was 'no money in book publishing', and little effort was put into publicity. It was frustrating, but I think part of the reason we didn't enjoy the same success in the States was because I didn't fit the profile of a typical diet and fitness guru. I was in my 40s and didn't look like a Barbie doll! I wasn't a film star and I wasn't 6 ft (1.8 m) tall or a size zero! I must have appeared quite frumpy to the Americans.

***

In 1989 the most important event was Dawn's decision to become a Christian. She had witnessed the transformation in our lives since Mike and I had both come to faith. One day she said to me, 'I want to be like you and Mike,' so when Billy Graham came to London in the summer as part of a live-link satellite event around the UK and into Africa, Mike and I took Dawn to the event in Loughborough. It was so inspiring to hear this great man of God preach, and at the end of the evening Dawn went forward to make a commitment. It was a very special moment, and since then she has trained and worked for many years for Christian organisations, and today is a minister and joint leader in her local community church and doing amazing work in her area.

Having enjoyed such astonishing success with my two *Hip and Thigh Diet* books, I felt it was time to create something different for my next book. The publishers were desperate for me to come up with another bestseller, so I decided to write my *Inch Loss Plan*. I thought it would be good to create a daily programme of diet and exercise lasting just 28 days, based on low-fat eating, with a progressive exercise programme as well as a daily motivational message. It involved a lot of work, but I was confident that it would be very effective for anyone who followed it.

The *Sunday Express* magazine serialised the new book over a dozen or so pages. It was amazing. I was on the front cover in a royal-blue catsuit, and inside the magazine were fabulous photographs of successful slimmers who had followed my new plan, as well as recipes and extracts from the diet. The book was another instant number-one bestseller and went on to sell over 800,000 copies.

Our life had now utterly transformed. The royalties were flooding in, boosted by the amazing sums paid for the serialisation rights. I learned that any newspaper that serialised my diets added around 100,000 sales to its circulation, so it wasn't surprising that newspaper publishers were queuing up to buy the rights to my next book. I was wined and dined by editors to ensure that I would offer my next book to them.

After the success of my original *Hip and Thigh Diet*, I was approached by a small film company to produce a fitness video to support the book. The owner of the company seemed a very pleasant guy and the prospect of producing a video was very exciting. I had previously produced audio tapes of fitness routines (not an easy task without visual images, apart from the accompanying poster) and had enjoyed some success with these, so I thought that creating an exercise programme for video would, by comparison, be significantly easier. I had also learned the nuances of obtaining music clearance (permission) for the use of pop music – a challenge not for the faint-hearted. It is time-consuming and frustrating as one has to get 'permissions' from the composers of the song lyrics and the music, as well as from the publisher and the artist who performs it. It is also expensive.

As I had been teaching exercise for over 10 years, I was confident that I could perform to the camera. The video would be 'produced' by the company, which would oversee the filming and editing into its finished form. The film set was the lounge at the Old Parsonage. To say the production values were minimal is an understatement. At one point, you could even hear an ambulance going past with its sirens blasting! We were, after all, right next to the A6 trunk road. There was a section on 'eating low-fat' and I had some prepared food ready in the fridge to illustrate low-fat meals. The only problem was that the roast chicken I had prepared had been left in the oven for too long and resembled a Danish pastry more than a chicken! We carried on regardless. This was a low-budget video.

We sold the videos by mail order initially through an offer on the back of Ryvita packs – the same way we had previously sold our audio tapes. The Ryvita crackers were in a sealed pack with a band of packaging around each pack. The reverse side of each band was blank and I was offered this rather useful promotional space free of charge. I would not receive any royalties on the sales of the videos until the production costs had been covered.

A year later, we recorded another video in London on a set created in the grimmest of studios in the centre of a derelict building behind St Pancras station. It was filthy and was just like the set of a gangster film! This second video was based on the *Inch Loss Plan* which, again, we sold by mail order.

Then the guy who ran the video company I had worked with invited me to London to meet a couple of other guys in the industry. We met for coffee at the Savoy and I was introduced to two men from a video distribution company, with a view to letting them take the videos to the shops for general sale. I have to admit I wasn't totally impressed with the slightly shifty characters who were persuading me that they were the 'best guys in town' to promote my videos, but it seemed that I had little option so I approved the deal. I would get £1 for each video sold and they paid me an advance of £30,000 against royalties, which, of course, was great. However, sadly, despite the fact that the videos sold over 500,000 copies over the following couple of years, I didn't receive a penny more. We took legal action, even consulting a barrister, but the view was that because the company was such a small enterprise, it would go out of business if it were to pay us what we were due (around £500,000); therefore we were unlikely to succeed. It was a tough lesson learned.

After the enormous success of my books and videos, I decided to approach the BBC to see if I could be considered for my own TV series. Within four months, *Rosemary Conley Diet and Fitness* was on BBC1 daytime television. We also recorded a video to accompany the series. *Rosemary Conley's Whole Body Programme* went on to sell 400,000 copies in a few months, and this time I did get paid for every single one. God bless the BBC!

***

My books were selling like crazy, my videos continually topped the video charts and we were making so much money it seemed unbelievable. Life was frantic, so we decided to buy ourselves a weekend 'get-away cottage' in order to escape from the office on a Friday evening and enjoy a couple of days a week to relax.

When we went to view Bay House in Rutland, the front door was opened by a very welcoming and bubbly woman called Gill Todd. Gill took us around the house, and in the dining room she showed us her cupboard full of cookery books – 'and this amazing new diet!' she proudly announced, waving a copy of my *Complete Hip and Thigh Diet* in the air.

'Do you know about it?' Gill enquired.

I smiled. When I explained that I had written it, she gave me such a big hug! It was a special moment.

Bay House was a chocolate-box-pretty thatched cottage in Rutland, the smallest county in England, and it took us just an hour to drive there from the Old Parsonage. We eagerly went ahead with the purchase. Gill, and her delightful husband Bill, kindly left some furniture for us. We also asked if we could buy a beautiful corner cupboard that looked wonderful in this quaint but quite spacious cottage. They explained that, for sentimental reasons, that would not be possible; but when we finally went over to collect the keys, Bill presented us with an exact replica which he had made for us! That was the sort of people they were and we became true friends.

I had great fun buying furniture and miscellaneous items from an auction house in Leicester, and soon Bay House looked very welcoming as we flopped in there every Friday evening. There was a pretty garden, almost an acre (0.4 ha), so most weekends were spent gardening, which provided us with much-needed relaxation.

On one Monday, Mike drove to Bay House to collect something I had left behind on the Sunday, only to find that burglars had been in and selected their 'treasures', leaving them all lined up ready for collection later. Fortunately, Mike had got there first!

We had also treated ourselves to a couple of very nice cars: a Ferrari for Mike and an XJS Jaguar sports for me. Not new ones, but they were lovely cars. On top of that, I managed to bid successfully for a special number plate – ROS 1E – which I bought from the DVLA. It had never been issued before and I was thrilled to secure it, even though it cost more than the car!

Not surprisingly, Mike and I were enjoying our very exciting life together, but I was so desperately busy all the time. Mike worked in the office with Di and Angie, while I was dashing all over the country doing interviews and TV and attending events. It was hard work to organise my life so that I could get home every night to see Mike (except on Mondays when I did my classes) and to keep weekends as clear as possible. Dawn came over when she could, but by now she was a teenager, studying for her exams and growing up fast.

Despite finding our life hard to believe – because we remembered so well what it was like to have very little – what I enjoyed and appreciated most was that people *loved* what I produced, and that what I produced worked for them. My books and videos were changing people's lives and that was priceless. I loved receiving letters every day from grateful dieters who had transformed their health, including a handwritten one from the then Bishop of Bath, the Rt Revd Dr George Carey. He explained that he and his wife had followed my *Hip and Thigh Diet* and both had reached their respective goal weights. He also wrote: 'Thank you for a splendid book which has made all the difference to us – and thank you for declaring your Christian roots so unashamedly in it!'

Some time later, of course, George Carey became Archbishop of Canterbury, and when the news of his enthronement was featured in the national press there was also a feature on how the new archbishop had slimmed down for his new role by following my *Hip and Thigh Diet*! Apparently, his son had told the press!

Among the many letters I received every day there were some very special ones. I will never forget the letter that came from a couple who wrote to tell me that they had been trying for a family unsuccessfully for years but, having lost weight on my *Hip and Thigh Diet*, they now found themselves with a beautiful bouncing baby boy. Their consultant had said that losing weight had made the vital difference.

Recording my TV programmes was enormous fun but, of course, a very steep learning curve. Nevertheless, I enjoyed the process. We had good viewing figures and the BBC was happy – until we hit on a problem. Some fitness experts contacted the BBC, saying that it was obvious that I wasn't qualified to teach exercise and that some of my explanations of 'which exercises were doing what' to our bodies were inaccurate. Something had to be done and it needed to be done fast if my career on television was to continue.

'Every cloud has a silver lining,' as the old saying goes, but sometimes the opposite is true: 'Every silver lining has a cloud.' In this case, a cloud of criticism.

8

Quorn House
1991–3

Thankfully, one of my critics, a fitness professional who had written to the BBC, turned out to be an angel in disguise and offered to work with me until I became qualified. The Royal Society of Arts (RSA) had recently accredited an 'Exercise to Music' teacher training course, created for people like me who wanted to teach exercise in the community safely and effectively. I honestly believe that none of the exercises I had ever taught would have done any harm to anyone, but becoming qualified was very important to me, especially given my high profile.

It was certainly challenging to fit into my desperately busy working life the hours required to study and train to become a qualified fitness professional. Taking the RSA Exercise to Music course is not for the faint-hearted. It requires a significant amount of time studying anatomy and physiology, as well as the practicalities of choreography and teaching safe and effective exercise. But it was vital that I achieved this. I had never been very good at exams, so to help me learn I created a list of dozens of questions I thought I might be asked on the theory paper. Mike became my personal tutor, firing these questions at me as I prepared the evening meal. I'm surprised I didn't start thinking about aerobic chickens or Yorkshire pudding press-ups, but the dinner-time revision routine worked extremely well! The course was extensive, involving both practical and theoretical exams, and I needed every bit of help I could get.

Thankfully, I passed. I felt very pleased that I was now a great deal more knowledgeable when appearing on TV, or writing my diet and fitness books, or recording my fitness videos. Even my loyal class members were impressed.

***

Having enjoyed a holiday on a narrowboat one summer, Mike and I decided to buy one for ourselves and moor it on the River Soar, which ran close to the bottom of our back garden. We designed and commissioned it from the local boatyard and it was fun for us all to sail up and down the river near the Old Parsonage. It also provided a very tranquil environment where I could write my next book: the *Metabolism Booster Diet*. This was a book that would comprise eight different diet plans, one of which proved to be of great value to ITV a few years later. At that point, an author tried to sue ITV for naming my TV show in 2001 *Eat Yourself Slim*, because he had a successful book published with the same title. The ITV lawyers were getting quite worried but were greatly relieved when I was able to tell them that I had previously published a book of this title in the early 1980s. However, because it was now out of print, apparently that didn't count. Thankfully, I remembered that one of the diets within my *Metabolism Booster Diet* book was also called Eat Yourself Slim, and that very much *was* still in circulation. The claimant disappeared quietly because the tables were turned. Now I could sue *him*! I let it all pass, but it was an amusing outcome from a potentially serious situation.

Every new book led to a three-week publicity tour around the UK visiting radio stations, book signings and events, which I did in between recording the next TV series. By early February 1991, I had four books in the top 10 of the *Sunday Times* bestseller list. The *Metabolism Booster Diet* went straight in at number one, knocking my *Complete Hip and Thigh Diet* off the top slot from the week before, after two years in the chart. At number five was my *Inch Loss Plan*, which also had been in the charts for all of the previous year, and at number seven was my *Diet and Fitness Action Pack*, which had involved writing and recording an audio fitness programme as well as a diet booklet and weight- and inch-loss charts to accompany my TV series. It was a crazy situation.

Almost as soon as I had finished one book, it was time to write the next one. In between the various diet books, I had also written a couple of low-fat cookbooks with Patricia Bourne. Patricia contacted me after losing weight on my *Hip and Thigh Diet* and asked if we could work together to produce a low-fat cookbook. In 1992, version two was published. I also wrote my *Whole Body Programme* book, which was published jointly by Arrow and the BBC.

In readiness for my second BBC series, I created an 'Action Band Workout Pack' to sell off the back of the programme. What the BBC hadn't realised was that I could sell the serialisation rights for the pack, and a significant sum was paid to the BBC for the privilege. Unfortunately, the pack didn't sell as well as expected and the BBC very kindly gave me all the unsold packs to dispose of how I wished. This proved very helpful to us, as will be revealed later.

Next, a new and exciting invitation came from the Editors of *Radio Times*. Would I write a six-part, eight-page series for them? This was quite a big project but I felt honoured to do it, and with the fee I received we bought a cottage on The Green in Mountsorrel, quite near to the Old Parsonage, and named it Times Cottage after *Radio Times*. We renovated it so we could rent it out. A couple of years later, Mike suggested we let Dawn live in Times Cottage because by then her dad had remarried. It provided her with the perfect opportunity to set up a home of her own.

***

Mike and I had loved living at the Old Parsonage and having our charming weekend cottage in Rutland, but at the end of 1991 we decided to move. We gave our horses to Vicky, our volunteer groom, much to her delight, and we rented some offices across the road from the Old Parsonage where Angie and Di, a couple of other staff members, and Mike and I could continue to work. It was a converted cottage, but it served us really well.

One day, the telephone engineer came to install a new phone system and walked into the office that I shared with Mike. I said hello and left to go to an appointment. Apparently, the engineer, now sitting opposite Mike at his desk, asked in a somewhat astonished voice, 'Was that Rosemary Conley?' Mike said yes, it was, to which the guy said, 'Really! Honestly? So you actually know her?'

To this very amusing response Mike couldn't resist leaning across the desk and saying in a hushed voice, 'Yes, I know her very well *and* I get to sleep with her!' The guy was flabbergasted until Mike added, 'Actually, she's my wife!'

During our house hunting, we found a smart-looking old rectory in the south-east of Leicestershire which was in a most amazing position, overlooking miles of open countryside. It had also been beautifully refurbished.

As soon as we viewed it, we fell in love with it as everything had been designed and fitted out to such a high standard. It had a couple of acres of land, a swimming pool and a magnificent kitchen-cum-sitting room. There was even a built-in alcove where Nik and Sheba would be able to sleep in the kitchen.

This was a very happy time. However, there was one problem. My health. As soon as I accidentally ate something high in fat, I felt very nauseous and the after-effects lasted for a couple of weeks. It was really getting me down. I decided I should have my gallbladder removed after all, but this time by keyhole surgery – a procedure that was very much in its infancy at the time. This would be so much less intrusive than the standard operation, which would require a 10-in. (25-cm) cut across my abdomen and about 10 weeks for recovery. By contrast, the recovery time from keyhole surgery is only a few days.

We managed to locate a surgeon in Hull who was happy to perform the surgery privately and I was told that I would be back to normal in a week. So we went for it. Mike drove me up there and collected me the next day, but what I hadn't anticipated was the excruciating pain caused by wind! To perform keyhole surgery the surgeon has to blow gas into your abdomen so that he or she can locate the offending gallbladder, which is situated to the centre-right of your torso, underneath the ribs, and isn't easy to access. After the operation, I was presented with a video of the procedure and a jar containing my gallbladder! It made interesting viewing!

Within a week I was almost back to normal and it was a great relief not to have to be so paranoid about the fat content of my food. The temptation was to start eating food that was higher in fat; but I enjoyed being able to manage my weight so easily by eating a low-fat diet, so I stayed with it.

Having completely recovered from my operation, it was time to start thinking about the next fitness video but, because I was so mentally extended by everything else I was creating, I decided that I needed third-party input to help me with the choreography. I engaged the help of a fitness professional, even though I was now qualified myself. A friend introduced me to Janet Thompson. Janet ran courses to train fitness teachers as well as teaching her own classes. She lived with her family in the south of England, but she was happy to stay with us in Leicestershire for a few days to help me work on my next video.

Recording videos with the BBC was a joy. We had a great team and we always had fun. The BBC always invested generously in my programmes because my previous videos had sold so well, and this allowed us to use original music tracks, which I felt was important. I wanted everyone who worked out to them to really enjoy doing so, not just once but time and time again.

The Director, Nick Patten, went on to produce the majority of my videos over the years and we always had a blast. Nick had directed the memorable celebrity chef Keith Floyd in all his series, as well as working in live television for much of his career, and what I loved about him was that he was great fun to work with. He was bursting with energy and brought sunshine to any production. Mike once watched him directing and recording one of my videos and smiled as Nick capered all over the 'gallery' (recording facility) and danced as he selected which shot he wanted from which camera. It was a hilarious performance, and his skill was such that he could edit the video as we went along.

I always used successful dieters as my 'backing dancers', and these women had to be found and auditioned. Their success stories always featured in the videos and they made the programmes real and inspiring to those who followed them, but of course their involvement had its challenges too. There were occasions when Nick would suddenly appear on the floor from the gallery, waving his arms around like an impresario but in his amusing style that always made me smile. He would say, 'Hello, campers! Are we all doing the same programme here?' This was another reason for having another fitness professional observing our every move.

***

One day when Janet was staying with us at the Old Rectory, working on my next video, she noticed in our local newspaper an advertisement for a country house for sale – Quorn House. This amazing Georgian mansion was being offered for sale at what could only be described as 'a snip'. While still costing a vast amount of money, it did include 147 acres (59 ha) of magnificent parkland, had its own lake and a gatehouse, and was situated in the heart of the highly desirable village of Quorn near Loughborough. Without question, it appeared to be amazing value. I had always loved big houses. One day when I was in my early teens, my mother and I went to a garden party at a country mansion, and I remember sitting on a blanket for our picnic and looking at the magnificence of the architecture and the grandeur of the size and imagining what it must be like to live somewhere like that – and Quorn House caught my eye and my imagination. So much so that I called the estate agent the very next day. Mike thought I was bonkers but agreed to a viewing, just for the fun of it.

We viewed the property the following Saturday afternoon. I was very excited as we drove past the gatehouse and over the bridge that spanned the lake and up the most magnificent tree-lined drive to see the impressive Georgian building that was Quorn House. But when we realised that we were the 10th potential purchaser to view the house that day, we acknowledged that it would be quickly snapped up. In addition, as we walked around the property, we realised how much work needed to be done. Wallpaper was hanging off the walls, there was obvious damp, the wiring was old and it was clear that it would not be right for us to live in. And anyway, why did we want to move? Our Old Rectory was immaculate. Why on earth would we want to leave a house where everything that could be done had been done by the previous owners and take on a property that needed so much work? So we dismissed the idea of Quorn House and got on with our very busy lives.

Some six months later, Quorn House was advertised again, now with £100,000 shaved off the asking price. Apparently, various potential buyers had been unable to get planning permission for whatever they were hoping to create, and the property simply had to be sold.

The Farnham family had lived in Quorn House since it was built in Georgian times. In addition, earlier generations had lived in a previous house on the same land for the last 800 years. Sadly, the family now urgently needed to sell.

I don't know what it was but, somehow, I knew we were meant to buy it. I rang the estate agent to find out what was happening and then I blurted out, 'I don't know what we're going to do with it, but I'm sure we're going to buy it. I'll get back to you.'

I discussed it with Mike and he thought I was crazy, but I just couldn't let it go. I lay in bed each night racking my brains as to what we could use it for. Perhaps I could run loads of classes there? Perhaps we could make it into a place where people could stay to lose weight?

Almost a week of restless nights followed. Finally, on the Saturday night, it came to me: we should create a national network of franchised Diet & Fitness Clubs, and Quorn House would be the training centre. Quorn House was perfectly placed in the Midlands. Everybody wanted my diet books and fitness videos; now we could take my diet and fitness plans into the community with fully qualified franchisees! *That was it!*

I hardly slept that night because I was so excited. As soon as Mike stirred next morning I blurted out, bursting with enthusiasm, 'I think I've mapped out our future! Why don't we start a franchise of Diet & Fitness Clubs and use Quorn House as the training centre? Janet could be our Teacher Trainer and it could be amazing!'

Thankfully, Mike immediately saw the potential and loved the idea. He offered to drive me to Harrogate where I was to appear at an event and, on the way, we rang Janet and put the idea to her. She was very excited too, and the following day I called our accountant, Stewart Collier (who was a partner in the accountancy firm where I used to work as Mark Rees's secretary all those years ago), and then our family lawyer, to ask for their opinion. They thought it would be a great idea too! Our lawyer suggested we talk to a Franchising Consultant he knew: Dr Brian Smith.

Dr Smith lived in Leicestershire and was one of the original founders of the British Franchise Association and was highly respected. We invited him to talk to us and we explained our idea.

'And how many franchises do you expect to sell in your first year?' he asked.

'About a hundred,' we suggested.

He laughed. 'I've worked in franchising for over 30 years and the most franchises ever sold in one year is 12. But, despite your over-optimistic forecast, I think you could make a great success of this because you already have a lot of experience in running classes and, with your diet and fitness programmes proving so popular, I think this would do very well.'

Having given his first hour of advice free of charge, Dr Smith went on to explain that he charged £1,000 a day for his services. We were very fortunate that we were in a sound financial position and so we were happy to invest. We wanted to get this right. We were very encouraged by Dr Smith's constructive advice and opinion. We also felt we would be in safe hands. Dr Brian Smith had been a franchisee and a franchisor in his long and distinguished career so could not have been better qualified to help us. He also lived locally and we liked him. He was amusing, always telling us anecdotes and stories of his experiences. One explanation he often gave was about commitment. He explained that 'commitment is a bit like an English breakfast – the hen's involved but the pig's committed!' We enjoyed Brian's company and soon became firm friends with him and his delightful wife Rika, who had also been a successful franchisor in her own right.

Before we leapt into buying Quorn House, Mike felt we should test the market, despite the fact that our financial advisers felt sure our idea would work. I was frustrated because I just wanted to jump into making an offer, but Mike, quite rightly, saw it as a big commitment and not a decision that should be taken in a hurry. We also needed to see if anyone would be interested in taking a franchise.

Our first step was to place an advertisement in the *Mail on Sunday* in early January 1993. It read along these lines:

Franchises available
Rosemary Conley Diet & Fitness Clubs
For more information write to . . .

Within a week we received over 300 requests for more details. The *Sunday Express* called and asked if we would like to place an advertisement with that newspaper too. We did and we received hundreds more enquiries. It was so exciting.

Initially, we wrote to everyone who enquired with a letter saying, 'Thank you for your interest in our franchise. We will be in touch shortly.'

Surely now, we could proceed with the purchase of Quorn House? But no. Mike was having second thoughts about it on all levels. Even to the point of looking at other houses instead! This we did over the coming weeks, but nothing came close to the suitability of Quorn. In the meantime, it was reported in the local press that Quorn House was going to be turned into a school! Oh no! 'Please, God. Don't let that happen,' I prayed.

With so much interest in our franchised Diet & Fitness Clubs, we had to swiftly prepare a prospectus. Brian Smith worked with us and we carefully went through the whole process of what we needed to include so that we could charge the potential franchisee appropriately. Then we needed to investigate the equipment and marketing campaign he or she would need to launch the business successfully – and everything else required to run it, including a professional music player (there was no wireless technology in those days), a music licence, insurance, advertising, leaflets, and so on and so forth! It is important to remember that this was before the development of social media, and even mobile phones weren't commonplace.

It was decided that the initial package for franchisees would include the licence fee for operating under the Rosemary Conley name, their accommodation while they attended our training course (which would take place over several months) and everything else they needed to launch, and initially run, their business. In addition, they would pay us a fee for each class they ran, and they had to run a minimum of nine classes a week.

If there was one important lesson I had learned from my IPC experience nine years earlier, it was that we should charge the franchisees a flat fee per week per class. If they were very successful, the franchisees could earn a lot of money but we would also get a fair return. And our share in their success would be a small margin made on the New Member Packs that they would be contractually obliged to buy from us.

Of course, it would take time for someone's business to build and, under the terms of the Franchise Agreement, he or she would not be allowed to have another job. This was why we always checked that new franchisees were financially secure to the point where they could afford not to work during their training period and the business-building stage.

We were particularly careful in selecting people who we believed would excel in their business. For example, we had to turn away caring fathers who were ready with their chequebooks to set up their daughter in what they believed would be 'the perfect business for her', except that we knew it wasn't. The last thing we wanted was for anyone to fail, and we did everything we could to avoid that.

The reason we insisted that franchisees should run a minimum of nine classes a week was to ensure they could earn sufficient income. These classes would be held within a designated territory which included a certain number of people, and this territory would be exclusive to them.

Brian was golden in his advice and worth every penny of his substantial fees. He recommended a specialist franchising lawyer, Gordon Harris of Wragge & Co., to create a fair and robust Franchise Agreement. In addition, Stewart Collier, our accountant, helped us with our business plan, not just for the prospective franchisees but also for us. In total, we invested no less than £50,000 in advice before we launched our business. As you only have one chance to make a first impression, we were determined to get it right first time.

Having carefully created our prospectus, we then wrote to all those who had shown interest in the franchising opportunity, explaining the cost and the time commitment. If they were still interested, they were invited to a 'presentation day' in late February. The prospectus also explained that potential franchisees attending the presentation day would be asked to participate in a short fitness class in order that they could be assessed for their suitability as exercise teachers. This may sound unusual, but if you are going to teach exercise to music it is fundamental that you can move to the beat of the music. And some people simply can't, which can frequently be noticed on a dance floor! To teach nine classes a week our franchisees needed to hear the beat naturally, have rhythm and be able to cue the next move while still executing the last one.

At the end of February we welcomed 60 potential franchisees to our presentation day at the Holiday Inn in Leicester. We explained every aspect of the business, and all our advisers were there to answer any questions – our accountant, lawyer and, of course, Dr Brian Smith. Janet Thompson had agreed to come on board as our Fitness Teacher Trainer and, while I led a short programme of exercise, Janet assessed each participant's movement quality.

For those attendees who were still interested in progressing further, there was then a brief interview to quickly assess their suitability. If they met our criteria, they were invited to attend a full interview with Mike and myself. Some 26 eager potential franchisees, from this first presentation day, returned for their interview, after which Mike and I would make our decision. It would have been so easy to accept everyone, but it was very important to us to only offer our franchise to people who we honestly thought would have the right personality to attract and retain their members, be good ambassadors for the brand, work hard, be successful at running their own business and genuinely care about their members. It was a lot to ask, but we were confident we could achieve it. In the end, 19 out of the 26 signed up to be our first franchisees.

The interviewing process was exhausting. Over the following couple of weeks, Mike and I took a meeting room at the Holiday Inn. Each potential franchisee was invited with a husband or partner, and we would spend three hours following a protocol laid down by our franchise guru, Brian. It worked. Occasionally we would have a difference of opinion, but Mike always won and I couldn't question his wisdom when later he explained why 'Suzy' or 'Sally' wasn't suitable. He has always been very good at making intuitive judgments, especially of people's characters.

On some days, we were doing three or four interviews and, as we drove home, we would always call Brian and tell him how we had got on – 'There were two good ones today, Brian! Really fabulous women!' – and Brian was like a proud father. He was always so supportive, so interested in our lives and our business. He cared a great deal and gave us continual encouragement. I have come to realise that choosing the right people as your advisers, inner circle of friends and trusted professional colleagues is one of the most important secrets of success.

9

Launching the Clubs
1993

In the middle of all this frantic activity, Mike and I had been invited to stay with Nancy DeMoss (the person behind the *Power for Living* book) in the United States. This had come about because we had been introduced to the Argentinian evangelist Luis Palau, who was speaking at an event in Birmingham. When we explained to him that reading *Power for Living* had made a tremendous impact on us, he said that he knew the people behind the book, and he then relayed the message to Nancy DeMoss in the USA. Soon afterwards, we were invited to afternoon tea with Nancy DeMoss in London.

It was wonderful to meet Nancy in person and we enjoyed a delightful tea together. Later that afternoon, Nancy invited Mike and me to stay with her in the United States and asked me to speak at some 'brunches' that she would organise. I had never spoken publicly about my faith before, but Nancy assured me that she would give me guidance on how I might do it.

A few months later, Mike and I flew to the States to stay with Nancy and to speak at the first event that she had arranged. To be honest, we were completely astonished at the response to my testimony of how God had changed my life, and we were all very encouraged.

After a second memorable brunch in Tampa where I shared my experience with another enthusiastic audience, Mike and I left Nancy to fly to Atlanta, Georgia, to visit some friends. The plan was for us then to fly on from there to Philadelphia for the final brunch organised by Nancy.

We arrived at the home of our friends, Flo and George, and spent a very happy couple of days with them. However, we woke up on our last day, 13 March 1993, to find that overnight a freak blizzard had hit the city. Snowfall in Atlanta didn't usually exceed 1 in. (2.5 cm) in a year, but this event had broken all records. It was described as the 'worst blizzard of the last hundred years' and is still talked about in terms of 'Where were you in the blizzard of '93?' The city almost ground to a halt as the snow was so deep! And on top of that, our scheduled flight to Philadelphia had been cancelled. Fortunately, another flight suddenly became available; at the time, this seemed almost miraculous. We made it to the final event, against all the odds, and yet again it was a remarkable occasion.

Through these wonderful events, many people prayed the same prayer that Mike and I had prayed some years earlier. Nancy was very moved by the response and so were we. She suggested that I should speak at similar events throughout the UK. A British version of *Power for Living* was printed to include my testimony, and I was able to give out copies to many people who came to those events and were eager to hear how God had changed my life.

Nancy was such an encouragement. Over the many years that followed, I spoke at numerous churches on all manner of occasions, and the *Power for Living* book was always given out to everyone attending. I still very much enjoy speaking at events to share my faith journey – and handing out copies of *Power for Living*. (For more information, see p. 334.)

After our amazing experience with Nancy, we flew back to the UK in something of a daze at what had happened over the previous couple of weeks. We had been made so welcome by everyone we met and had found a very special friend in Nancy.

***

Meanwhile, back in the UK it didn't take long to launch our first three franchisees: Hayley Humphries in High Wycombe, Mandy Skeggs in St Albans and Kim Imerfreys in Wolverhampton. As they were already qualified to teach exercise to music, their training course only needed to cover how to run their business. These three fabulous women launched their franchises after Easter to eager new members who were flocking to their classes. It was so exciting for them and for us. It was also encouraging for the remaining 16 franchisees who were undergoing their lengthy training.

We were holding our training courses at a local hotel and it didn't take long for Mike to see that the business was working; so, at last, he suggested we make an offer on Quorn House. Mysteriously, it seemed to have waited for us! The school owners who were interested in buying it had changed their mind, and our offer was accepted.

As the lawyer went through the process of the property searches, a previously unknown fact emerged, and this explained why the price was so low: the property did not own the mineral rights for the granite that was under the 147 acres (59 ha) of land.

Emotionally and physically, we felt we had gone too far to turn back, so when we were told that we didn't own the mineral rights I wasn't too concerned and, thankfully, Mike didn't seem unduly worried either. We considered that the quarry half a mile away would never get planning permission to mine on the land, so we reckoned it was a risk worth taking.

It was decided by our accountant that it would be less strain on the company if we were to purchase Quorn House ourselves through a personal pension fund. This would mean the business would only have to pay rent, and it would give us an opportunity to invest in our long-term future.

In between all this excitement, my life continued to be ridiculously busy and my *Complete Hip and Thigh Diet* remained persistently on the *Sunday Times* bestseller list. My BBC TV series was commissioned for just a couple of years and then I went on to *Pebble Mill at One* with Anne Diamond and Nick Owen, but soon I was approached by ITV to join the team on *This Morning* with Richard Madeley and Judy Finnigan. The only problem was that the show was transmitted live from Liverpool – four hours' drive away.

This Morning was, and still is, a massively popular programme, so it was exciting to become part of it, and it was perfect timing for me to have weekly exposure on terrestrial television just as we were launching the Clubs. I managed to negotiate, as part of my fee for my weekly slot, a special arrangement for transport: a car would collect me from home at 5 am to take me to the studio by 9 am, and then, after the show, I could have the use of the car and the driver for as long as I wanted for the rest of the day.

When we originally launched the Clubs, I promised the franchisees that during the first year of operation I would visit every single one of them at one of their classes. Having a car and a driver at my disposal once a week was fantastic. We have to remember that this was years before laptops and tablets had been invented; so, with books to write longhand and copious amounts of mail to deal with (I would dictate my responses into a small Dictaphone), this arrangement meant that in a day I could achieve a huge amount of work in the car and then, in the evening, I could visit one of our franchisees. The members loved seeing me, particularly after I had been on TV in the morning and, of course, the franchisees appreciated my interest.

While they were long days, they were great fun too. On one particular day, after a 5 am start I didn't get back home until one o'clock the next morning because we'd visited a class in Surrey that evening. Fortunately, my driver was a joy; he seemed perfectly happy to get such a big driving job and he had a sleep in between my appointments so that he could drive safely.

Meanwhile, the Editors of two leading Sunday magazines were pressing me to sell them the serialisation rights for my next book. Usually, serialisation rights are sold by the publisher, but I had such a good relationship with the press that I continued to take on this role myself. In return, I asked for a bigger percentage cut of the serialisation fees paid to the book publisher, and they were happy to agree to that.

I was writing a book called *Shape Up for Summer* – a small paperback that would help people to shed a few pounds ready for their holiday and give them some exercises to do on the beach. The *Mail on Sunday's You* magazine and the *Sunday Express* magazine both wanted it very badly, so I asked them to place their best bid in a sealed envelope to arrive by 12 noon on Thursday the following week, and to include in their offer 12 pages of colour advertising for our new Diet & Fitness Clubs in their magazine – to be taken within the next 12 months.

The *Sunday Express* came back with a six-figure sum for the serialisation but was unable to offer the free advertising. The *Mail on Sunday* came back with a slightly lesser figure but agreed to the free advertising, so I accepted that offer. This was just what we needed to help us launch the Clubs and it was the perfect audience too. To justify the investment, the editor asked me to undertake some *You* magazine 'Roadshow' days which they would organise. They were great fun and a real pleasure to do over the following 12 months. The *Sunday Express* was disappointed but understood why I had taken the option with the *Mail on Sunday*.

Selling serialisation rights usually involved appearing in a TV commercial for that week's edition. This was always great fun too. For *Shape Up for Summer* I walked into a studio in a normal building that had been turned into a very realistic beach! The unlikely star of the 30-second ad was the comedian Les Dawson, which was a wonderful surprise. What a charming man he was! I didn't have to do much – just say a couple of sentences, which thankfully were on autocue. TV advertisements were always exciting to do as they had such high production values. No expense was spared and they seemed to have a crew of thousands!

With TV advertising to promote the serialisation of *Shape Up for Summer,* and advertisements for our Clubs placed in the magazine and reaching a national readership, this was just the exposure we needed to launch the Clubs. It had a significant impact and everyone was very happy.

***

The process of purchasing Quorn House involved getting planning permission to convert the Grade II-listed building from a domestic dwelling into offices. Apart from moving the entrance from the road by a few yards, which proved no problem, we had to set about finding a builder, electrician and plumber to renovate the house so that we could turn it into offices and a training centre. We allocated a budget of £250,000 to the whole renovation work, including the decoration. Remarkably, and thankfully, all the tradespeople kept to their quotes and everything was done within budget and on time.

We were very grateful to the fashion and homeware company Laura Ashley, which sponsored the decorating and furnishing of the drawing room and of the main hall situated in the centre of the house. With its magnificent cantilevered oak staircase, and high glass ceiling allowing natural light to fall on the oak panelling throughout the hall, you couldn't help but admire the architecture of such a fine building. In fact, the hall had such a high ceiling it took one whole roll of wallpaper to run from the top to the bottom of the staircase at its highest point.

A stylist from Laura Ashley, Alison Brind, designed the interiors (curtains, soft furnishings, wallpaper) throughout the whole house, and I bought all the furniture and pictures at auction. I didn't have time to attend the weekly sales, but I viewed the lots every Thursday evening prior to the Friday sale and placed my maximum bid on any item I thought would work within the house. I developed a great relationship with the auctioneer at Churchgate Auctions in Leicester, who helped me select special items and gave me guide prices for anything that took my fancy. Then it was enormous fun when, on the following Monday, the auction house delivered my successful bids. The items would be cleaned up and positioned around Quorn House, and soon the rooms looked elegant and welcoming. There was even a large bust of Beethoven rather appropriately placed above the carved fireplace in the library where our students would learn how to become qualified diet and exercise-to-music teachers.

The house looked amazing, yet it was furnished on a shoestring. Our massive boardroom table cost £10, and the sideboard in the drawing room, £30. The magnificent library had beautiful oak shelving – but no books; so I ordered 1,800 volumes from a book dealer with the only stipulation that their covers should be red, blue, green or yellow to tone in with the original, and valuable, William Morris wallpaper that had adorned the walls for the last century. I realise that book-lovers may feel that a 'designer library' like this, perfectly colour-coded, is somewhat questionable from a literary point of view – but it looked fabulous. Everywhere you looked in Quorn House, there was improvisation and impact, achieved at remarkably low prices. The huge table where our students would sit as they were taught everything from anatomy to accountancy was a converted snooker table costing just a few pounds.

When it was all completed, the final refurbishment was featured in the *Mail on Sunday*'s *You* magazine with an acknowledgment to Laura Ashley.

The exercise studio required little furnishing because we needed empty space in which to train our franchisees how to teach exercises, but the room featured a most magnificent fireplace and was also adorned with elaborate coats-of-arms denoting the Farnham family's ancestral marriages dating back to the 1400s, all encased within the oak panelling that surrounded the room.

The kitchen was redesigned as a TV kitchen so that cameras and lighting could fit around the cooking area. And upstairs there were 10 bedrooms, a mezzanine floor, and an attic where presumably servants had lived in times gone by, all of which became our offices.

The whole project took seven months, but we were able to move out of our Mountsorrel office into the first two refurbished rooms within a couple of months. With so much work going on, not surprisingly it was very dusty and grimy, but gradually Quorn House was taken back to its former glory and emerged as a magnificent training centre and headquarters for our exciting new business. It seemed very strange moving from our tiny two-up, two-down offices in Mountsorrel into a mansion, but it didn't take long before the staff numbers grew significantly.

As soon as the Quorn House sale had been agreed, I rang Martin, our painter friend, to invite him and his wife Dolores and family to live in the gatehouse at the entrance to the property. Martin and Dolores lived in the centre of Leicester and, knowing their love of animals and the countryside, we felt the gatehouse would be ideal for them. They moved in soon afterwards and it worked wonderfully for them and for us. It meant we had someone on site all the time and they could enjoy the grounds – all 147 acres (59 ha). Dolores became our housekeeper and Martin combined his decorating activities with duties as gatekeeper and general handyman. They were terrific and helped us with the numerous tasks that presented themselves over the next 21 years.

***

Meanwhile, the *Shape Up for Summer* book was given unbelievable promotion by the Editors of the *Mail on Sunday*. At the same time as the book was hitting the headlines by being serialised in *You* magazine, they also promoted the fact that I was appearing on *This Morning* every day the following week! Each day on the show, I gave a separate message from the book: creating poolside cocktails on one day, exercises for the beach on another, cooking healthy summer recipes, and so on. The benefit of this cross-fertilisation was quite extraordinary, and the book, like its predecessors, topped the charts.

Some time later, the editorial team at *The People*, another Sunday newspaper, asked me to write a weekly column for their *Yes* magazine. Mike and I went down to London for the meeting at Canary Wharf and met the Assistant Editor, Geri Hosier. She explained what they were looking for and I said that I was happy to do a weekly column but that I would require a very substantial figure plus, of course, free advertising for the Clubs.

At this point, Mike chipped in with, 'Don't worry – you'll get your money's worth!' I was very grateful that I had such a supportive husband.

Unlike most freelance contributors, I explained that I wanted to write my column in the paper's own offices. I would go to London one day a month, compile my recipes and meal planners, design my exercise programmes and find the photographs to illustrate them, and respond to readers' questions for the column. This idea was accepted – and it worked. In my crazy life I needed to be away from the rest of my world to concentrate on the job in hand. The magazine's food stylist and photographer would shoot the food and, just like magic, a comprehensive double-page spread would appear every Sunday! After a while, we decided to create a book from some of my columns, so *Be Slim, Be Fit* was published and again did really well.

But perhaps the most enjoyable part of my whole enterprise with *The People* was getting to know Geri Hosier. She was sparky and funny, with a great personality, and we just hit it off. I knew she didn't suffer fools gladly, but I was amused by her creative way with colourful language and we got on like a house on fire. Geri was always entertaining and fun and there was mutual respect between us.

Apparently, the increase in circulation was notable, so much so that a few weeks into my column being published, the Editors at *News of the World* approached me to write a column for them and asked, 'What would it cost us for you to break your contract with *The People*?'

I told them they could offer me £1 million but I wouldn't break my contract; however, I said they could contact me in nine months to have another chat. And indeed they did. I got a call from Rebekah Wade, the Features Editor, inviting me to go to lunch along with Phil Hall the

Deputy Editor, and the Editor Piers Morgan. They took me to The Ivy and we negotiated a very generous deal, and then, of course, I asked for some free advertising. I enjoyed writing my column for them for a couple of years or so once my contract with *The People* had expired, and I had a great relationship with them.

***

One of the disadvantages of moving from the BBC to ITV's *This Morning* was that the BBC could no longer produce and market my videos. I had recorded nine titles with the BBC, but now I was in a quandary. Mike and I decided we would create our own video, with Nick Patten (who had produced all my BBC productions) as a Freelance Director to produce it. We hired a mobile gallery and recorded the workout in the drawing room at Quorn House. But then we had a problem: we didn't have the ability to distribute and retail it through the shops. That's when I called Paul Hembury, from Video Collection International (VCI), for some help. Paul was a Director of an independent company and had contacted me previously, but I had told him I wasn't interested as I was already with the BBC. Now I picked up the phone, holding a great big piece of 'humble pie', and asked meekly if he could help us. Thankfully he did and the video was launched. It was not as successful as previous ones, but it didn't matter; we had now forged a new working relationship that would span many years into the future.

Meanwhile, my publishers wanted to release my next book, *Rosemary Conley's Flat Stomach Plan*, that autumn, and the discussions commenced regarding serialisation. With my weekly column in *Yes* magazine, which was the colour magazine supplement to their Sunday newspaper, the Editors at *The People* were keen to take first serialisation rights; but because the book was a 28-day plan, they decided to do a collaboration with their sister paper, *The Mirror*. It was a massive undertaking as they serialised an edited version of the text for all 28 days! To support it, there was a TV advertising campaign. Then the *Mail on Sunday*'s *You* magazine bought second rights and did it all over again! The book could not have been given a bigger launch.

In the meantime, ready for the following January, we had produced a new video programme. It was given massive publicity by the people at VCI, who appeared to be really glad to have me on board, and Paul Hembury could not have been more supportive. They launched a comprehensive TV advertising campaign, and on *This Morning* we did a daily strand based on the video, again for a whole week. Both the book and the video were number-one bestsellers and sold hundreds of thousands of copies.

Life was frantic. Exciting. Writing books, appearing on TV every week, creating my column, recording videos, recruiting and training franchisees, running the business and moving forward with the refurbishment of Quorn House – but still also taking my Monday evening classes. That was important to me. Mike and I were working flat out, and Mike was fully supportive and accommodating of my travelling and activities, and looked after things while I was out or away.

To help us separate home life and work life, we did three things.

1 We always changed when we arrived home, getting out of our smart work-clothes into casual gear.
2 We didn't talk about work at home.
3 We tried very hard to keep our weekends free to recharge our batteries.

I think this was the only way we survived.

It was an extraordinary time and it seemed as though everything we touched turned to gold. The Clubs were flourishing and I remember one franchisee calling us after her first class. She had turned up at her venue, a community centre, only to find the car park full. She was very worried about where her members would park, assuming that there was another function taking place in the same building. But no, she walked into her room to find 70 eager members queuing down the corridor! Such was the demand for our classes.

Ever since I was a child, I had loved raising money for charity. When I was asked to lead the warm-up for the first Race for Life in London, it occurred to me that we could encourage our members to participate in raising funds for cancer research. It took off wonderfully and the franchisees loved encouraging their members to take part. Not only did they enjoy raising thousands and thousands of pounds, but they were also thrilled to see how their weight loss and increased fitness had enabled them to achieve this. Many of our franchisees were asked to lead the warm-up in their locality before each race, which was an extraordinary privilege and they loved it. Some years later, we were presented with an award from Cancer Research UK because our franchisees had raised over £2 million for the charity!

***

Meanwhile, the royalties continued to flow in from my books and videos and all my other ancillary activities. While they were flowing, Mike and I made the decision not to take a salary out of the Clubs business but rather to leave that money in the company to invest in the continuing growth of the franchise. When you suddenly find yourself in an incredibly fortunate financial position, the question is where to invest wisely, and we decided to invest in property. After Mike and I had so enjoyed the challenge of buying Quorn House and refurbishing it, and had pulled it off without any disasters, we realised we weren't frightened of taking on an old and large property. Because of this, we decided to look for another big house somewhere nearer to Quorn than the Old Rectory – a 40-minute drive away – which might be an exciting challenge and at the same time become a beautiful place in which to live.

We started looking at a few interesting historic properties on the market as a bit of a weekend hobby. Ultimately, if we did find somewhere we liked, we hoped it would also be a good investment. The only problem was that it seemed that with every house we viewed, there was a major drawback – it was either too near the road, or structurally unsound (one house had a huge crack all the way down it!) or we just didn't like it.

Then our estate agents, Savills, told us about Ashby Folville Manor. It had only just come on the market and there were no printed details yet, and they weren't sure what the price was, but they felt it would be somewhere near our budget. We drove around the pretty village of Ashby Folville near Melton Mowbray and could only see the back corner of the house from the service entrance. It was a really grey and miserable day and the house looked dismal and uninviting from what we could see from the road.

We rang Savills and said no, we didn't like the look of it from the road in the centre of the village.

The agent immediately launched into a protest: 'Oh, but you *must* go to see it. It's a magnificent property! Please, just view it first before you say no.'

After such enthusiasm, we agreed to meet his colleague at the property the following weekend. When we met, we had to follow her out of the village and then up a magnificent chestnut-tree-lined drive for a quarter of a mile . . . over a beautiful bridge – and there it was. A property of fairy-tale proportions and beauty. Yes. It really was magnificent. Grand. Majestic. Extraordinary.

As we approached the fine front door, I asked the agent, 'Before we go in, we must know the price?'

To my disappointment, but not total surprise, the sum was way beyond our budget. I was glad I'd asked. My heart sank, and Mike immediately realised it was a no-hoper, but I suggested that we should still have a look around despite the fact that it was far above our limit.

As soon as we stepped into the vast and magnificent hall, with its exquisite staircase, enormous fireplace and chandelier, I was mesmerised. It was amazing. As we walked around all three floors, including the charming ballroom with an enchanting minstrels' gallery on the first floor, the beautiful 10 bedrooms, six bathrooms, including a flat, with views from every window over its 40+ acres (16+ ha) of garden and farmland, and a proper lift, I was entranced. But there was more. There was also a substantial two-bedroomed cottage in the grounds. We realised that this house was unlike any house we had ever seen before. In fact, it was truly a fairy-tale house, but sadly not for us.

We drove away inspired by the beauty of Ashby Folville Manor but deflated by the outcome. As we crossed the elegant bridge, I thought of the film *A Bridge Too Far*. Our dream house was just that – a dream.

10

The miracle of Mary

1993–5

One Friday night at the end of 1993, I was invited on to a late-night show on Central TV. *Central Weekend* was a bit like *The Jeremy Kyle Show* where the producers picked a subject, invited guests from opposing sides, put them in a room together and threw in a metaphorical grenade! Of course, when you are invited, it is not portrayed like that. 'We would love to have you on to talk about your very successful fitness videos,' they said and, on the basis that the programme was made nearby in Birmingham, I was up for the challenge.

As we waited in the green room, someone pointed out to me the fitness supremo Mary Morris, who was one of the founders (and now Chief Verifier) of the RSA Exercise to Music qualification. To me, as a newly qualified Fitness Instructor, Mary Morris was like a 'fitness god'. I was utterly in awe of her and, at the same time, felt really scared! Maybe she was one of those who had written to the BBC when I was teaching on my own show and giving wrong information? Oh, my goodness!

Soon it was time to be led in to the studio. Diana Moran (known as the Green Goddess), who was another fitness video celebrity, Jane Irving, who had become famous as a weather forecaster, and I were seated on the stage; opposite were two other people who had been brought in to 'oppose' us! Mary Morris was sitting in the front row of the audience, not on the stage. I learned later that Mary was supposed to be on the stage but had refused to do so when she realised that the plan was to 'rubbish' our fitness videos.

The presenters introduced the programme with some footage of the supermodel Elle Macpherson, whose exercise video, *Elle Macpherson: The Body Workout*, had received some criticism in the press. The point for discussion was 'Are fitness videos presented by unqualified celebrities dangerous?'

Of course, Diana Moran and I had both now qualified, so we were outraged that we were being questioned.

'Jamie', one of the 'opposition' guests, laid into me with accusations about the harmful effects of the fitness videos that I had recorded before I was qualified – which I knew were false.

I was incensed and leaned towards him, waved my finger at him and shouted, 'You show me *one* person who has been injured by any of my videos!' (Dawn told me afterwards, 'Mum, I've never seen you so cross!')

Jamie didn't ask me any more questions for the rest of the programme.

Diana was brilliant, of course, and between us we fought our corner robustly. However, after the programme was over, we were all very disappointed and felt that we had been 'stitched up'. There was a discussion about whether or not we should take action, but I was against it. It wasn't worth the effort or the energy. We'd all learned a lesson and survived.

Some weeks later, I was welcoming our new trainees for the last training course that would be held at the Holiday Inn, as Quorn House was fast approaching completion. All the RSA Exercise to Music courses were appraised by a verifier from the RSA Examination Board and I knew to expect the verifier any time that morning. Before we started each training course, it was our custom to collect payment from all of our trainees for the purchase of their franchise. On this day, just as the 12 trainees were handing me their cheques, who should walk in but Mary Morris, Chief Verifier! I don't think I have ever felt so embarrassed. I swiftly stuffed their cheques into my briefcase and then hurried away, leaving our Head of Training, Janet, in charge of the trainees.

Much to my astonishment, the following day Mary called me. She wanted to have a meeting with me as she had a business of her own, FitKid, and wanted to pick my brains about it. I was so surprised and, of course, delighted.

A few days later, Mary came to Quorn House and we chatted through her business activities. Apparently, she had seen how we operated our franchise and, after seeing me collecting the cheques from our trainees, instead of being shocked she had gone home and said to her husband,

Rod, 'We've done this all wrong. We should have charged our FitKid trainers money up front for the training and licence, just like Rosemary has!'

Mary and I chatted for a couple of hours. As we parted, I wasn't sure how helpful I had been, but at least I now realised that Mary was 'normal' and not an unapproachable 'fitness god' after all – just a lovely woman who was passionate about exercise and wanted it taught safely and effectively. And, no, she hadn't written to the BBC!

Recruiting new franchisees wasn't difficult. By the end of the year we had recruited 64 people and by January 1994 over 600 weekly classes would be running. The classes were proving so popular that our franchise opportunity was an obvious option for any potential entrepreneur with an interest in diet and fitness. We ran several training courses in that first year, and almost everyone launched a very successful business.

In December 1993 we decided to hold a Christmas party for all our franchisees and their partners at Quorn House, and it was like a house-warming celebration. With everyone dressed in full evening dress the event was spectacular – particularly as all our very fit franchisees looked so glamorous dressed up to the nines. And Quorn House looked magnificent too, its Grade II Georgian grandeur enjoying the glamour and hospitality that no doubt had been experienced as part of the lifestyle of the aristocratic family who had lived there in bygone years. The rooms were now decorated with Christmas trimmings, and a huge Christmas tree stood proudly in the corner of the central hall. Quorn House was such a happy place to be.

After all the extravagance of the festivities, we were grateful to have opportunities when we were reminded about what was important. In early 1994, Mike visited India with our special friends, Ian and Ruth Coffey. Ian was then a Baptist minister and the couple had lived nearby when we were at the Old Parsonage. Soon after we had become Christians, we started having Bible study evenings with them, together with some other friends. Ian and Ruth had connections in India, and they invited Mike to join them on one of their trips. Mike had always wanted to visit India, so this was the perfect opportunity. What he hadn't expected was to have the privilege of meeting Mother Teresa (now Saint Teresa of Calcutta). This was an amazing moment in his life – to be in the presence of such a loving and humble person. Some people reflect the beauty and character of God, and Mother Teresa was one of those people. Now, a beautiful photograph of Mike, Ian, Ruth and Mother Teresa hangs in our house, reminding him of that special day and, quite apart from that, a very memorable three-week trip. Mike had fallen in love with India and the country would always be in his heart.

Meanwhile I was at home, occupied with a variety of matters to do with promoting our business, but I have come to understand that there is no separation between business and faith, private and public activities; everything belongs together.

One day, I was in the office when I received a phone call from a repre-sentative of Kellogg's, inviting me to produce a fitness video for their Special K brand of breakfast cereal. Consumers would collect a number of packet tops and, for a very small sum, be sent a copy of the *Rosemary Conley Special K Health and Fitness Workout*. Kellogg's would pay me generously for my efforts, and the contract was signed.

Janet, who by now had relocated with her family to Leicestershire and was working full-time at Quorn House as our Head of Training, helped me choreograph the fitness programme for Special K, and soon we got into full rehearsal mode. For this video it was just me, so no backing dancers were required. Kellogg's hired the studios at ITV Central in Nottingham and off we went to record it.

All appeared to go well until three days later when I received a phone call from the video producer. The client, Kellogg's, was unhappy with the production as there appeared to be a black outline around my body as I exercised and they wanted to re-record it – soon! Presenting an exercise programme is really hard work and the very thought of redoing it was beyond belief! I didn't have time. I didn't have the energy. And it wasn't my fault. But they were adamant. So, after some reflection, I agreed to do it again, but I said they would have to pay me another 50% of the fee and they agreed. My diary was bonkers and the only day I could do it was the following Monday, but Janet wasn't free then because it was exam day for our trainee franchisees and they were all set to launch their businesses the following week.

Whenever I recorded my videos after I was qualified, I insisted that Janet would oversee it to ensure that I did everything technically correctly and to check that my instructions were clear and accurate. I didn't know what to do. Then I remembered Mary Morris. Having spent time with Mary to help her with her business, I felt comfortable about calling her and asking if she would step into the role of my Fitness Consultant the following Monday.

I learned later that she had a completely full diary that day but cleared it immediately to help me. We met at Central TV and I proceeded to present the fitness programme to camera.

Working with Mary was bliss. We worked so comfortably together and, while she made a few improvements to the programme, I was able to implement them easily. At the end of the day we felt very pleased with the enhanced finished product. But I hadn't anticipated what would happen next.

After we finished re-recording the programme, Mary and I walked back to the dressing room, and I thanked her profusely for everything she had done and told her how much I had enjoyed working with her. She had given me enormous encouragement and I hadn't been used to that.

Mary commented: 'The difference is I don't want to be in your place.'

Yes, it was a breath of fresh air for me to be working with someone who didn't yearn to be in the limelight. The Special K video was a great success and the Kellogg's bosses were happy, but best of all I had made a new friend.

I wasn't a natural exercise teacher despite my notable success. Ever since I was a child, I had struggled with memorising anything. I can recall standing in front of my class when I was five or six and being asked to say the days of the week; I was petrified as I struggled desperately to remember them. I have a good memory for facts, but memorising poetry, the words of a song, or a script – I just can't do it. I think that bit of my brain must be missing. I soon learned that the only way I could memorise anything was by endless repetition, so remembering things like the Lord's Prayer or the National Anthem is fine because I have said them so often. Consequently, I had to work really hard at memorising the exercise routines and the only way I could do it was by endless practice. I think this had often frustrated our Clubs' Fitness Trainer, Janet, who couldn't understand why I found it so difficult when she could remember things instantly. I also think she struggled with the fact that this somewhat mediocre Fitness Instructor was starring in very successful fitness videos; she would have given anything to be in my place. What Janet didn't understand was that maybe it was my mediocrity that made the difference. It was what the women who followed my videos liked. I was more like them.

I have always said that our franchisees were better teachers than I ever was, and I was always inspired to see them take their classes. Janet was an excellent trainer and our franchisees were testament to her skill.

***

Appearing weekly on *This Morning* brought many benefits, but perhaps the most exciting was being sent to faraway places to record series of 'strands' for the programme. This involved flying to some exotic location with a crew and then recording interesting facts and ideas in the form of six-minute films which would be shown each Wednesday on *This Morning*. In 1994 I was asked to visit the USA and the task was to investigate various brand-new weight-loss and fitness trends. 'Spinning' classes and 'line dancing' were among them.

While staying in Santa Monica, just outside Los Angeles, we would be filming on the beach and in gyms and exercise studios. When the Editor of *You* magazine for the *Mail on Sunday* found out I was going to LA, they asked if they could film my next TV commercial for their up-and-coming serialisation of my next book, *Beach Body Plan*. The producers of *This Morning* agreed.

On the day of filming, I was shown to my Winnebago next to the beach where my hair and make-up artists were waiting, surrounded by all the paraphernalia that accompanies making a television advertisement. We all prepared ourselves for a busy day.

The storyboard for the ad was that I would be carried on the shoulders of two Chippendale-type hunks while I delivered my lines to camera encouraging viewers to buy the *Mail on Sunday* that week if they wanted a beach body in time for summer. To my amazement the props team had even planted extra palm trees on the beach – even more perfect than the natural palms – to enhance the already idyllic image. These were the days when newspapers had big budgets! Next, I was introduced to my two hunky guys. I felt a bit uncomfortable, to be honest, as I think they were expecting an 18-year-old, size-zero supermodel, but instead they got me – a 47-year-old diet author.

These productions take for ever. The crew mark out where we will walk. Rehearse for lighting. Rehearse the camera angles. Rehearse the words. Eventually, they start recording – then they want to shoot it 20 times! On this occasion I had no problem remembering the words as I had to repeat them so often.

Unfortunately, what the recruitment team hadn't realised was that 'No.1 Mr Hunk' had a bad back and 'No.2 Mr Hunk' had a bad shoulder! I think they were expecting a Kylie-type, super-light slip of a girl, but alas they had to carry *me* on their shoulders! I felt like an elephant, despite only weighing about 8 st. (51 kg)!

To go with the serialisation of my *Beach Body Plan*, *You* magazine also did a photoshoot of me on the beach. It was all good fun.

The next part of the trip took me and the *This Morning* crew to the Golden Door – an exotic and exclusive health spa near San Diego in California. It was the most extraordinary place where the rich and famous went to relax and shed a few pounds. We really enjoyed filming in such an exquisite location. While I was there, the management team kindly invited me back for a week's holiday.

Having taken up their kind invitation, a few months later I was luxuri-ating on my own at the Golden Door among the palm trees, marvelling at the hummingbirds flickering their wings a million times a minute, when my phone rang. It was Mike.

Apparently, Janet had taken the opportunity while I was away to ask Mike if they could go for a curry. She wanted to tell him that she had decided to resign as our Fitness Trainer because she wanted to start up her own fitness club with her husband.

When Janet and her husband relocated to Leicestershire, as part of the package we had offered him a job too. He worked with us as our administrator but didn't stay long. He had been used to running his own business and now he wanted to do it again – but this time with his wife.

This was devastating news as we had to have a Fitness Trainer. In desperation I immediately rang Mary Morris. I didn't know who else to call. I knew she was attending a convention for fitness professionals the following week and I thought she would be the perfect person to find us a replacement for Janet. She knew what we did and the standards we maintained, so who better to ask?

Much to my astonishment, the next day Mary called Mike to say *she* wanted to apply for the job herself! I couldn't believe it. Not only was she one of the best Fitness Trainers in the land, but I had already worked with her and we had got along so well. I knew I would love to have her on board, although I still couldn't imagine that she would want to give up her current job of running her own health club with her husband. But apparently she did. We paid a very generous salary for this important position in our company, and Mary could see the practical sense, and a great opportunity, if she were to join us.

Mary is completely unselfish in her attitude to fitness. She is passionate about getting the British people off their sofas, and when she co-founded the RSA Exercise to Music course it was to help more Fitness Trainers to teach safe and effective exercise to the unfit community. She saw Rosemary Conley Diet & Fitness Clubs as the perfect pathway to reaching tens of thousands of people, and this excited her. What impressed her most was the fact that in our organisation *every* instructor was professionally qualified, unlike other companies where just one professional instructor would be employed and that person would pass on his or her knowledge to the fitness-training staff.

When Mike told me the news, I just couldn't believe Mary Morris would be working for us! In fact, I didn't believe it until the day Mary walked through the door at Quorn House to take up her new role as Head of Training and Development. Her husband and daughters, both Fitness Instructors, would take over the running of their health club and Mary would be working full-time for us. I was so excited.

After my luxurious time at the Golden Door, I stayed overnight in a hotel in San Diego in readiness for my flight home the following day. The hotel was enormous. I had never seen such a vast dining room; when full, it must have accommodated around 800 people. There were only about 20 people having dinner when I was there and I relished the fact that, having spent a week eating super-healthy diet food, I could now treat myself. I might just have a dessert! The carrot cake looked particularly enticing, so I decided that, because I was safe from onlookers who knew who I was, I would indulge. This was something I couldn't do in public in the UK because it would cause comment.

I enjoyed every mouthful of that cake and revelled in the feeling of freedom from 'big brother' – no-one was watching this dieting guru breaking all the rules. It was strangely liberating. The carrot cake was utterly delicious and I treasured the taste of every crumb as it slipped down my throat.

Next morning, the courtesy bus was ready to transport passengers to the airport. As I sat on a long seat looking at the passengers on the opposite side, a woman smiled and said, 'It's Rosemary Conley, isn't it?'

I smiled back and said 'Yes', to which she said, 'I thought it was you – we saw you in the restaurant last evening.'

Oh no! I thought, riddled with guilt!

She went on, 'I go to one of your classes in Essex.'

A feeling of shame swept over me as I imagined her regaling her next class with the tale of my devouring a giant piece of carrot cake. In fact, I remember that feeling every time I'm tempted by a carrot cake today!

***

Having Mary join us meant that our franchisees were going to get the very best training available and our teachers would be among the best in the UK. In addition, I was going to have a new choreographer for my videos. I knew we would work brilliantly together.

Mary created a new training programme specifically for our members, adapting the course to ensure that our franchisees could safely and effectively teach a class full of members with very mixed abilities. After all, someone who weighs 18 st. (114 kg) will find some exercises difficult, so adaptations would be necessary. All the participants would need to be taught appropriately, no matter what their age or fitness ability, within a class environment. To assist in the training and to help the franchisees fully understand the potential challenges of exercising when overweight, we bought 'fat jackets' weighing 20 lb (9 kg) for the trainees to wear while they exercised. Mary was determined to produce teachers to the highest standard and, as a company, we were right behind her.

Quorn House was now fully functional, so we held our presentation days (when we met potential franchisees) and franchisee training courses there, which made life much easier. Our staff numbers had increased significantly, but time was our enemy when it came to recruiting staff. Brian said we now needed Franchise Support Managers to help manage our network, as well as a General Manager, as it was all getting too much for Mike and me. At Brian's suggestion we called on the services of a Recruitment Consultant, who handled the advertising and initial interviews and then presented us with his shortlist of candidates. It was a very effective way to recruit staff for key roles.

By now I had a very lovely Personal Assistant (PA), Louise, who brought sunshine into our already glorious offices. Louise had won prizes for elocution at school and was full of personality. She had a wonderful telephone manner, lots of confidence and was perfect for organising my hectic life. She had worked as PA to the Managing Director (MD) of a major book publisher in London and had moved up to Leicester to live. As the business had developed, my original secretary, Di, moved over to run the administration office and Angie, who had joined Mike and me in our office at the top of the Old Parsonage six years previously, was now running the accounts office as that was her area of expertise.

The company was growing very fast, and my workload with it, so we soon appointed Melody as my secretary. She helped type up my books and lots more. This was still before the age of even laptops, let alone tablets, and I always wrote my books in longhand or dictated them. Despite the lack of time-saving technology back then, I had learned to become very efficient with my time and not a moment was wasted. Whether I was being driven in my car, or travelling by train or on a plane, I worked. Since the original *Hip and Thigh Diet* was written, I had written 10 further books and presented 11 fitness videos, and these were created in between all my many other activities, including my weekly appearance on *This Morning*, which was always a highlight. I loved it all and I didn't mind working my socks off.

I adored working with Richard and Judy on *This Morning* as they were consummate professionals. Every programme was fun and exciting, and I loved meeting the amazing celebrities who appeared on the show. One morning, I was walking through the studio to prepare food that I would be cooking on air later, only to see Michael Ball, just a few feet away, singing 'Love Changes Everything' from the popular musical *Aspects of*

Love. It was truly a magical and memorable moment that I will never forget.

Mike had taken over the franchisee-interviewing process, which he did with our new General Manager, Simon Ford. Simon had been the MD for Esso Tanzania but was now living in the UK; he quickly grasped the ethos and the principles of our business and we worked very well together.

Fortunately, we had no trouble recruiting staff. We paid well and were considerate employers, and we didn't expect people to work beyond their hours. In addition, Quorn House provided an idyllic environment in which to work: fabulous architecture, newly decorated offices upstairs, with views out of every window across our magnificent expanse of land and lake called Quorn Park. With swans on the water, and foxes as large as German Shepherds (because they had the park to themselves) trotting across the fields, it was glorious. Not surprisingly, there was a delightful atmosphere and the whole place was buzzing, particularly when TV or video filming was happening. It was especially exciting when the occasional celebrity visited us to be interviewed as part of a TV show I was presenting.

One day we recorded *Cash in the Celebrity Attic* with Gloria Hunniford. Any cash raised from this episode was given to Steps, a charity of which I am Patron. Because the surroundings were so impressive, and the miscellaneous goods which I had acquired from the auction house were varied and interesting, the episode proved very popular and was shown on TV about six times! I think it was because it all looked so grand.

About 18 months into the franchising business, Mike and I, having not taken a salary, decided to treat ourselves to a company car each. Mike bought a brand-new BMW. I chose a second-hand Bentley, which looked very fine with the ROS 1E number plate I had bought some years earlier. The royalties and advances from the books and videos, the fees from the various serialisations, plus my weekly column for the *News of the World* meant that our income was a bit bonkers and we didn't need to take money out of the Clubs business. We weren't running the franchise operation with a view to making a fortune; we just wanted to do it because there was a demand for what we were offering and we wanted to put Quorn House to work and, of course, we felt there was a good business opportunity.

While I felt self-conscious about my Bentley initially, it turned out that the staff and the franchisees liked to see that the company was doing well. It gave them confidence. I soon fell in love with that special car because, despite its size, it was effortless to drive and made my many long journeys significantly more pleasurable. I didn't think twice about going shopping in it and, quite apart from me, Nik and Sheba loved sitting on their specially made seat cover. On one occasion when I had parked in the centre of Leicester, I was just coming back to my car as my time on the parking ticket was about to expire. The traffic warden was hovering and, as he came close to the Bentley, Nik went crazy, barking ferociously at him. Thankfully, he quietly slipped away. I never did get a parking ticket on that car!

Because of my increased need to travel and my ever-growing workload, having a freelance chauffeur was invaluable. I was being invited to various Christian events all over the UK to speak about my faith and how God had changed my life. However, attending such events often meant I was out late, and Mike was much happier that I had a professional driver looking after me on these occasions. My driver, David, took all the strain, and I used every second of my journeys to dictate my letters, write my column or work on my next book.

Everything was turning out wonderfully well. Mary, as Head of Training and Development, was amazing and we loved working together on the choreography for my next video. Despite such a hectic life, I still enjoyed taking my own classes on a Monday evening and they proved to be a perfect testing ground for each new video. If my members could follow the routines, we knew they would work for people following the video at home. Teaching my classes also helped me to memorise the choreography so that, when it came time to record the videos, the moves appeared more natural.

Mary and I also decided to write a script for each new programme which I would then read off on autocue. Not only would this prove less stressful for me than trying to remember all the routines, but it also meant that we could include more teaching points. This was a significant undertaking and took us two days to prepare, but it was worth it. We both recognised the importance of giving clear instructions for every move and action. This made the videos a more enjoyable experience for the viewers, like participating in a 'class' – but in their living room. Our backing dancers were trained to demonstrate the moves at varying degrees of intensity to accommodate all the abilities and fitness levels of our viewers. A fitness video programme has to be enjoyable and effective, and I also recognised that it shouldn't be irritating, so I always recorded mine very 'straight'. No jokes or funny bits, because after the first couple of times of hearing those quips they quickly lose their humour. I wanted people to be happy to follow my programmes dozens of times, not just once or twice – and I know they did.

While we had done some Roadshows before, they reached a whole different level when Mary came on board. Just to explain, our Roadshows involved inviting franchisees and their members to join us for a day in a large venue where they could work out and learn more about diet and fitness. Mary and I gave motivational talks and provided education on weight loss and fitness, and the participants joined in a couple of workouts led by both Mary and me. What I hadn't realised was that Mary is a natural entertainer! She was so enthusiastic in the way she educated our attendees, and she was really comical in the way she delivered her health messages – like an actor. Everybody loved her. I wasn't surprised to learn some years later that she had won a place to study at the Royal Academy of Dramatic Art (RADA) in London, but she decided to pursue a career in teaching and qualified in physical education instead.

The crowds adored Mary, and our Roadshows became popular, energy-filled, happy days for everyone. Our Franchise Development Managers manned the stall, selling my books and videos, and members queued up for autographs and photographs. It was lovely to meet, face to face, the people who had benefited from our diet and fitness programmes, and it was a credit to our franchisees that they had achieved so much weight loss and such fitness. At the end of each Roadshow, we would invite everyone who had lost 3 st. (19 kg) or more to join us on the stage. We weren't minimising the importance of losing less than 3 st., but there wouldn't have been enough room for them all! It was so rewarding to hear the members announcing how much weight they had lost – sometimes as much as 10 or 12 st. (63.5 or 76 kg)! It was truly astonishing and they looked amazing. Toned up and fabulous. And that was the key to our success. We were teaching diet *and* fitness, both through the classes and through my videos. Regular exercise toned everyone up as they lost weight, and they were not left with saggy, baggy bodies when they reached their goal weight. The whole experience was uplifting for the franchisees, the members and particularly for Mary and me. And it was fun.

Then I couldn't help wondering: what next? We must be able to do more!

11

A magazine, M&S and *This Morning*
1995–6

Amazingly, in September 1995 my *Complete Hip and Thigh Diet* was *still* in the *Sunday Times* bestseller list. My various other books had been and gone, but that title carried on, now in its seventh year!

It was around this time that the Editors of *Woman's Own* magazine asked if I would write a column for them. While doing so was a weekly commitment, fortunately it was relatively straightforward because I had so much material available from my books, plus questions and answers from our members.

My visits to Liverpool to appear on *This Morning* were always a thrill. On one memorable day, I was sitting in the green room awaiting my time slot and there was great excitement that Hugh Grant was going to be interviewed. He was promoting the film *Four Weddings and a Funeral*, but up to this moment I hadn't even heard of him.

Hugh was sitting with his publicist across the room from me when the programme menu appeared on the TV in front of him: '. . . and at 10.50 Rosemary Conley will be . . .' At this, he turned to the researcher who was looking after us and asked, 'Who's Rosemary Conley?'

Looking rather embarrassed, she waved her hand towards me and explained, 'This is Rosemary Conley – she's our fitness expert.'

Immediately, Hugh leapt off the sofa and came over to me, shook my hand and kissed me. Having since watched his many films, many times, I now treasure that memory!

Another notable occasion was the day when Robson & Jerome were to appear on the programme. Robson & Jerome were an English pop duo who were active in the mid-1990s, consisting of two very handsome actors, Robson Green and Jerome Flynn, who had risen to prominence via the British television series *Soldier Soldier*. They had recorded the classic song 'Unchained Melody' and were promoting it on *This Morning*. There were just the three of us in the green room awaiting our respective slots when they got a phone call to tell them their song had just reached number one in the charts! We all just hugged and jumped around in joy. Such was the wonderful atmosphere of *This Morning*, and when I had the privilege to appear on it again, 20 years later, it was no different. There is something really special about that programme.

However, not everything went perfectly with those memorable trips to Liverpool.

As I have mentioned, it was not unusual for me to be invited to churches around the country to give my Christian testimony, and on one occasion I was invited to a church attended by some special friends in Surrey – John Blackburn and his wife Annette. I had dated John when I was about 16, before going out with Phil, and John was our best man at our wedding in 1968. His wife, Annette, was the very kind girlfriend of John who had encouraged me to lose weight when she called round with him in 1970 – a meeting that motivated me to stop gorging myself and start losing weight – a moment that, in fact, changed my life.

So now I was invited to speak at John and Annette's church, stay with them overnight and then fly up to Liverpool to appear on *This Morning* the next day.

By 5 am the taxi had still not arrived and, when it did finally turn up, the driver explained that he had been looking for a petrol station as he was almost out of fuel. Without success.

He drove me to the airport, but painfully slowly – 'to conserve fuel'! I seriously considered whether this was a Noel Edmonds 'Gotcha' set-up, but I had already been the victim of one of those practical jokes only a couple of weeks before (more on that later), so I knew this was real. And I was panicking. My stomach was tied in knots and I found myself with a sense-of-humour bypass. The driver then admitted that this was his first day as a taxi driver. It was truly like a comedy sketch, except that I didn't find it at all funny.

When we finally reached the airport, I ran to my departure gate only to find it had closed five minutes earlier. I burst into tears and explained my predicament to the ground staff, but they were unsympathetic and said I would have to wait for the next flight. Fortunately, there was another plane to Liverpool an hour later and I finally reached the studio with just minutes to spare.

For my item on the programme that day, I was to cook a three-course healthy meal in about three minutes. It was grilled grapefruit, grilled pork chops with vegetables, and a light dessert. As my slot arrived, Richard and Judy stood next to me as I explained the menu to the viewers.

Suddenly Richard said, 'Shouldn't you cut off the fat from the pork chops?'

'Yes!' I quickly replied. 'Well spotted, Richard! We absolutely should. Sorry about that! I've had a hell of a journey this morning and I hadn't noticed it.' That just about capped it.

However, this unfortunate blip did not tarnish my golden memories of working on the fabulous *This Morning* for all those years!

***

As soon as the original *Hip and Thigh Diet* had hit the headlines, I was asked to endorse a variety of products, from vitamin supplements to thigh-toning gadgets, but I turned them all down. I wasn't in the business of endorsing products that I didn't believe people would use in the long term or whose effectiveness was questionable. But when I was asked to launch my own range of leisure- and fitness-wear with Dash, which looked amazing, and a full range of home gym equipment with Kettler, I was excited. All of these activities involved some input from me and, of course, took up more of my time for photoshoots and promotion. But it was fun, and the products were good and enjoyed moderate success.

Meanwhile the Clubs were flourishing, and in 1995 we submitted an entry to the British Franchise Association (BFA) for their annual awards. After the meteoric growth of the Clubs, we felt confident that the BFA would take us seriously. We had entered the year before and were very disappointed that we didn't win, but apparently the BFA was concerned that our franchise operation was overly dependent on me as an individual. 'What would happen if you were run over by a bus?' they asked. It was a fair question but, as time went on and we continued to go from strength to strength, it became obvious that the power of the product was in the brand, not the person. My name attracted members to join a class, but it was the individual franchisee's personality that attracted those members back, week after week, year after year, not Rosemary Conley the person.

We were told that we were finalists for the Newcomer of the Year category, so we booked our table at the awards dinner in London. Our accountant Stewart Collier, our lawyer Gordon Harris, plus Brian, Mary, our General Manager Simon, and Mike and I went along. And amazingly we won! We were thrilled!

Winning this award was very important. It gave us credibility in the business world and gave confidence to potential franchisees. As a result, our Diet & Fitness Club business continued to flourish.

***

Amid all the glamour and glitz of our success, normal life continued at home, and that involved my phoning my stepmother, Mabel, regularly. By now my father was suffering from Alzheimer's disease and life must have been very tough for her; the least I could do was to give her a daily phone call and some moral support. One day, I learned that Father had poured tea into the sugar bowl; on another occasion, he had decided to chop down their next-door neighbour's trees, causing, unsurprisingly, a serious issue with said neighbours. Thankfully, Mabel seemed to cope very patiently.

However, the challenge for me was her attitude to life. Comments such as 'All women are lazy! They don't get up until midday and then they sit around all day watching television!' was not an unusual Mabel observation.

I remember on one occasion she happened to repeat her view of women at a time when I had been working unbelievably long hours. I asked her if she thought *I* was lazy.

'Well, no. Not *you*. But most women are!'

Strangely, I didn't mind the daily challenge of holding court with my stepmother. It was good training for business; it taught me to think on my feet and fight my corner as she came out with her daily criticisms of people.

As time progressed, my father's dementia inevitably became worse. Mabel stoically nursed him through Alzheimer's disease for five years until, in the end, he had to be admitted to a geriatric psychiatric unit.

This was necessary for her and his safety. She visited him every single day he was in the hospital. She could not have been more devoted. It was a heartbreaking time for everyone but particularly for Mabel. I continued to ring her every day to give her moral support and a sympathetic ear, as well as an opportunity for her to 'sound off', and I went over to see them both every six weeks. But it wasn't long before I began to dread those visits. It is the saddest thing when your own father, who has loved you for the whole of your life, looks at you as if you are a total stranger. There wasn't the slightest flicker of recognition. It was devastating. And I feel for anyone experiencing this. It is the cruellest of diseases for everyone involved.

In the midst of this sadness, we were blessed with some joyful news. My wonderful daughter, Dawn, became engaged to Ben, a talented musician. The wedding was planned for September the following year. By now, Dawn had moved into Times Cottage in Mountsorrel, which we had bought some years before. It was close to where she worked as a PA and, with a lodger to help with the running costs, she was really happy there.

***

With so many successful slimmers emerging from our classes and with the franchisees going great guns, and my books and videos selling like hot cakes, it became obvious to me that we should create our own magazine. But there was a problem. We had never published a magazine before and I wasn't sure quite where to start. Mike could see the potential so was supportive of the idea. All I knew was that I wanted us to publish it ourselves, not through a third-party publisher, because I wanted to retain full editorial control. It was important to me that everything we printed was safe, effective, accurate and technically correct.

Thankfully, I had become friends with Geri Hosier through working with her on *Yes* magazine at *The People*, despite my moving over to the *News of the World* to write my weekly column. I mentioned to her our plans for a magazine and she suggested that Mike and I should meet her husband, Mike Ryder, who worked for Mirror Group and had been in publishing for decades. Maybe he would be able to point us in the right direction.

As we chatted over dinner in a restaurant in London, Geri's husband explained that the key starting points were finding a distributor and a printer, so he put us in touch with his contacts and we set off on one of the steepest learning curves of our lives. But we knew it was the right path to tread.

One of these contacts was Comag, a major magazine distributor which, crucially, had a very useful 'Beginner's Guide to Magazine Publishing' with one key piece of information: *Expect to sell only half the number of magazines you print!* For us, this put a totally different complexion on the cost implications, but Comag's Manager, Lynette Jillians, was very encouraging and quietly confident that our magazine would be a great success because the brand had such a high profile and a massive following. She was very keen for us to work with Comag.

After we had created our business plan, I needed to find an Editor. Geri Hosier was the obvious choice but, unfortunately, she couldn't join us because of her existing commitments. However, she was able to point us in the direction of some other potential members of our team. Geri knew a talented designer, Tim Harrison. Tim became our Art Director, and Jan Bowmer, who had edited most of my books and was a master at manoeuvring text into perfect, flowing English, became our Subeditor. Jan was now working freelance so was our perfect choice, and I was the Editor.

Our first staff appointment was Linda Stevens, plus a Junior Assistant, and over a period of a few months we started putting together our very first issue of *Rosemary Conley Diet & Fitness* magazine. Linda was an extraordinary talent. She had the ability to coordinate all the different elements of the magazine as we began this journey into the unknown. She had to think on her feet because I was stretched in so many other directions, but she knew when she could just get on with it and when to come and ask for my advice. I really admired her for that and I completely trusted her judgment. Linda was the linchpin of the magazine and she knew where we were with everything at any one time.

Mary Morris became our Fitness Consultant, putting together the exercise features, and we commissioned experts we knew to write their own columns. I had met Dr Hilary Jones while writing for the *News of the World*, while Mary introduced me to Dr Andrew Prentice, a world authority on obesity, and Dr Kevin Sykes, a leading expert and author on exercise physiology. Both Andrew and Kevin later became professors, which serves to explain their level of expertise, for which I was most grateful. They were all delighted to join the team and I felt I had lined up the very best group of experts in the land. For the recipes, the co-writer of my *Hip and Thigh* cookbooks, Patricia Bourne, was also very happy to be involved. I had become friends with Hilary Talbot when she worked as a journalist on the *Sunday Express* magazine, but now she was freelance and was my first choice to write up the interviews with our successful slimmers. Other freelancers put together pages on healthy foods, beauty and fashion.

Our franchisees submitted 'before' and 'after' photographs of their successful slimmers. From those, we selected the women who had achieved the most impressive transformations, and they were invited to Quorn House for a makeover and photoshoot. We hired a wardrobe stylist, make-up artist and professional photographer.

Our photoshoots were very exciting occasions and soon became the favourite part of my entire job. I loved meeting the members and witnessing with my own eyes how brilliantly they had transformed their body as well as their health and fitness. These individuals were inspirational and were living proof that my diets worked, and clearly the exercise classes, taught by our franchisees, had toned them up very effectively. Often their franchisee accompanied them, adding even more excitement to the day. And when the 'models' saw their photographs, they couldn't believe how fabulous they looked. 'I can't believe that's me!' they would say, often shedding tears of joy in utter disbelief. I know from experience that it takes a while for the brain to catch up with the new size of a body when significant weight has been lost; but, for these slimmers, seeing themselves in those photographs drove the point home. Yes! They *were* slim and they *were* beautiful! It was such a delightful privilege to be able to make this happen.

The franchisees loved having their members featured in the magazine, and this also led to local publicity for them, so everybody won. With a directory listing all our classes at the back of the magazine, it was a wonderful means of promoting their franchise.

***

At the same time as we were planning our first issue, someone from Marks & Spencer contacted me and invited me to meet their team at Baker Street in London to discuss their food ranges. They asked if I would become their Consultant and help them create a healthy food range. I was thrilled as I had always been such a fan of M&S. I had never done anything like this before and it was yet another exciting project.

The M&S team explained that up to this point they had a selection of products with a variety of healthy messages on different items – 'low fat', 'low salt', 'low sugar', 'high fibre' – but I could see immediately that there was no cohesion from the customer's viewpoint. My recommendation was that they needed to put all these products into a single range and decide what the main factors needed to be. In my view, the approach should be based on 'fat' and 'calories', with the fat and calorie values printed clearly on the front, as well as full nutritional information on the back of a pack. This is common practice today, but no-one did it back then. I suggested they call the range 'Healthy Choice', and that is exactly what they did.

The people at M&S were very excited about my new magazine and took two double-page spreads in the first few issues. They also put up posters publicising the magazine, and my association with them, in their food hall in Baker Street. I created diets for them by going to their Baker Street store and putting every product they had that fell into the 'less than 4% fat' category into a shopping trolley. The items were signed out and then taken back to their offices where I used them to design meals and create a calorie-controlled diet. It was such an easy way to do it as I could see the products placed around the floor of the office, grouped in individual meals, and I could tell at a glance whether there was enough protein, carbohydrate, fruit and vegetables in each day's menu. The diet was then written up and printed into a leaflet which was given away free in store. It was the perfect method for putting a diet together! The M&S bosses and their customers loved it, and three million of the diet leaflets were taken.

I worked as a Consultant for M&S for four years and, in that time, created a Rosemary Conley fitness-wear range and produced an M&S fitness video. They were such happy times and included M&S Roadshows, which were also great fun.

The Roadshows were held in very smart venues to which M&S customers were invited. They were given snacks and drinks, and a team of us put on the entertainment. M&S had asked some employees to help present a game based on the popular TV quiz show *Who Wants to Be a Millionaire?* The winners would receive M&S prizes. I gave a talk on the principles of weight loss and fitness, and explained my association with M&S. There was also a generous goody bag for everyone, plus a raffle.

At one event, I had finished my talk and had gone backstage to change into fitness-wear so that I could demonstrate exercises later in the show. I then heard shrieking laughter coming from the audience. Apparently, a guy from M&S was on stage drawing the raffle and, when a woman held up her hand waving her ticket in the air, he said: 'Ah! The winner is . . . the lady with the peroxide hair!' I often wonder if he ever recovered from making such an inappropriate comment in front of a roomful of women!

Of course, at the same time as all this was happening, I was writing my column for the *News of the World*. The Features Editor was very supportive of our magazine and took a double-page spread in each issue for six months, advertising the fact that I was writing for them. I was also appearing weekly on *This Morning*, which had now moved its studio from Liverpool to London, so it worked perfectly for me to tie in my visits to M&S head office in Baker Street with my appearances on TV earlier in the day. *This Morning* also proved to be the most wonderful environment to meet celebrities who were happy to be interviewed for our magazine. Everything was slotting into place and it was beyond exciting!

Appearing on *This Morning* every week was an extraordinary privilege. Richard and Judy were incredible and the whole team was delightful. And I *still* use the make-up artist, Jane Tyler, who looked after me then, for my own photoshoots today.

***

By the end of November 1995, our Art Director Tim and Subeditor Jan had settled in as part of the magazine team. They both lived in London and came up to Leicester for meetings with me and Linda Stevens who ran the magazine office. Soon, our launch issue was ready to go to print.

We realised we needed to advertise the launch, so our advertising agents suggested we take some billboards. They managed to secure a deal for around a hundred 96-sheet posters. They were huge! Their shape was a long rectangle, so they decided the image on the posters should be a photo of me lying face down on top of the words 'Diet & Fitness' while holding open a copy of the first edition of the magazine. And it worked. We even had one of our posters in shot in an episode of *EastEnders*! It was slightly bonkers but it was effective. When the magazine was launched, the first issue flew off the shelves and sold 260,000 copies!

The next bit of good news was that at the end of 1995 Geri Hosier decided to leave Mirror Group and accept our invitation to become our Editor. This was a huge relief for me and it meant that I could hand over the everyday running of the magazine to her. It was so great to have Geri on board as I respected her immensely and I knew we worked well together.

Then came a big surprise. As is the case with most publications, we included a subscription offer. We offered readers the opportunity to take a subscription for one year at a reduced cost and to receive a free T-shirt, but if anyone wanted to subscribe for *two* years, we would send them one of the Action Band Workout Packs – the products that had been donated to us by the BBC as unsold stock after my last BBC TV series. Much to everyone's astonishment, we sold 9,000 subscriptions in the first month, and most of them were for two years. This gave us the liquid capital we needed to fund the magazine and we had no need to use any of the overdraft facility offered by the bank. It was an astounding result.

After such a successful launch, we were scratching our heads as to what to do to make the second issue really exciting. Mike suggested that I could ask to be photographed with Cliff Richard.

The year before, I had been invited by Cliff to do a workout at his famous charity tennis tournament. This was a massive event held in an indoor arena where 10,000 of his devoted fans would arrive for the tournament during the day, and then he would sing to them in the evening. I had met Cliff before and he knew that I had become a Christian through the *Power for Living* book in which he was featured. It was a real privilege to be invited to contribute to his event.

As all the members of the audience would be sitting down, I devised, with Mary's help, a suitable 'chair workout'. So, sitting in the centre of this huge stadium in Birmingham, with Cliff next to me, the vast audience participated in a 10-minute workout. It was amazing!

Because of this experience, I felt comfortable about approaching Cliff for the magazine photograph. It was a brilliant idea from Mike, so we set about trying to contact Cliff's office. Thankfully he said yes, but we had to go to his office and we would have just 10 minutes in which to take the photographs. We all drove down to the headquarters of the Cliff Richard Organisation in Surrey and met our photographer, Alan Olley, to set up for the photo session. Cliff, of course, was charming and so helpful, and I came away on cloud nine! It was a great coup for us, and the second edition of the magazine was hugely successful, just like the first, so we felt we had properly arrived in the publishing arena. This was confirmed when the following year we received an award for Best Launch Magazine in 1996 at the national PPA Awards.

It wasn't long before my daughter, Dawn, joined the team at Quorn House Publishing – the name we had chosen for the company that published the magazine. Initially, when Dawn left college, she had worked as a temporary secretary / PA to the Chairman of a local company but, after she became a Christian at the Billy Graham live-link evangelistic event in 1989, she had a real passion for her faith and decided to take a year out from employed work to be placed with a church. At the end of her year, I persuaded her to join the Quorn House Publishing team.

It was great to have Dawn on board as she had grown up understanding the philosophy of my diets and knew the principles inside out, and I knew her work ethic. Who better to place on the editorial team of my magazine? Dawn looked after the consumer side and spent many an hour trawling through supermarkets looking at suitable products to feature (this was before the days when every product was available to view online). She also organised taste tests and all the food photography.

The magazine team had its own offices at the top of Quorn House, and our monthly editorial meetings were fascinating. Geri, Tim and Jan would come up from London and the whole team would sit around our vast boardroom table (the one I bought for £10 at auction) trying to come up with topics that would interest our readers. We also thoroughly enjoyed selecting our successful slimmers for the next photoshoot – and we had so many to choose from as we had around 50,000 members attending weekly at our nationwide network of classes. We were spoilt for choice.

We were now employing significantly more staff to help run the Clubs and, while Mike and I were very much involved in the decision-making, the day-to-day responsibilities were left to Simon, who was doing a great job as General Manager. I was involved with the magazine as Editor-in-Chief and took on the responsibility of proofreading the whole magazine before it went to press; I often did this while being driven around to events or late into the evening after Mike had gone to bed.

Throughout the life of our Clubs we tried to support various charities, and one good cause that we loved was Children in Need. One year, we launched a major fundraising initiative supported by all the franchisees. We also held an 'aerobathon' on the lawn at Quorn House at which Simon, our General Manager, dressed up as Pudsey, the Children in Need mascot – a role which revealed his undoubted talent as an actor! We had a fabulous day, and overall we raised a very significant sum. Because of the success of our efforts, some of our staff members went down to London and handed over a giant cheque live on BBC1 on the night of the Children in Need telethon. The following January, I was invited to Broadcasting House to a special 'Thank You' reception for those who had been responsible for raising a lot of money that year. It was such a privilege to meet Terry Wogan and his beautiful wife Helen, and to chat with them. What a lovely couple they were and what a thrill it was!

***

In an attempt to give ourselves an interest outside of work, and to do something together, Mike and I decided to take up horse riding again but this time to have proper lessons. I had always loved riding and, of course, going pony trekking was how we had met in the first place in 1983. It was also some years since we parted with Splash and April, the horses we had at the Old Parsonage.

A friend introduced us to a local stable where event riders Gary Parsonage and his then partner Gemma Burton kept several horses and gave lessons. Both were talented riders in the horse-eventing world, and

Gary was being considered as a member of Team Great Britain for the 1996 Olympics in Atlanta on a horse called Magic Rogue.

To be a 'Three-Day Eventer', a horse has to be able to be competent at dressage, cross-country and show-jumping. First created as a way of training horses in the military, 'dressage' was designed so that horses could learn to follow the rider's instructions very precisely and with great discipline to prepare them for formal occasions such as Royal Parades, for example the event known as 'Trooping the Colour' as we might see it today. On the other hand, 'cross-country' teaches the horse to be brave and to trust its rider. Over several miles of rugged countryside, and against the clock, a cross-country race involves riding a horse over a track that includes a variety of very challenging jumps over obstacles that are often solid in construction or multifaceted. Trust between horse and rider is essential because many times the horse has to jump while not knowing what kind of surface or terrain might lie on the other side of the fence. It could be water, or a downward slope, and often the horse is faced with another jump a couple of strides further on! The original idea of cross-country trials was to train horses to have the stamina and agility to fight in a battle where the landscape was unpredictable. The third element of eventing is show-jumping, which was designed to train horses to jump high in a restricted space to avoid danger.

In Three-Day Eventing the rider and his or her horse form a partnership, and together they must execute all three disciplines over a three-day period. It is tough but exhilarating, and it is only possible to do it with a horse who loves to do it and a rider who is very skilled and courageous – and enjoys a massive adrenalin rush! It is one of the few sports where men and women compete equally.

Gary was spotted as having great talent when he was a young rider entering competitions and was encouraged to make it his career. And here he was, being considered for the Olympics.

We instantly became friends with these two horse-lovers, and we both looked forward to our riding lessons – Mike with Gary, me with Gemma. We also enjoyed meeting them socially and had a lot of fun attending events where they were competing; this was a whole new world of excitement, expertise and extreme danger! If you have never been to an event such as Burghley Horse Trials or Badminton, you are missing a treat. For those who like horses and being out in the countryside, I wholeheartedly recommend it.

It soon became obvious that Gary's chances of being chosen for the British team would be enhanced if he had a sponsor, so we stepped in to help and our magazine company, Quorn House Publishing, became his official sponsor. By providing him with horse blankets and livery emblazoned with our logo, we gave Gary greater standing in a very competitive field. A few weeks later, Gary called us to say he had been selected for the Olympic team! We were all so excited and decided that we would fly out to Atlanta to support him.

As Mike became more and more interested in riding, and we were still looking to move, we decided we would try to find a house with stables. Despite looking at a variety of properties, however, nothing had appealed so far. The Old Rectory, where we had lived for five years, had been on the market for a while when suddenly we found a buyer, so we decided to rent. We discovered 'The West Wing', which was part of a mansion called Burley on the Hill (not to be confused with Burghley House at Stamford), situated on the outskirts of Oakham in Rutland. I managed to persuade Mike that we should make this our temporary home.

The part of the property we were renting was on four floors with extremely high ceilings and had 78 stairs to our bedroom! When we first went to see it, I thought it was amazing as it was well decorated and the views were stunning. What I hadn't realised was that, because it had no carpets or curtains, the sound resonance was extreme and we could hardly hear each other speak if we were more than 2 ft (0.6 m) apart! The views were spectacular over Rutland Water but, in reality, it was not an ideal home. Nik and Sheba enjoyed the walks in the park surrounding the house; however, living in that building was far from comfortable.

Then one day, I went to look at a house – very similar to Quorn House – that was located near Uppingham, also in Rutland. It was a charming place, but the noise from the A47 was overwhelming so I knew it was out of the question for us. As I chatted to the estate agent, I explained that the only house we had really fallen in love with was Ashby Folville Manor but that the price was prohibitive.

Immediately she said, 'Make a silly offer! I bet you'll get it and what have you got to lose?'

12

Houses, horses and heartache
1996

I rushed back to the office and called Mike straight away. He sounded surprisingly interested. I thought he had gone off the idea of Ashby Folville Manor, but he suggested we go back to the agent. It was now almost two years since we had first viewed this house and the agent was pleased to hear from us, particularly as we had sold our property and were cash buyers. He explained that the vendors were keen to sell and that he would be prepared to put our significantly reduced offer forward and also to explain that we would like to view the property again.

A meeting was set up with the vendor for 5 pm the following day, but when we arrived the vendor was somewhat shocked to see us. Apparently, he had told the agent he wasn't interested in our offer and that there was no point in our coming. That day, for some extraordinary reason, I had forgotten my mobile phone so I never received the message.

'Well, we're here now, so can we discuss it with you?' I said to the owner.

We were invited in and wandered through the amazing hall and onwards to the magnificent drawing room, chatting. It was fabulous to be in the surroundings of such a fine building.

We learned that since we had last viewed, the National Rivers Authority had implemented a flood alleviation scheme. This involved moving the position of the river that flowed through the garden of the Manor and constructing a weir and various overflows, with the result that part of the lawn and the land on the other side of the river had been rebuilt. As it happened, and to our good fortune, this had been such a major construction that it had made the property virtually unsaleable. I imagined that it must have looked a bit like a motorway construction site for most of that time. But now it was finished, and we didn't care one jot that there was brown soil waiting for the grass to grow on the banks of the relocated river.

Thankfully, we agreed a very satisfactory price from our point of view and proceeded with the purchase. But, as with most house moves, it wasn't to be straightforward.

***

Meanwhile, my work life had taken on a new dimension as Granada Television had collaborated with Sky Broadcasting and launched a satellite channel, Granada Breeze. This was split into four groups of programmes, one of which was Granada Health & Beauty. The Director of Programming, James Hunt, had to fill seven days a week with programmes and called me to his office. I knew James from when he was Editor on *This Morning*; he had commissioned me to appear regularly on the programme when I first joined it. This was the beginning of the explosion of additional channels in the UK. More options became available and the situation was a far cry from the days when it was just the big four: BBC1, BBC2, ITV and Channel 4.

Because of my experience on *This Morning* where I demonstrated healthy recipes and taught exercise, together with my books and videos on diet and fitness, it seemed that I would be ideal to help fill a lot of the airtime on Granada Health & Beauty. I also suggested that some of our franchisees would be suitable as exercise presenters on the channel. The producers loved the idea and soon we were organising a screen test at which interested franchisees auditioned.

The franchisees were very excited and flocked to the studio, all looking really glamorous. I was very proud of them as they taught their short exercise routine in front of Dianne Nelmes, Head of Daytime Programming at ITV, and me. Of course, they couldn't all get through, but dozens of them did, and recording dates were arranged for them to come into the studios.

I was delighted by it all and went along to my own first recording day in Manchester, close to the set of the long-running soap *Coronation Street*.

A team of trainee studio technicians had been recruited and, under the supervision of an experienced programme-maker, we started putting the programmes together. What fascinated me was that, on one day, trainees David and John would be on cameras, Dan was on sound, Gill was on lighting, Sean was a runner and Ritchie was taking the role of Floor Manager. The next day, they all changed jobs! It was remarkable to see how they switched around, but also to see where natural talent was coming through.

On the first day, Ritchie was Floor Manager and was a natural in that role. He had authority but was calm and reassuring; he just had an air of confidence and of being in control. And I told him so. A few years later, I was thrilled to learn that Ritchie was Floor Manager on *This Morning*.

To make the programmes, I recorded 10 cookery demonstrations and then moved on to another element and recorded multiples of that. Ultimately, they would be edited together to make cohesive half-hour programmes. These would appear at different times throughout the day.

As well as recording cookery demonstrations, there was a series of interviews with experts and sometimes with successful slimmers. The producers also wanted me to respond to viewers' questions. This was a fascinating exercise. They took questions that had appeared in my magazine, prompted me with a subject by putting a one-liner clue on to the autocue, and then I gave a two-minute answer straight into the camera. I would do about 40 of these straight off the top of my head, which was great experience for answering random questions off the cuff and getting used to speaking into an inanimate object. The whole experience was exhilarating.

I did these recording days regularly, but one day in the middle of the afternoon I was suddenly taken into the studio set of a quiz show. I had no idea this was on the agenda. It was all very makeshift, and the buzzers for answering the questions were just fake versions, but it looked all right on the screen. I was handed a bunch of cards holding the questions and answers and was suddenly a quiz host. With no training or experience whatsoever, it proved to be one of the more stressful elements of my TV career and, while we completed the experiment, it was never repeated.

Recording for Granada Breeze was undoubtedly hard work but I enjoyed it. On a couple of occasions, we did two consecutive days and that was brain-numbing, but it stood me in good stead for later in my career and I look back on those days very fondly.

**

The excitement of moving to Ashby Folville Manor was palpable, even though my ridiculous workload was making it difficult to find the time to actually move! But I was so thrilled at the thought of living in such a splendid property that somehow I found the motivation to work even harder.

We agreed a date with the vendor and booked the removal company. However, the vendors were proving challenging and, even on the day of the removal, we still hadn't exchanged contracts, let alone completed the sale! In addition, Mike was due to go to Badminton Horse Trials with Gary and Gemma for the weekend. I insisted that he still go because, to be honest, I had lived with Mike long enough to know that he doesn't handle stress well and I really didn't need someone else stressed on the scene. It was easier for me to sort it out on my own.

The poor removal men must have been exhausted as they trundled up and down the endless flights of stairs in the West Wing and then carried our furniture into their van. By the time they were all packed up, I was *still* waiting for the call from our solicitor to say the sale had gone through. Having explained the situation to the removal guys, I asked if they had ever had to take furniture back into a house.

'Oh yes,' they said cheerily. 'It's not uncommon at all!'

I didn't want to even consider that scenario, so we set off for Ashby Folville Manor, praying that everything would be 'all right on the night'.

I had the dogs in the car, and the boot filled to bursting. The guys carefully manoeuvred their removal van through the back gate of the property because we didn't dare take the very heavy vehicle over the bridge at the front of the house. Some friends met me there, together with Martin (our decorator friend) and his wife Dolores, as well as Ken and Mary, our gardener and housekeeper – all prepared to help us move in.

The son of the vendor met us and apologised for the delay in finalising the deal but their bank was proving difficult. Our lawyer, Carol Hodges, was a star. As 5 pm arrived and her law firm closed for the weekend, she had to sit in a partner's office so she could have a private line for the vendor's bank to call. When the official finally phoned and told her the bank was closing and we would have to deal with it on Tuesday, as Monday was May Day, she shrieked down the phone, 'My client is on the doorstep with her furniture! You *have* to do this today!'

Thankfully, Carol's persuasive powers did the job. Fifteen minutes later we got the call saying, 'The house is yours!'

Hallelujah!

I called Mike immediately and he was *so* relieved!

There were cheers all round, the son of the vendor handed me a bottle of champagne and the removal men were all smiles as they unloaded the furniture. Our friends helped unpack the basics and get us sorted, and we were soon making it look like home, even though our furniture looked lost in such a huge property. By nine o'clock our kind friends had left and the removal men sat down with me to an Indian takeaway at the kitchen table. It was a special moment of celebration.

We had managed to get the master bedroom pretty straight and a bed made. I slept well because I was exhausted, despite also being incredibly excited. We were finally, finally, 'in'. I couldn't believe it. I was so happy!

The next morning, I was awoken at five o'clock by Sheba, who had found her way upstairs looking very distressed. I followed her down, only to find Nik almost unconscious and haemorrhaging badly. It was such a distressing sight. I called the vet immediately and he came straight away.

A month previously, while we were walking around the park at Burley on the Hill, Nik, now 13 years old, had chased after a rabbit as though she were a two-year-old. We joked, 'If she has a heart attack now, she'll feel it was worth it.' But she was fine. However, the following morning I went downstairs to make a cup of tea and realised that Nik couldn't walk properly. We knew there was something seriously wrong, so we took her to the vet and he kept her in for tests. Later, the vet called us to say that Nik *had* had a heart attack and that she also had advanced-stage breast cancer. He explained that there really was no option but to put her to sleep there and then. Thankfully, Mike asked him to wait so that we could both go and see her after I returned from London in the early evening. We both felt we wanted to see her to say our goodbyes.

When we arrived at the surgery, Nik greeted us with body language that said, *I'm OK! Don't put me to sleep. I'm fine!* And she did appear to be better – a totally different dog. We pleaded with the vet to allow us to take her home, even if it was only for a few days or weeks. He agreed.

Over the following month, Nik was given so much love, so many strokes and cuddles, but now, on this Saturday morning, her time had come. The vet came immediately, and our beautiful, loyal, full-of-character Nikki-Noo, as we usually called her, slipped peacefully away.

After calling Mike to tell him the sad news, I rang Martin and Dolores to ask them to collect Nik so that she could be buried in the grounds of Quorn House where she had spent such happy times with us all. Martin and Dolores were at the house by 6 am – that was the sort of friends they were. Martin planted a magnolia tree beside her grave in her memory and we created a little Garden of Remembrance which we could see from our office.

Nik had been with Mike and me from the very beginning and was such a special dog. We were both so upset to lose her, but also glad that we had had our four extra weeks with her to show her how much we loved her. Dawn, who had grown up with Nik and loved her, had at least had time to come to terms with the fact that she would not live for very long as she was so poorly. It was so sad.

On this 'day 2' of the move, I had arranged to meet the removal men at 9 am to collect the rest of our things from Burley. But I was so upset – and of course, I felt so sorry for poor Sheba who had lost her mum. When I told the guys about Nik, they were really sad too and very kind. What a mixture of emotions!

Over the next couple of days, our friends worked tirelessly helping me to place the furniture around the house and make it look welcoming for when Mike came home on Sunday evening. I was so excited about him coming back and arriving at our new home as I knew how much he hated living at the West Wing and how much he was looking forward to moving into the Manor.

It was a bittersweet homecoming because his beloved Nik had gone, but Mike was thrilled to drive to Ashby Folville and to feel that, at last, the Manor was ours.

***

The following month it was the Olympics, and Mike, together with Gary's parents and Magic Rogue's owner, flew to Atlanta. I followed a few days later because I was tied up with work commitments. It was an amazing experience and we had a fabulous time – a trip we will never forget. We all rented a house together near the Equestrian Park, which was some distance away from the athletics stadium. Soon, 'Team Gary' got to grips with the whole Olympic scene and by the time I arrived I was in the hands of experts.

Magic Rogue, Gary's Olympic horse, loved the excitement of the cross-country elements and the speed and challenge of the show-jumping, but he really didn't enjoy dressage and Gary had to work unbelievably hard to get him to raise his performance to a reasonable level. Just as people have different strengths and weaknesses, Magic Rogue was included in the British team because of his flair and talent for cross-country and show-jumping. He was a good jumper. Because it was a team event, and marks were given across the performances of all four competitors in each team, his weaker performance in dressage would hopefully be absorbed.

Great Britain came fifth overall in the team event, which was a commendable result, and we were all very proud of Gary and Magic Rogue who did amazingly well. Most importantly, they were both safe and fit, which is always a relief. Eventing is a very dangerous sport, and injuries to horse and rider are not uncommon.

Almost as soon as we were home, Magic Rogue's owner called to ask if we would like to buy him, which we did. And so we met our next challenge: we needed to build our own stables.

The Manor already had a large barn and there was a perfect area suited to constructing a suite of stables. Of course, we had to get planning permission, but within a few months Mike had designed and organised the construction of a beautiful eventing yard with 20 stables and a manège (horse exercise arena). It looked fabulous, and Gary and Gemma moved into our gatehouse cottage within the grounds.

Gary rode for several horse-owners, as well as for us, and he and Gemma also had their own horses, so at one point there were 17 horses stabled in the yard. As they grazed in the fields in the front of the house it was a glorious sight – a fulfilment of a dream for me. I have always adored horses, but these equine athletes were nothing short of magnificent.

Moving into the Manor was a big undertaking. We needed two gardeners – Ken 1 and Ken 2! Ken 1 had looked after our garden since we were in the Old Parsonage, and Ken 2 joined us after his wife Mary came to clean for us at the Old Rectory. But now they were going to move in to live in the flat at the top of the house and be our gardener and housekeeper. They were such a delightful couple and we loved having them with us.

Mike and I always tried to give ourselves a weekly treat on a Friday evening by walking to The Carington Arms, the charming traditional pub in the centre of the village of Ashby Folville, where excellent meals were served. The villagers were very welcoming to us as we moved into the Manor, and we soon settled into our new life there. The only problem was there just weren't enough hours in the day. Mike and I discussed what we could do to help us cope with the workload.

'What would be the most help to you?' he asked.

Having given his question careful thought, I came up with a solution. I wasn't a fan of ready meals, but if someone could cook us four low-fat meals a week so that all I had to do when we came in from the office, or wherever, was to put them in the oven or boil some rice or potatoes, that would be a great help. We asked the owners at the pub if they knew anyone in the village who might be able to do it. They suggested Millie Eggleston, who had previously cooked for them but had stepped back from the long hours that the job had entailed. Millie is a farmer's wife and a qualified cook, and she lived nearby. Thankfully, she was delighted to take on this new task, although low-fat cooking was different from what she was used to. Furnished with my low-fat cookbooks, Millie soon got to grips with the principles of low-fat eating and created fabulous meals for us. Not only that; she also did any incidental shopping we needed. This was the perfect solution and it transformed my life.

We also decided to get ourselves a new German Shepherd, and in August a little bundle of black-and-tan fur joined the family. We called her Max. However, Sheba, now 11 years old, wasn't at all impressed and, despite all our efforts to help her adjust to Max, spent most of her time asleep upstairs, only coming down for mealtimes. This lasted for about six months and then gradually she relaxed and seemed to tolerate Max.

As the house needed rewiring, the electricians were soon tearing up floorboards and climbing about in the roof space. It took eight months and 12 miles (19 km) of cable to complete the job. It was a great relief when they finally packed up and left.

The same interior designer from Laura Ashley who had designed the furnishings at Quorn House took on the task of redesigning some of the rooms – but not all, because in quite a few rooms the curtains were already beautiful. It was a big job and it took months to complete, but by the time it was finished the house looked amazing. In the meantime, I went back to the auction house and started buying all manner of furnishings: pictures, chairs, tables, chests of drawers, rugs, a baby grand piano, an old organ . . . This was a house that needed 'stuff'. But there were certain items I had to buy from an antique dealer as they were specific for our needs. For instance, the dining room was vast and we needed to buy a huge table as anything smaller would have looked ridiculous.

Most of the furniture and items I bought from the auctions weren't valuable antiques, but they were carefully chosen and, when re-upholstered, looked beautiful.

My goal was to get the whole house furnished in readiness for my 50th birthday party in December. It was to be a great occasion and my guest list included all my close friends, including my former husband Phil and his wife Trish, and a few celebrities, which made it even more exciting. Richard Madeley and Judy Finnigan came with their nine-year-old twins, Chloe and Jack, along with Dr Hilary Jones and his wife, and Dr Raj Persaud and his wife Francesca, all of whom had become friends through *This Morning*, while I knew Dr Hilary because he was writing for my magazine. They all stayed over in our newly refurbished bedrooms. There were beds everywhere as we tried to accommodate everyone who had travelled a long distance. It was a brilliant experience to have over a hundred guests happily sitting around the vast hall, on the wide stairs or wherever they could find a seat. What a magnificent sight! I loved every minute of it.

On the day of my birthday I was at the office, and at 3 pm I was invited down to the library, where all the members of staff were gathered. What used to be an old snooker table (and was now the franchisees' communal training desk) was covered in bouquets, flower arrangements, giant cards

– one signed by the staff and another by the franchisees – and piles of gifts. There was also another huge card signed by all the members of classes in the West Midlands run by one of the original three franchisees, Kim Imerfries, with lovely messages. It was so special and I couldn't have felt more loved. Mike gave me the biggest bouquet I had ever seen in my life, full of scented lilies and white roses. But then there was another big surprise.

I was invited to sit down, along with the rest of the staff, to watch a large screen. I expected perhaps a montage of my life, but no. What followed was extraordinary.

Mike had asked each individual department in Quorn House to create a skit and Mike filmed it. In Louise and Melody's film (that's my PA and secretary) they were each trying on *my* suits and jackets (which Dawn had supplied from my wardrobe without my knowledge); Dawn and the team in the magazine office had a sketch where they pretended to turn down interviews with members of the Royal Family; and there was a scene where Martin was lounging in a wheelbarrow outside the front door pretending to be drunk and slurring, 'Rosemary, you don't realise that every weekend after you've all gone home, Dolores and I run a B&B here at Quorn House!' There were about seven scenes in total and it was utterly hilarious. I had tears streaming down my face, while my sides, and my face, were aching with laughter!

Mike had taken all his film footage to my Fitness Video Director, Nick Patten, who had edited it and put the whole thing to music. It was a masterpiece! I couldn't believe that everyone had gone to so much trouble just for me – and I could only imagine the fun they must have had recording it! It was incredible and very, very lovely.

After all the celebrations around my birthday, I was particularly excited about the following January when we were to announce our first magazine Slimmer of the Year. In the previous October we had looked at all the application forms received from our class members and produced a shortlist of 20 people. It was an astonishing sight to see so many successful slimmers and the remarkable transformations they had achieved. In the end, Geri and I decided to invite five of them for a photoshoot at Quorn House in November; from that, we would choose our final placings.

The day of the photoshoot included the services of a fashion stylist and make-up and hair artists, with the result that all the finalists looked stunning. Our photographer set up his kit in our exercise studio, and the four beautiful women and one handsome man were photographed in a variety of outfits. It was very exciting and immensely rewarding.

We decided on our winner, Helen, who had throughout her life always been overweight and now had shed 9 st. (57 kg) to look stunning in a swimsuit as well as in an evening dress. Her 'before' photographs, some dating back to childhood, were a dramatic contrast to the svelte and beautiful woman she now was.

In second place we put Sandra Lewis, who had lost over 6 st. (38 kg) and also looked fabulous. In fact, later, Sandra became a very successful franchisee for our Clubs. In third place was Althea Sutherland, who looked wonderful having lost 5 st. (31.75 kg). We then decided to create a joint fourth place for Julia Bunstone and Philip Partington, who had each transformed their lives. We were delighted that we had a male slimmer among our winners.

We emphasised to all the winners that they must not tell a soul that they had won until they had been officially announced at our awards ceremony, to be held at the Savoy Hotel in London in early January.

With photographs taken and announcements made, everyone went home excited about meeting up again in a couple of months, in January. However, when we did meet up, there was a big surprise – and not a good one.

13

A Gotcha, a wedding and a funeral
1997–8

After my exciting 50th birthday celebrations, I was looking forward to January immensely. I had, of course, organised Slimmer of the Year Awards in my long-gone SAGG days, but this year's event was to be in a whole new league. With our own magazine celebrating its first birthday, we decided to celebrate our first Slimmer of the Year event at the Savoy Hotel in London. Our top three successful slimmers had lost significant amounts of weight and we had photographed them in November so they could feature in the January issue of our magazine, with the winner on the cover.

The day before we held the awards ceremony, Mike and I drove over to Birmingham and hired an edit suite to allow my Video Director, Nick Patten, to edit a montage of photographs of our fabulous winner, Helen. This included lots of shots of her from when she was a very overweight child, through her teenage years and as an adult, interspersed with the fabulous 'after' photographs that we had taken at our photoshoot in November. The montage of pictures told an amazing story. It was impressive. I was so excited about showing the video of pictures prior to welcoming our winner on to the stage.

Next day, Mike and I drove down to London, and as I walked happily into the Savoy I was met by Geri, who was almost apoplectic!

'She's put loads of weight on over Christmas!' screamed Geri.

'Who has?' I asked, puzzled.

'The winning lass! She's gained loads!'

My heart sank. As I prepared to walk into the room where the girls were being made up, I spotted her; the poor woman must have gained at least a couple of stone (about 13 kg) since last we saw her. And she couldn't fit into the dress she was supposed to wear. It was a disaster.

Fortunately, I had another evening dress with me and she tried that on. Because it was stretchy – very stretchy as it turned out – she could just get it on. We had no option but to carry on as though nothing was wrong because she was on the front cover of the magazine – and it was already printed.

I tried to hold it together as I announced our lovely third-placed winner; then Sandra, our second-placed success story, who was even more slender than she had been in November; finally we showed the montage of the winner in all her slinky size-10 photographs, and then she walked on to the stage. Thankfully, everyone applauded and I presented the award, together with her £1,000 prize and £600 of gift vouchers from M&S. It all went remarkably well. After all, despite her recent weight gain, she had still lost a massive amount of weight.

Fortunately, we had photographs for the press to use from the November shoot and these were the ones they used in the papers the following day. We received excellent coverage and we all left the event feeling somewhat relieved.

The story behind the winner's weight gain was, in fact, very sad. She had lived much of her life with her grandmother and, not surprisingly, was extremely close to her. Over Christmas, Grandma had suddenly died, and our winner had turned to food for comfort. She hadn't even told her grandmother that she had won our Slimmer of the Year award. It was a heart-breaking situation.

Then came another unexpected setback. In the shock of the drama of the day, my asthmatic lungs reacted very badly and I quickly developed a severe chest infection. I could *feel* it. It was as though I had a brick in my chest. I was staying down in London as I had a meeting with M&S that afternoon and was due to appear the next day on *This Morning* (which by now had relocated from Liverpool to ITV's London Studios). I can recall sitting right at the end of a massive boardroom table in Baker Street head office for my meeting with just two M&S personnel, saying, 'I really don't want you to come near me. I'm really poorly!'

I then went back to the hotel and slept for 12 hours, before going over to the TV studio the following day.

I caught the train back to Leicester immediately afterwards, and I don't know how I drove myself home from the station – a journey of 15 miles

(24 km) – as I felt so ill, not helped by the fact that it had been snowing heavily.

The next day I called for the doctor. Mike was really worried about me. I had a raging temperature and could hardly breathe.

When the doctor arrived, he walked into our bedroom and rather surprisingly said, 'I've got to say, seeing this beautiful house covered in snow was magical – like driving into a Christmas card!' at which point I coughed so hard I threw up! I think that was when he realised I was really ill! In fact, I had pneumonia and was immediately put on strong antibiotics and steroids, and told to stay in bed, and he would revisit me in three days' time.

Gradually I got better, but progress was slow as I hardly had the strength to walk to the bathroom, which was right next to our bedroom, let alone do anything else. Dawn and Mike were brilliant, but by the following week I still wasn't well enough to go down to London to appear on *This Morning* so Richard and Judy rang me live on air. I was looking at the TV screen in the corner of the bedroom from my bed and could see a map of the British Isles with a pulsating spot on Leicestershire, signifying my location. It was very sweet of them and it did perk me up.

I cancelled all my appointments and publicity activities for my new book, *New Body Plan*, and just rested. Then I received a call from the producers of *Noel's House Party*. A few months earlier I had been 'Gotcha'd', and now they wanted to transmit my film.

Noel's House Party was a highly popular BBC1 Saturday night entertainment show in the 1990s and, in the 'Gotcha' segment, featured celebrities being 'caught out' by a crazy situation. The plot of my Gotcha was as follows: while I was doing a photoshoot at Ragdale Hall for our magazine, the fire alarm went off and we had to evacuate the building. As I went out to the front, a fire engine was already there with firefighters investigating the potential blaze – but I have to add that at this point I couldn't see any smoke. Soon I was spotted by one of the firemen, who invited me on to the appliance because his wife was a huge fan of mine. There I was, enjoying this new experience, when suddenly there was a 'shout' to attend an emergency at a nearby house. They wouldn't let me off the appliance, saying all the guys needed to pile in fast, and off we went! The house was only a mile away, so we all got off the fire engine to find that the problem was a cat stranded up a tree! Out came the fireman's ladder and, as I watched from the ground, I could see this very shaggy-looking cat near the top of the tree. As the firemen got close, it looked as though it would fall and I shrieked! When they finally rescued it, I realised it was a cat-shaped pyjama case! I was well and truly Gotcha'd.

It was all a bit of fun, and the guys were great. But now, a week after I had been diagnosed with pneumonia, the producers were calling to say that my film was to be featured on next Saturday's programme and I needed to be there. I explained I had been really poorly, but they insisted.

Mike drove me down to the studio. I slept most of the way and just rested. Upon arrival, they took me on to the set and explained, 'When Noel calls your name, we want you to run down those stairs and on to the set so he can present you with your Gotcha award.'

I still found walking more than a few yards difficult – let alone running! I said I would do my best.

I went through make-up and a rehearsal, which I took very slowly, and then it was time. I think the adrenalin of the moment must have just taken over because I managed to half-run down the stairs and then sit embarrassed as they played my film. Noel was great, of course, and I was presented with my Gotcha award, which I still treasure today.

But there were more surprises. After the show, it turned out that lots of my special friends had been invited too and we had a party. And from that moment on, amazingly, I recovered very quickly. It would appear there is nothing like a massive adrenalin rush from a live Saturday night TV show to pick you up! It was like a miracle.

***

Mike was now stepping back from the day-to-day business at Quorn House as we had more staff and he has the kind of personality that thrives on a new challenge but is not as motivated by more normal activity. We now had around 50 staff, and we had extended the existing double garage into a large warehouse selling my videos and books, as well as handling all the franchisee stationery orders. The business was running very smoothly, and when Mike did come into the office for Board meetings, or whatever, he always got on well with the staff. He had a real gift for that.

We were happy at home, settling into life at the Manor, and Mike and I were loving life, particularly going to three-day equestrian events and watching Gary and Gemma compete at weekends. Also, now that we were owners of competing horses, we were invited to the 'Welcome' cocktail parties in the stately homes hosting the events – Blenheim Palace, Badminton House, Burghley House – all stunning places with extraordinary estates. It was such a privilege and we really enjoyed it.

On one occasion, Gary was competing at Bramham International Horse Trials. Mike wasn't joining me this time, but I went with Gary's mum and dad, and I took our two dogs: Max and a rescue dog we had adopted, Rosie. They both loved going to horse events. They had fun seeing the hundreds of other dogs who attended, and Max was mesmerised by the horses galloping past as we watched the action.

Spectators can walk around the cross-country course, but the actual route which the horses follow is cordoned off for safety reasons. There are stewards at 'crossing points' where the public can walk across the course path, but this is carefully timed so as not to interfere with the horses galloping towards the next fence. To signal when a horse is approaching, a steward at the previous fence blows a loud whistle, and the steward at the following fence ensures the course is safe, clearing the spectators off the track and cordoning off the crossing point. One cardinal rule of attending a horse event with a dog is to always keep it on a lead. If a dog somehow got loose, it was seriously frowned upon.

Max had learned that when the whistle sounded, a horse was fast approaching – and she got very excited. Gary's mum and dad and I were watching along with their two and our two dogs when Max suddenly ducked her head, moved backwards and slipped her collar. With her big ruffle of fur around her neck it was impossible to have the collar too tight and she had never done this before, but now she was free and she was off! I handed Rosie to the others and ran across the course, feeling acutely embarrassed.

This part of the course at Bramham Park had four cross-country fences in a kind of zig-zag pattern, which meant that it was a great place to spectate as you could see the rider jump four fences. But now I found myself in the middle of the four with hundreds of people watching – and I knew they were thinking, *Stupid woman! Fancy letting her dog off the lead!*

I realised I shouldn't be cross with Max because, if I was, she wouldn't come back to me, so in a very light-hearted voice I shouted as loud as I could: 'MAX! GOOD GIRL, MAX! MAX! *GOOOOD* GIRL!' and thankfully she ran towards me. As soon as she was near, I launched my body into the biggest rugby tackle and landed on top of her, pinning her to the ground. Very unexpectedly the whole crowd broke out into spontaneous applause! I guess it must have been quite entertaining to the 500 or so spectators! Gary's mum said it was the funniest thing she had ever seen.

Later, I apologised profusely to the rider who was on the course during this exploit; but, as it turned out, she had been more concerned that Max would run on to the nearby road. She was in fact a vet, which explained her thoughtfulness.

***

Once our Clubs had been established, we joined the Association for the Study of Obesity (ASO) as a means of keeping up to date with the latest research on the subject of nutrition and weight loss.

As a diet and fitness writer and a broadcaster, I knew that many of the academics in the field of obesity were not my greatest fans. I was neither a qualified dietician nor a nutrition scientist, yet here I was – enjoying enormous success and showing good results from my methods. On the other hand, Professor Andrew Prentice was a real fan, and he asked me to speak at the Annual Conference of the ASO in London. I was flattered and scared at the same time.

Andrew could see that we were reaching a vast number of people through our Clubs and our magazine in addition to my bestselling books and videos. He asked me to create a pie chart of my audience reach, including the impact of my weekly newspaper and magazine columns, my weekly TV appearances (on *This Morning* and daily on Granada Breeze with my own show) plus my work with M&S where over three million of my Healthy Eating plans had been taken by shoppers. Andrew wanted to illustrate to his sceptical colleagues that I was delivering a sound diet-and-fitness message, very effectively, to millions of people every week.

I took a long time to write my speech, under the guidance of Andrew, and then put it into a document which everyone could take away. On the day, I was the last speaker at the event and, I have to admit, I had found it pretty heavy going. I wondered what on earth the assembled experts would think of me. We had all been sitting in the auditorium for hours so, as soon as I stood in front of the microphone, I asked everyone in the audience to stand up, do some squats and march on the spot. It broke the ice and gave me a moment to compose myself.

Afterwards, Andrew told me he was pleased with how it had gone, and later, in 1998, my speech was published as a paper in the *International Journal of Obesity*. This was an unexpected accolade.

As the years passed, Andrew handed over the mantle of working with our Clubs and magazine to Dr Susan Jebb, who later became a professor in her own right.

Both Andrew and Susan had helped us train our franchisees in nutrition and weight management. Mary and I loved working with them both, and they enriched our knowledge and understanding of nutrition science immensely.

***

I was having such a happy time in my work and home life. Dawn had come to live with us temporarily at Ashby Folville as she was buying a new marital home for her and Ben in Staffordshire. We were all getting very excited about their wedding in September.

Ben and Dawn got the keys to their new house a week before the wedding. We had given them some carpet we had taken up from the Manor to be fitted in time for when they returned from their honeymoon. Unfortunately, the carpet fitters said it would be impossible to lay it as the carpet had gone hard over time, even though it was in perfect condition to look at, and Dawn was panicking – there were only two days before the wedding. So, loving a challenge, we set about looking for a carpet supplier and a fitter. It was a case of searching through the Yellow Pages of the telephone directory back then – there was no Google – but after several phone calls I happened upon a fitter who had just had a job cancelled. Dawn and I went to select the carpets from a nearby shop, and then the fitter kindly collected them and fitted them all that day. We felt very pleased with ourselves.

While we were excited about the wedding and all the happiness that surrounded it, there was enormous sadness too because it was also the day of Princess Diana's funeral. Such a sad moment for the nation – if not the world – but we were still determined that this day would be a day of celebration for our daughter. Thankfully, the wedding was in the afternoon after the funeral was over. The marriage service was held at Dawn's old church in Mountsorrel and we then drove off to the reception at Stapleford Park Country House Hotel.

Dawn looked like a fairy-tale princess and we were all so proud. It was on occasions like this that we were all so grateful that Phil (Dawn's father) and I had stayed best of friends and that he and his wife, Trish, and Mike and I were able to chat away very happily without anyone feeling the slightest bit awkward.

The wedding was a beautiful occasion when close friends and relatives from far and wide all came together. Some of them I hadn't seen for decades, so it made the day even more special.

Meanwhile, my business life was as busy as ever and, later that year, I was totally shocked to be presented with an award: Top Female Video Entertainer of the Year 'for achieving seven of 1996's Top 75 best-selling fitness titles'.

Through all our personal and professional joys, our faith was very important to us, and Mike and I went along to church as often as we could. When we moved to the south side of the county from Mountsorrel, we had joined a church in Knighton in Leicester and, soon afterwards, they created a new sister church a few miles away in Wigston. We joined this congregation, Meadows Community Church, when it first opened in a local school in 1993. The hope was that one day the church would be able to move into a building of its own. Under the leadership of Geoff Baker, and supported by the elders of the church, the membership flourished and within a few years there was an urgent need for our own premises.

An old hosiery factory in Wigston came on the market in the late 1990s and it seemed perfect for us. The plans were drawn up to turn it into a church and community centre at a cost, including the refurbishment, of around £1 million. The church members were united in their desire to make this happen, so a management company was created and Mike was asked to be part of the team that supervised the whole operation.

A day nursery was to be set up as part of the business plan, and this would create income to help pay for the running costs. The church members gave very generously, the money was raised and work began. It was a very exciting project. It gave Mike an interest outside of our company and I think he enjoyed being part of it.

It was shortly after this, in 2001, that the church moved into its new and very impressive premises. Geoff is not only a gifted minister but is also a talented musician who writes worship songs and plays the keyboard. Geoff and his wife Jo took their pastoral responsibilities very seriously as part of their ministry, something that proved to be invaluable to Mike and me a little later.

Appearing weekly on *This Morning* was a joy, and each year I was asked to undertake more trips around the world to film a series of strands – six-minute films – which were inserted into the live programmes. As well as Santa Monica, I also went to Granada, St Lucia and Barbados in the Caribbean, and finally beautiful Bali. These trips were great fun and a tremendous experience. What a way to see the world! Most of all, I was so grateful that Mike didn't mind my going.

I felt I had such a privileged life in so many ways – a happy home life and a very fulfilling career. I loved the new experiences that came along and I particularly enjoyed working with M&S where we had developed a great working relationship.

My long recording days continued at Granada Breeze. The channel's bosses appreciated the fact that we included their programme listings in our magazine, and I enjoyed recording endless programmes for them. This is where I learned the art of talking to a camera lens as if it were a person.

We had created a TV kitchen at Quorn House and so, whenever the Granada people wanted me to record cookery shows for their food channel, a team would descend on our offices and I would record many half-hour shows each day. To meet such a heavy recording schedule, they commissioned a home economist to shop, prepare and guide me through the various recipes. Having done my Cordon Bleu cookery course years earlier, I had an understanding of how to cook, so thankfully I was able to pick up the method and techniques quite quickly.

Then one day a different home economist was there, setting up. He was in a different league from the normal home economists I had previously worked with. His name was Dean Simpole-Clarke.

Working with Dean was bliss. Everything was perfectly planned and laid out, and he explained it all fully to me. My job of cooking the food and chatting through the method to camera suddenly became very straightforward. I later realised that Dean was in fact a qualified chef, so that explained why he was so good.

Over time, we recorded over 400 cookery shows, and Dean took over as the chef for our magazine and created the recipes for all my cookbooks and diet books from then on. He even accompanied me to Barbados to create a series of mini-films for *This Morning*.

Dean also created the Low Fat Cookery Course which we published as a pullout part-work in my magazine to celebrate the new millennium. We later edited it into my *Step by Step Low Fat Cookbook*, which was a great success.

I loved working on our magazine. Our bimonthly editorial meetings were always great fun and very lively with Editor Geri and the team. As I have already mentioned, my favourite job of all was doing the photo-shoots with our successful slimmers from our classes all over the UK. Those days were always the most thrilling and satisfying.

In 1998 the Clubs were flourishing and we were very excited when we won the top award offered by the British Franchise Association (BFA): Franchisor of the Year. This is like getting an Oscar for Best Film but in the franchising world. It was an astonishing achievement for a small company like ours when you realise that we were competing against giants like McDonald's and Prontaprint. Apparently, the BFA liked us because we held such high standards in our selection of franchisees and in our extensive training. Our Clubs were gaining an enviable reputation.

Amid all the fun and frivolity of the late 1990s, there was also real sadness. At one of our Roadshows, Simon had called me on my mobile. I knew he wouldn't do this unless it was serious. Linda Stevens, who was the anchor woman in our magazine office, had been diagnosed with breast cancer. Mary and I were in shock.

Linda subsequently was treated in Glenfield Hospital in Leicester where she had a mastectomy. Despite undergoing a variety of treatments over the following months, very sadly the cancer spread, and Linda became so unwell that she was unable to work. Together with the staff, we did everything we could to support her through her dreadful illness. In these situations where one feels so helpless, the least we could do as a company was to commit to paying her salary for as long as she needed it, so that she didn't have to worry about covering her mortgage and household bills. Three years later, Linda was transferred to LOROS, our local hospice, and I went to see her. I just sat at her bedside, looking at this beautiful woman in her 30s with whom I had loved working on our magazine and who had become a friend. I fought back the tears as I realised this might be the last time we would meet. Linda was losing this hard-fought battle, and two weeks later we received the news that she had passed away. It was unbearably sad.

Many of our staff went to Linda's funeral service at the crematorium and tried desperately to celebrate her 30-something years with our memorable 'Linda-memories', but it was all so devastating. It seems unfair when someone so young falls victim to such a cruel disease. We tried to remember the laughter that had enriched our lives during the precious time we had enjoyed together, but it was no good; we couldn't hold back the tears.

14

Heartbreak, Honours and
This Is Your Life
1999–2003

After having had so many fabulous years when our marriage seemed to reach new heights, it came as a real shock when in 1999 Mike seemed to change. He had always been affected by fluctuating moods, and I had learned to cope with these, but in the great times when he was very affectionate and funny, he was amazing. The best husband anyone could wish for. I was always totally in love with him and I always knew that he was in love with me. But suddenly, a darkness seemed to fall on our marriage. Mike also became even less interested in the business and gradually isolated himself from everything to do with our life together.

As he became more and more detached, instead of being supportive in all that I was doing, he became disinterested and almost dismissive. I felt that whenever I spoke to him, I was treading on eggshells. It all became very painful. Perhaps worst of all, I just couldn't understand it. What had I done to make him feel this way? Yes, I worked very hard, but previously he hadn't had any issue with that. I always tried to get back home as quickly as possible from any events that occurred after normal office hours. I planned any evening commitments so there would be no more than one a week. We had everything we could have ever wished for – a beautiful home, a wonderful family – plus we had been together for 16 years and had lived and loved our exciting journey together. I could not understand why this was happening.

Thankfully, we were committed to our church. Having been part of the congregation that had moved from Knighton Evangelical Church in Leicester to 'plant' a new church, Meadows Community Church in the suburb of Wigston, we knew everyone and we all cared for one another.

We would all meet up on Sunday mornings for praise and worship. Our friends at church were supportive, particularly the minister and his wife, Geoff and Jo Baker, who had become close friends.

The congregation must have known there was something wrong between Mike and me as it was not unusual for me to start crying in the middle of the service and have to go out. A word of a song, a Bible reading or just a feeling in my heart would set me off. It was all so hard and my heart was breaking in the sadness. And I felt desperately helpless because I couldn't understand it.

As with many in this situation, we had to put on a brave face at the office and in public. In fact, it was better when we were with friends or colleagues because Mike behaved more warmly towards me; but, as soon as we drove away, the 'ice curtain' would fall and a veil of silence descended. It was back to walking on eggshells.

In the summer, we were following Gary and Gemma around the country at weekends to various horse events when Mike suggested that we buy a villa in Portugal. The now Non-Executive Director of our Clubs business, Dr Brian Smith and his wife Rika, owned a property in Portugal and had invited us to stay with them on a number of occasions and we had loved it.

I was immediately very excited as I thought this was a very positive suggestion from Mike and one which could potentially help our relationship. Dawn was thrilled with the idea, as were our various friends, so Mike and I flew over to the Algarve, stayed with Brian and Rika and looked at properties. We soon found a delightful villa not far from where Brian and Rika were now living for most of the year.

The property needed a new kitchen, so we decided to return once the transaction was completed. Unfortunately, Mike suddenly suffered a serious neck problem and, after being referred to a specialist, was told that the damage caused by his falling off a ladder a few years earlier had left him with quite a serious injury; the slightest wrong move could affect his spinal cord. He was put on strong painkillers and muscle relaxants, and was instructed not to fly and to do nothing while he recovered. This made life even more challenging, but at least he was being treated.

Mike suggested that Dawn and I should go over to the villa, meet the designer to create a smart new kitchen, and start getting the house into some kind of order. It is usual practice when buying a property in Portugal that the purchase also includes the contents, so our villa was already furnished. I really hoped it wouldn't be long before Mike would be able to join me and, hopefully, we could together enjoy our first-ever home abroad, though I have to admit it was something of a relief from the strain at home to be away with Dawn on my own.

It took weeks before Mike's neck improved, so it was a worrying time and, understandably, Mike became quite depressed. As a result, as well as having little to do with the business, he also lost interest in the horses, now rarely coming to events. Instead, he started spending a lot of time with a family from church. Life became increasingly challenging at home, but I was always hopeful that we could get through this 'sticky patch'.

Work, of course, was as busy and as crazy as ever. To be honest, I was glad to be in the company of positive, friendly and supportive people when out of the house. It gave some relief from the atmosphere of home. I realised that my working so hard would have had an effect on our relationship and that Mike must have felt at times that work was more important to me than he was, and I regret that. In fact, that was never the case. However, things were going from bad to worse and life was becoming unbearable.

Looking back, I now see that when a couple go through a tough time in their relationship, both parties can react in unfortunate ways. I became super-controlling – 'Where are you going?' 'Who are you going with?' 'Why are you doing that?' – and as I was so stressed, I guess I must have become quite unpleasant to live with too.

Then one day, I went into the office as usual only to be met by a very excited Louise, my PA.

'Look at this!' she said, beaming from ear to ear.

It was a letter from the Lord Lieutenant of Leicestershire, inviting me to become a Deputy Lieutenant (DL). I wasn't even aware such a position existed, but I was flattered and felt highly honoured. I, along with other new deputies, was invited to dinner at the home of the then Lord Lieutenant, Tim Brookes. As Mike was away on that date, I went with Dawn. We new DLs all had to swear allegiance to Her Majesty the Queen, and then we were presented with a certificate. The role of a Deputy Lieutenant is to support the Lord Lieutenant, who is the Queen's representative in that county, and to fulfil various roles as determined by the lieutenancy office. Deputy Lieutenants, and there are quite a few of them, are there to stand in when the Lord Lieutenant is unavailable to attend an event, and it is a role for life. I felt very privileged to have been given this honour and it was a big ray of sunshine on a rather gloomy horizon at the time.

Unfortunately, by Christmas our relationship was going from bad to even worse, and on Boxing Day Mike called me at home from our friends' house to say that he had decided he wanted to have children of his own. This came like a thunderbolt. Having had a hysterectomy years before we met, I felt my heart sink. His words crushed me to the core. This really was the end, then. I was stunned and didn't know what to do or what to think. It was heartbreaking news.

Mike came home and explained that it wasn't anything I had done. It wasn't my fault. It was just how he felt. It was all so desperately sad and I felt completely helpless. There was nothing in the world we could do to rectify this. What he wanted I couldn't give him.

Life, of course, had to carry on and we behaved in a civilised manner, but the air was icy cold. I did my best to hold myself together even though it was unbearably difficult. It must have been hard for people around us as we drifted further and further apart under this never-ending black cloud of unhappiness. Here was the man I had loved passionately for so long, a man I absolutely adored, but now he wanted to find someone else with whom he could start a family. Part of me couldn't believe it, while the other part of me was processing the consequences of our splitting up – moving house, sorting out the business, and so on.

As we had already invited guests to a celebration meal on New Year's Eve, the eve of a new millennium, I busied myself with the preparations. We rarely entertained in our formal dining room because the table was so huge, but for this once-in-a-lifetime event it provided the perfect setting for 16 of us to sit around our table celebrating this momentous occasion. Mike sat at one end, and I at the other. It said everything about our relationship. We were poles apart.

As the evening progressed, Mike was ensuring that the 20th century would go out in style, and he celebrated into the small hours with his friends. It became increasingly obvious that he didn't want me to be part of his life in the next century. I felt so isolated and bereft. There was no doubt that he had become emotionally detached from me and emotionally attached to this other family – people who had once been my friends. I felt betrayed on every level.

In the January of 2000 Mike would be marking his 40th birthday and, at the same time, as it turned out, I was going into the menopause; so I suppose it was not surprising that we were both going through a strange stage of our lives. After his birthday meal, which we shared with friends, we had a blazing row and I declared that I couldn't live like this and that I wanted a divorce. As a result, he moved out of our bedroom up to the next floor of the Manor.

The next day, I arranged to meet a solicitor to discuss the possibility of divorce proceedings. I said I didn't want to do anything yet but I needed to know where I stood. I am glad I had that meeting. It helped me to understand, and come to terms with, the implications if we were to make such a major, life-changing decision.

In the meantime I went to my GP to explain that I felt very low and unable to cope. He did a blood test and found that I was indeed in the early stages of the menopause and immediately put me on to hormone replacement therapy (HRT). Within a couple of weeks, I felt much better – so much so that I went back to the doctor to ask him to increase my dose of HRT, and I have remained on it ever since. It transformed my confidence and enabled me to deal with our domestic situation significantly better.

Somewhat surprisingly, Mike and I managed to live together relatively amicably, albeit separately, under the same roof – the blessing of a very large house. I was getting accustomed to the cold atmosphere and sadness between us. You can always tell when a relationship is struggling by the absence of eye contact, and the lack of endearing touches or affirming comments. Everyone around us was now aware of the situation.

Developing my sense of independence, in the spring I decided to go over to the villa in Portugal for a week on my own. I needed a break from the pressure of our home life and felt a holiday would do me good. It was such a relief just to get away. I loved the villa, and our kind taxi driver, Antonio, whom Dawn and I had first met some months before, drove me from Faro airport. Antonio was so helpful, appreciating that this was the first time I was to stay on my own. He checked the car that came with the house, and suggested that his sister could take me shopping the next day to buy a kettle and various other items to match our newly fitted kitchen. I have experienced so much kindness from the Portuguese.

A couple of days later, I drove to the shops in our car but, before I had driven even a couple of miles, was pulled over by the police. The car had UK number plates and apparently it had no legal standing to be driven in Portugal. The police officers didn't speak English and I didn't speak Portuguese, so it was an interesting conversation. They wanted to see my proof of ownership. The only documentation I had was the sale–purchase contract for the villa, which included the car. I ended up driving two policemen to the villa and then, while they waited outside, I desperately rang the estate agent to get his advice and ask him to speak to the police officers for me, which he did. I showed them the contract and they were very unhappy about the section that said the car had been purchased for £1 as part of the deal. After much conversation between the two of them, not a word of which I understood, I was told to present myself and the car at a police station some 10 miles (16 km) away at 3 pm prompt that afternoon.

I was scared to death and dreaded driving through the main city of Faro and out the other side to Olhão police station. I set off early and I couldn't help saying to myself the words, 'I'm in trouble with the police and my husband doesn't love me any more!' with tears streaming down my cheeks.

When I finally arrived in Olhão I found a police station and parked up – but it was the wrong one. The staff rang through to the other station and put me on to 'my' police officer from earlier.

'Ah, Rosemary!' he said in a cheery voice, and then proceeded to give me further directions in very broken English.

I finally arrived to find my Portuguese policeman 'friend' waving at me outside the station and inviting me in. He and his colleagues were polite enough and told me that I must not drive the car again as it was illegal, and that I must pay a £300 fine! They were quite pleasant despite my misdemeanour, and off I drove home.

I rang Mike who, while sympathetic, thought it was quite amusing. Later I called Dawn, who was at a Christian conference with a few friends. When I told her of my adventurous day, I heard her turn to her pals saying, 'My mum's been arrested!' Everyone thought it was hilarious. I suppose you have to see the funny side but, at the time, I felt so scared and lonely.

To complete the story of the car, we ultimately sold the vehicle to a dealer who drove it back to the UK.

I enjoyed my time away once I was past this hiccup, and I rested and relaxed. I could do my writing and catch up on my mail while sitting on the balcony in the sunshine. It did me good.

***

Mike and I continued to exist together, but it all seemed so hopeless. Some days I could see a chink of light when he was nice to me and on other days it was unbearable. I felt such a deep sense of rejection that I became very insecure. So much so that I ended up making a decision I later came to regret. When I went down to London one day to appear on *This Morning*, my slot on the show was suddenly dropped, despite the fact that it was included in the programme menu and everything was prepped and ready to go. I know this can happen in television but, after it happened a second time, I felt that perhaps I was being eased out of the show. So, in fear of further rejection, I decided to resign. In hindsight it was the most stupid decision I have ever made, but that was how insecure I felt at the time. In my letter of resignation I thanked Richard and Judy for the seven very happy years and all the amazing opportunities the show had given me, but said I believed it was time to leave as I felt they wanted me to. They wrote a very kind letter back to me saying that was not their intention but they would honour my wishes. They were lovely people and I missed everyone on the show after I left.

That summer, Mike went away to our villa in Portugal with the family with whom he had become very close friends and with whom he spent so much of his time. He would spend the first week with them on his own; then I was to arrive for the second week. Because they were a family of four, they needed three bedrooms, so there was no alternative but for Mike and me to share a bed – for the first time in months. As we tried to go to sleep, I loved being near him even if we were lying back to back. I loved him so much but hated the situation we were in, and there seemed to be nothing I could do about it. Just being in the same bed with him was amazing – I felt a kind of electricity between us and hoped that our skin might touch and we could become close again, but sadly it was not to be. There were no loving vibes coming in my direction.

While we were away, Mike's uncle telephoned. Mike's father had died suddenly. It was such a shock because, while we knew he had had some health problems, there was no sense that this could happen. We immediately decided to leave Mike's friends at the villa and return home to be with Jeanne, Mike's mum. I was very happy to leave.

The earliest flight was the next morning. We travelled in silence, but it wasn't a cold silence. It was a compassionate, sympathetic quietness.

The next few days were busy as Mike organised the funeral and looked after Jeanne, who was remarkably stoical. She had adored Philip throughout their long and devoted marriage, but I knew she had always hoped that Philip would pass before her, and now he had. He was only 75 when he died. He was a real gentleman and I was very fond of him.

Thankfully, my relationship with Mike seemed to improve slightly and sometimes we got on relatively well – with no further mention of his having children. In fact, over time, Mike even returned to the marital bed.

Also in 2000, we had launched a new *online* weight-loss Club called Slim with Rosemary. A Nottingham-based IT company had launched a similar site for men called Fat Man Slim. The company was owned and run by three young guys, Phil, Oliver and Neil, who were now looking after all our IT needs. It made sense to create a female version of Fat Man Slim, and so Phil and I adapted the programme. I recorded the messages to accompany the audio programme and, once it was all completed, it was very exciting to appear on *Steve Wright in the Afternoon* on BBC Radio 2 to talk about both Fat Man Slim and Slim with Rosemary. Steve Wright is an extraordinarily talented broadcaster and I came out feeling exhilarated.

That year, our friend Revd Ian Coffey (who was only too aware of our marital challenges as he and his wife Ruth were among our closest friends) asked Mike if he would accompany him to Uganda to make a film illustrating the building of an extension at an orphanage. The money had been raised at the annual Christian convention Spring Harvest in the previous year and amounted to an extraordinary £1.2 million to be spent on four children's projects around the world. One of those projects was to build an extension to an orphanage, Jaja's Home, which means 'Grandma's House'. Mike had a good eye for photography and film-making and, together with a young man, Lloyd Parsons, he and Ian spent a week compiling a film report of the construction, as well as meeting the children who would ultimately benefit from the extra facilities. I think Mike felt enriched by the whole experience and loved meeting the children – and they loved him.

As Mike was having little to do with our business except attending Board meetings at Quorn House, he decided to become a Justice of the Peace. He has always had a very good brain and a strong desire to see justice done, so he was ideally suited to this role as a local magistrate. Mike was sworn in on the very same day the planes crashed into the Twin Towers in New York on September 11, 2001. No-one will ever forget that day.

Meanwhile, I never gave up on our marriage. I was always hoping and praying that things would sort themselves out over time, despite my somewhat impetuous consultation with a solicitor about a divorce at the beginning of 2000. Then one day, I noticed Mike was no longer wearing his wedding ring. I was shocked and stunned. Why had he removed his wedding ring? Was he making a statement that he was looking for another relationship? Was there really no hope for us after all?

So I asked him, 'Where's your wedding ring?'

He responded with, 'I've just decided not to wear it any more.'

Once again, I was utterly devastated. I also felt a bit stupid and naive for thinking we might be able to rebuild our marriage. I was truly shocked and couldn't believe he would do that.

On top of all of this, my father's health was deteriorating. He had been quite settled in the geriatric unit in North Walsham in Norfolk for five years when he started showing signs of distressing deterioration, so he was transferred to the Norfolk and Norwich University Hospital. I went to visit him, having collected Mabel from their bungalow. As he lay in bed, we tried to feed him but he just choked. I then heard the doctor make the decision that from now on he would receive 'nil by mouth'. I understood how difficult it must be for the medical staff to take such a drastic step, but he wasn't even able to swallow a mouthful of the creamy yogurt that he loved, so in a way this was a kindness.

As we were about to leave, Father looked me in the eyes, smiled and gestured for me to kiss him. It was a very special moment because for the last couple of years he hadn't even recognised me. I treasure this memory so much. Two days later, my father finally passed away. At 88, he had lived an eventful life and had listened to God and found a wife who had been utterly devoted to him until his final day.

Mabel was quite stoical about his passing and asked to have his body at home, and so he lay in his open coffin in his bedroom for four days. Mabel's father had been an undertaker and she had been brought up with dead bodies around their premises, which I have to say was difficult for me to comprehend. But, for Mabel, Father was now at home, and every morning she went into his bedroom and had a cup of tea with him!

My brother Robert and his family, and Mike, Dawn and I all attended the funeral, which, while lovely, was of course extremely sad. My father had been so kind to me when I was such a frail little girl, and I will always remember him giving me piggyback rides and rubbing my back to help me breathe more easily. He was a warm-hearted and generous man.

For the first few weeks I continued to call Mabel every day, but then I weaned her down to every other day. She missed Oswald enormously and seemed to have lost the reason to live. She no longer needed to drive every day to sit with him in the hospital for two hours. Now the days had no purpose and it proved very difficult to keep her spirits up. This is a situation that many elderly people find themselves in and it must be very difficult. My heart goes out to them.

Life at home continued to be grim but, just as I was reaching even greater depths of despair, I had another big surprise. I was contacted by an official at Leicester City Council offering me the honour of being the first woman to be given the Freedom of the City of Leicester; would I be happy to accept? This is the greatest honour that can be awarded by any city and I was flabbergasted! Previous honorary freemen included such notable people as Richard and David Attenborough, and Professor Sir Alec Jeffreys who discovered DNA fingerprinting. I was thrilled to be asked but nervous about telling Mike. However, Mike was kind and supportive and was pleased for me.

On the day of the ceremony, when I and a local philanthropist, Frank May, were honoured, Mike, Dawn, my brother Robert and sister-in-law Jane all came along. No-one would have known that Mike and I were struggling in our relationship and all appeared well. It was on these special occasions that I so wanted us to be happy again.

Very gradually, things seemed to improve a little and we began to cope better. Maybe this latest honour had given me some much-needed confidence.

***

In the following year another, quite different honour was to take me by surprise. Apparently, the team that ran the TV programme *This Is Your Life* had wanted me to be a mystery guest for some time, but my TV agent June Ford-Crush, Dawn and my PA Louise all knew of our marital problems and had tactfully put them off. As time progressed, things did seem to improve in that area and, with the programme-makers pushing to get me on, it seems Louise spoke to Mike and persuaded him that they should be allowed to do it. As I was going to stay with Nancy DeMoss in the United States for a week on my own, this presented the perfect opportunity for the production team to meet up with Dawn and Mike and also to film and interview Gary Parsonage, our horse event rider, at home.

Of course, I knew absolutely nothing about what was going on. One day, I was in London at the Slimmer of the Year event for 2002 and, while our winner was being presented with her award, suddenly there was a loud gasp in the room. I thought someone had fainted. No, the presenter of *This Is Your Life*, Michael Aspel, had appeared with his big red book!

It was such a shock yet so exciting at the same time. I ran over to Mike and gave him the biggest hug, as I realised he must have agreed to this happening and I saw it as a massive turning point in our relationship.

I was overwhelmed after the announcement but explained to the programme's producers that I needed to look after my Slimmers of the Year first, before going to the studio, because it was such a big day for them. They were very accommodating and said I could take all the time I needed.

Rosemary in the garden of her family home
in Countesthorpe, Leicestershire, aged 2.

Rosemary playing with the rabbits
in her school uniform, aged 6.

Rosemary with her brother Robert, and her father
and mother in the garden in Countesthorpe.

Rosemary, aged 18, attending the Good Grooming course at
night school with Tutor Kathy Parker in 1964.

Phil and Rosemary's first car in 1965, which cost £10.
It was a 1937 Hillman with an interesting registration plate!

Rosemary, aged 20, being photographed for her first modelling job in Leicester.

Rosemary gaining weight (see Chapter 2) in 1970.
Pictured with Pyrenean Mountain dog Sheba.

Rosemary with her daughter Dawn, just a week old, in 1975.

Mike and Rosemary's first home together –
the Old Parsonage in Mountsorrel, Leicestershire – in 1983.
It was a bargain at just £42,000.

Mike and Rosemary on Bondi Beach
during Rosemary's Australian book tour in 1988.

The sequel to Rosemary's original *Hip and Thigh Diet* book. This follow-up book went on to sell 2 million copies worldwide.

PAPERBACKS

THIS WEEK	General	LAST WEEK	WEEKS ON LIST
1	**Rosemary Conley's Metabolism Booster Diet** (Arrow £4.99) Eight 30-day diet plans for eating more of the right foods and staying slim	—	1
2	**Rosemary Conley's Complete Hip & Thigh Diet** (Arrow £3.50) The updated version of Conley's original method of losing weight	1	97
3	**A Year in Provence / Peter Mayle** (Pan £4.99) Writer's witty account of how he and his wife moved into an old French farmhouse	2	38
4	**Seasons of My Life / Hannah Hauxwell** (Arrow £3.99) Solitary Daleswoman's account of her life without modern comforts	5	27
5	**Rosemary Conley's Inch-Loss Plan** (Arrow £4.99) Another of Conley's astonishingly successful slimming series	4	49
6	**Families and How to Survive Them / Cleese & Skynner** (Mandarin £5.99) John Cleese and his psychiatrist on coping with domestic upheaval	3	4
7	**Rosemary Conley's Diet and Fitness Action Pack** (BBC £7.99) Tie-in to Conley's Daytime TV Fitness Club includes diary, wallchart and exercise cassette	7	2
8	**The Time of My Life / Denis Healey** (Penguin £6.99) Labour politician's highly readable autobiography is also a post-war history of Britain	6	15
9	**Lose 7lbs in 7 Days / Miriam Stoppard** (Headline £3.50) How to lose weight by eating six times a day	—	1
10	**The 1991 Good Pub Guide / ed Alisdair Aird** (Ebury £10.99) Ninth edition of this tour of the country's best hostelries	8	3

THE SUNDAY TIMES
27 JANUARY 1991

The *Sunday Times* non-fiction bestseller list on 27 January 1991.

Ashby Folville Manor, near Melton Mowbray in Leicestershire,
where Mike and Rosemary lived from 1996 to 2016.

Rosemary and local philanthropist Frank May being granted
the Freedom of the City of Leicester by the Lord Mayor,
Councillor John Allen, in 2001.

Michael Aspel surprising Rosemary for TV show *This Is Your Life*
during her Slimmer of the Year Awards in 2002.

Rosemary receiving her CBE at Buckingham Palace in 2004,
accompanied by daughter Dawn, husband Mike and mother-in-law Jeanne.

Completion of the Steps Conductive Education Centre TV makeover challenge in 2007.

Some of the dogs who have won Rosemary's heart over the years

Rosemary's favourite childhood dog,
a Sheltie crossbreed named Sue.

Dawn aged 18 months with Pyrenean Mountain dog, Beauty.

German Shepherd Nik and one of her pups, Sheba.

Another German Shepherd, Max,
enjoying the snow at Ashby Folville in 2006.

Waise (pronounced 'Visor'), a stray whippet–lurcher cross
Rosemary and Mike adopted in 2007.

Mike and Rosemary on the bridge at Ashby Folville Manor in 2008.

Rosemary with her professional ice-skating partner Mark Hanretty
for ITV's *Dancing on Ice* in 2012.

Rosemary enjoying a workout with a wonderful crowd of women.

My driver, David, then took me to the studios on the outskirts of London, and there I was asked to stay in my dressing room until the live filming of the show. Dawn had brought about 20 different evening dresses and outfits from my wardrobe to give me a choice of what to wear, but in fact I wore the suit I had worn in the morning – a favourite suit that I had bought while staying with Nancy DeMoss in the States.

I was kept away from everyone until the programme began. The producers had very kindly kept my make-up artist from the morning event, so at least I had a friend with me during the afternoon. Then it was time. Apparently, the guest is never discussed by name, only by a code name, so that the audience has no idea who will be revealed. My code name apparently was 'Herb'.

I was so excited – on many levels. It was a tremendous accolade to be chosen, but also I knew it would be a lovely experience. I had no idea who would be featured, so you can imagine my surprise when, apart from my family of course, there were tributes from Terry Wogan (because our Clubs had raised loads of money for Children in Need); Cliff Richard (because it was partly through him that I had become a Christian); Richard and Judy, chef Brian Turner and agony aunt Denise Robertson, all because of my time on *This Morning*; actor Patrick Mower who had voiced one of my early fitness audio tapes (in the days before videos); Dr Hilary Jones (whom I knew through our magazine); and Revd Steve Chalke, founder of Oasis Trust, a Christian charity we had supported. Then they also brought on my three Slimmers of the Year – Helen Jary, Rachel O'Hara and Louise Irvine – which must have been so exciting for them! There were more personal films of Gary, our event rider, and also my best friend from school, now living in Australia, Lizzie. It was extraordinary. My mouth was parchment-dry with adrenalin and Michael Aspel was a sweetheart. Such a very lovely, gentle man.

After walking through the sliding doors for the big reveal of the night's celebrity, I sat on my chair. Mike was next to appear on the show and sat beside me. Sitting opposite were my friends from years gone by: the original women from my first slimming class held in our kitchen; Geoff and Jo, and Ian and Ruth, our very close Christian friends; John Simons, on whose programme on BBC Radio Nottingham I had regularly appeared and from which I recruited trialists for my *Hip and Thigh Diet*;

my first boss, architect Roy Bordoli; Dawn and Ben of course, my brother Robert, sister-in-law Jane and one of my nieces, Nicky . . . and so the numbers went on! All of our staff members were in the audience. It was mind-blowingly exciting.

Apparently, the planning had been a nightmare for Dawn, Louise and Mike as they tried to put together the pieces of my life without my knowledge, but gradually it took shape. On the day before, after Mike and I had left to go down to London for the Slimmer of the Year Awards, there was a loudspeaker announcement at Quorn House when the receptionist said: 'ROSEMARY HAS NOW LEFT THE BUILDING!' and everyone could breathe a big sigh of relief! They could now prepare to travel to London themselves to attend the programme the following day.

After the show was recorded, which was an utterly joyous experience, we all went backstage to find that ITV had laid on a fabulous party for my guests. It was amazing. They spoilt us with a delicious buffet and unlimited drinks. It was such a wonderful surprise, and as I looked around I realised that everyone in the room meant something very special to me. Once all my family and friends were assembled, I stood on a chair and addressed them. I think I said something like: 'Thank you all so much for being part of this extraordinary day. I want to thank ITV so much for making the programme, and while I feel immensely flattered that so many celebrities said such lovely things, it is you, in this room, who have really formed my life. Please don't leave before I have had a chance to say hello to you all. It is such a thrill to see you.'

In fact, it was a bit like attending my own funeral while still being very much alive.

After it was all over, a few of our closest friends went out for dinner, though I wasn't hungry at all and just wanted to sit down quietly. Later, Dawn and Ben and Mike and I went back to the hotel, but I couldn't relax. My head felt as if it was going to explode. So much emotion. So many memories recalled. It was difficult to comprehend it all. I hardly slept a wink, and next morning I told Dawn of my sleepless night.

'Good!' she laughed. 'I haven't slept for a fortnight stressing about it! I slept really well – at last!'

She went on to explain that the production team had emphasised throughout the planning process, which had taken months, that if the celebrity found out what was happening, the programme would be pulled. No question.

After all the excitement of the recording day, the staff were buzzing in Quorn House. The programme would be shown in a couple of weeks' time on ITV and everyone was looking forward to seeing it. Of course, there were some people who had not been invited on to the show and were disappointed, but there was nothing I could do about it as I had known nothing about it anyway.

Appearing on *This Is Your Life* gave me a tremendous confidence boost, which helped me feel happier for a while; but unfortunately the slight improvement in our marriage was short-lived. As the weeks and months passed by, Mike became less and less interested in me and the business. When the team from Quorn House went down to London for the finals of Franchisor of the Year 2002, Mike didn't want to come, which was a shame because we won the top award – *again*! When I called Mike from the car on the way home to tell him, he really wasn't interested. It was very disappointing.

Living together was proving so unpleasant that I dreaded going home each evening. We would sit down to eat, but I just couldn't swallow. Something was breaking in my heart and the weight fell off me. I started eating chocolates and crazy food to try to get some concentrated calories into me. I didn't know what Mike was doing half the time, and by now we were behaving like strangers, living separate lives.

Mike also decided that we should bring to a close our interest in Three-Day Eventing. This was a shame, but I had to admit it was an extremely expensive hobby. We gave Gary his Olympic horse as a gift and he was very grateful. The other horses were sold, but we made sure they all went to good homes. Gary moved up to the north-east of England and continued his career. It was a time of new beginnings for Gary and Gemma as they both went their separate ways and forged new relationships. Both are now married and have children, as well as continuing their careers with horses.

Our own relationship seemed so hopeless. I think what hurt most was how charming and delightful Mike could be to everyone else, at church or wherever, and how he seemed to make a real effort to be unpleasant to me. One day we came back from church after he had been particularly charming to a female member and I just couldn't take it. That same day, a friend had given back to me a very large crystal cut-glass vase which I had loaned to her, and when we arrived home I got out of the car and threw the vase as hard as I could to the ground, smashing it into a million pieces. I wanted to somehow demonstrate how stressed and upset I was at Mike's behaviour. It was killing me.

Six months later, Mike decided to move out completely. He had found a house near to where his friends lived and he wanted to buy it. I didn't have a problem with that but, as it turned out, I had little to do with it as he and his friends furnished it and redecorated it. I absolutely hated going there and never stayed over. Looking back, I think this was the worst bit. I felt such an unwelcome outsider. Not only to my husband but also to this family – people I had considered to be my friends but who had turned their back on me.

I had loved Mike so much and believed he would be my soulmate for ever, but now he was gone.

15

Onwards and upwards
2002–6

Thankfully, for the sake of the business, Mike and I had to carry on as if nothing was different. If he went to Quorn House, it meant that I still saw him occasionally – which was good. He was still a Director of the company, and whenever we needed him at Quorn House he would be there and we always appeared to get on well. But we rarely spoke, and at the end of the day we drove home our separate ways.

The Manor was a big house for one person. Our housekeeper and her husband no longer lived in the flat on the top floor, but I had the dogs to keep me company and so I rarely felt lonely. Dawn was amazingly supportive, which was such a blessing. Everything continued as normal, but it was desperately sad that our personal relationship had come to this. I adored Mike and I couldn't imagine life without him.

Mike had always been so supportive of my work commitments, never complaining if I was away filming on the other side of the world with *This Morning*, or working my socks off recording my next fitness video, or shutting myself away to write my next book. He had supported me in anything and everything I ever did, and I honestly do not believe I would have enjoyed the success I achieved had I not had Mike's unconditional love and encouragement behind me. There was no doubt that I was driven and highly motivated by my work and I derived an enormous reward from it, and I am not talking financial reward here. It was immensely gratifying to produce diet books and fitness videos, and lots of other things that people seemed to want and which apparently changed their lives. I also acknowledge that I may have given the impression to Mike that he wasn't as important to me as he actually was. I utterly adored him and he fulfilled my life beyond my imagination; but, as I have said, I recognise that he may not have always felt that. I didn't mind that he wanted to work less in the business, and he knew he had a completely free rein to pursue whatever interests he chose, such as becoming a magistrate, learning to fly a helicopter or playing golf whenever he wanted. It had been a wonderful marriage of respect and love – but now that had all gone.

The staff at Quorn House were like a family, and those who were closest to me, and knew about Mike's departure, were very supportive and kind. At more formal events, I had to put on a bright and calm face to the world, whether it was a presentation day for new franchisees or a Roadshow for the members of our Clubs, or even an evangelistic evening where I spoke of how God had put Mike and me together, which felt very weird as we were now living apart. Such evenings did, however, act as a reminder that God had told me to marry Mike in the first place. There were times when I wondered how I would manage to face the audience as I felt so sad at how it had all gone wrong. However, I still loved Mike and I was there to speak about my faith. Geoff, our minister, and his wife Jo were wonderful, as were our other friends, Revd Ian and Ruth Coffey.

I think now would be an appropriate time to apologise to anyone and everyone who had to put up with me during this period, when I was so often discussing my marital problems, asking for advice and needing people to lend me an ear or a shoulder to cry on. I must have been such a drain on everyone I considered a close friend. Thank you so much for your patience, your love and your support, because without it I don't think I would have survived.

It's really hard when you love someone so much and don't know, and don't understand, why that person doesn't love you any more. At a loss to know what to do next, in desperation I called Nancy DeMoss in the USA, and she was so sympathetic and supportive. She suggested that I keep some booklets and Bible verses in the bathroom and next to my bed and on my desk to read when I could, and to listen to inspiring Christian music in the car, in the bathroom and so on. In other words, she was encouraging me to feel God's presence everywhere I went to protect me and support me through this awful time. And that's what I did. It was very calming and comforting, and I certainly felt that God was protecting me everywhere I went.

But there was another form of divine help too. It seemed I had been sent an army of guys, some from church, some just friends, who were truly looking out for me. It was amazing how, at crucial times of desperation, one of them would ring out of the blue, simply call to say 'How are you doing?' Their care and kindness made a massive difference. They knew how I felt about Mike and there was never a hint of anything other than simple thoughtfulness and support, and it made me feel as though someone understood and cared about me. It is difficult to put into words how much I appreciated that. It was like honey to my soul, a healing power. Our minister Geoff Baker was amazing, as was Ian Coffey. I felt God was sending me this army of support, and I felt he was also sending personal positive 'signs' to help me feel I was OK and to know I could 'hold on' and have faith.

It was now in our fourth year since our 'troubles' began, and during this period I had been given awards and honours I had never even dreamed of, but none of these accolades could mend a broken heart. Our relationship, while polite, had reached an all-time low. Then, at the end of 2002, it all reached a crescendo and I decided I couldn't take it any more. The constant coldness from Mike wore me down and I am sure my response to him wasn't very warm either. Suddenly, it dawned on me: I didn't love him any more. It was then that I decided it was all over.

I know I am not the only one to have gone through such times – there are millions and millions of others who have – but I had experienced the most utterly destroying feeling of rejection and I felt bereft. However, now, I felt resolute. Enough was enough and I was prepared for a new life on my own, with all the sacrifices that would inevitably bring, and I felt brave enough, at last, to face it.

At times like this we find our true friends, and I don't think I could have survived without the support of Dawn, who was outstanding, as well as Geoff and Jo, and Ian and Ruth. As I consulted with them all, they completely understood my decision, and sympathised with it. Then it was decided that there should be a meeting at Geoff's house. Ian would drive up from Plymouth, where he was the local Baptist minister, and he and Geoff would meet Mike to address the crisis in which we found ourselves. Half an hour later, I was invited to join the discussion to explain my decision.

When I arrived at Geoff and Jo's house, I have to admit I was slightly disappointed when Ian greeted me with the question, 'Do you think there is any way whatsoever you might be able to reconcile your differences and save the marriage?' It had taken me a long time and a lot of soul-searching to reach the decision that I had and, to be honest, I was almost looking forward to being free from all the stress of the last four years. To me, our relationship was irretrievably lost, but I went into the meeting to see how Mike reacted.

I made it very clear that for me it was all over. After further discussion, Mike and I went back to the Manor to talk. He wanted to stay there and try to rebuild the relationship. I had no objection to his staying, but I was totally serious that we had reached the end of the road as far as our marriage was concerned. I felt too damaged and exhausted by it all. I hadn't come to this decision lightly and I wasn't prepared to change my mind now.

From then on, we slept in separate bedrooms with separate bathrooms. Over the next few days, Mike went to a great deal of effort to persuade me to change my mind about ending the marriage. He left romantic messages on my pillow and kept telling me how much he loved me in an attempt to keep us together. It was nice to be in the company of this man who had suddenly transformed himself into the delightful guy I had originally married, but I was not to be persuaded. I remained in the other bedroom and was resolute in my decision (but I have to admit I did enjoy his care and attention).

The following Saturday, I was invited on to ITV's hugely popular live TV show *Ant & Dec's Saturday Night Takeaway*. It couldn't have been worse timing. The idea was that I would surprise a woman who regularly worked out to my videos by suddenly appearing in her house. At one point, I had to smile at the camera for what seemed like five minutes, awaiting the moment when I would appear on 10 million TV screens! I had never felt less like smiling.

David, my driver, drove me down to London and, inevitably, as with any live TV show, there was a lot of hanging around. David had become a very kind friend and one of my 'supportive army' and was very aware of the problems Mike and I were having. To be honest, it was good to get out of the house on that Saturday – weekends are very long when you are in a bad place emotionally with your partner – and I remember asking David to pop into a fish and chip shop to get me a bag of chips after the show. My weight was so low, barely 7½ st. (47.6 kg), and I knew I could do with the calories. The chips were delicious and a real treat!

Mike called after the show had gone out live and told me how great I was – but it was too little, too late, and the next day I decided I'd had enough. I was exhausted and resolute in my decision. Mike had to go.

Mike pleaded with me to give him another chance and he promised he would change. I wonder how many partners have had those words said to them. I knew he could be nice and kind, but I needed time to be convinced and, in the meantime, I desperately needed a break.

***

Care for the Family is a Christian charity with which Mike and I were very familiar. Its founder, Rob Parsons, is a personal friend of both of us and had spoken at our Annual Franchisee Convention on at least two occasions. When Rob learned of our problems, he drove over from Wales to chat with us. I recall a conversation he had with me in our kitchen.

'Is there anyone else involved?' he enquired of me.

'Absolutely not,' I said.

I had been faithful to Mike for the whole of our marriage. I had not even considered a relationship with anyone else, even at our darkest times, and I wasn't even thinking of the possibility of looking for another relationship now. Mike had been my life since we met 20 years previously, but I was damaged, hurt and exhausted and I needed a complete break.

Care for the Family is based in Cardiff, and Rob very kindly offered Mike a job there for six months, which he accepted. This was ideal. It would be helpful for both of us. In fact, it was a perfect solution. Mike would be among good people whose whole purpose was supporting families in difficulties. I would have a break from him, and I was prepared to see how we got on over the following months.

That weekend, we travelled down to Cardiff to find Mike a flat, and within a couple of weeks he moved in. I felt an enormous sense of relief and I began to rebuild my energy and my life. We spoke regularly on the phone and he came home at weekends. Our relationship was certainly a bit better and Mike did make every effort to be kinder and more loving towards me, but it would take time to heal from my side.

Then something surprising happened. Mike took it upon himself to apologise for his actions. He not only profusely apologised to me for the hurt and heartache he had caused me, but he visited Dawn, as well as our friends who had been so supportive over the last four years, to tell them he was sorry for the sadness and the trouble that his behaviour had caused. To be honest, I felt that it took guts on his part to acknowledge his mistakes and to face up to the consequences of his actions. I know everyone else involved felt that too. Some years later, he told me that he hadn't been looking for someone else. He didn't know who he wanted to be with. At the time, he said, he didn't even want to be with *himself*. He just felt lost in his own life.

In late January 2003, Mike and I were due to fly off on a skiing holiday that we had booked months before. However, for me, it was too soon for us to go away together. Instead, Dawn went with me, and she and I loved and cared for each other and also had fun.

Dawn was amazing and did everything she could to support me. Incredibly sadly, later that year, she had her own heartbreak. Her husband of six years decided to leave her. It was the most awful news! While we knew there had been some issues, this was a total shock. Dawn was devastated and so were we. Having just gone through our own horrific journey, we knew first-hand how painful this was going to be for her.

I did everything I could to support Dawn and she reciprocated. The good that came out of this whole ghastly situation was a very special bond between us which is still as strong today. Like us, Dawn had the support of her church and some wonderful friends; at times like these, such friends are golden.

Over the following few months Mike continued to be very loving – albeit at a distance – and he came home at weekends. Amazingly, gradually, we did begin to rebuild our relationship. Lessons had been learned on both sides and we both needed to make changes. I knew it wasn't all Mike's fault but, my goodness, those four years were the worst in my life and remain so to this day.

As time moved on, we began a new journey, and slowly, day by day, we developed a new and different relationship. I don't believe you can go through four years of rejection and not suffer some personal psychological damage, and I couldn't pretend everything was fine and dandy because it wasn't. I felt scarred, betrayed, let down – there are any number of words to describe how I felt. The bottom line was that the man I loved hadn't wanted *me*. He later explained that the time he spent so closely involved with the family from church had made him think he wanted children of his own, but he now acknowledged that he didn't. It was just how he felt at the time because he was in such a mentally confused state. I accept that, but he couldn't expect me to say, 'OK then. Let's forget it ever happened!'

If we wanted to get back together and into a solid and stable marital partnership, it would take time and effort. Lots of effort. Mike and I did work hard, very hard, to rebuild our marriage. The relationship between us was good, but it took a long time before I felt what I would call 'secure' in our relationship. There were rows. There were times of despair as we tried to mend this shattered marriage, but with God's grace, good friends, and patience and determination on both sides, we gradually and successfully re-established our relationship. It took a long time and yet we both felt it was worth the effort because, underneath all the hurt, the rejection, the disappointment and the desperation, we knew we were meant to be together. The challenge was how to navigate along that path to the ultimate goal of total trust, unity and happiness with each other.

It's never easy to rebuild a relationship after such a traumatic period of life. And to be honest, the majority of marriages don't survive this kind of episode. But when you stop and think about what you have to lose, it can seem worth the effort, and that can make all the difference.

I believe in slow-motion miracles. Many people think that an amazing transformation is like a fairy godmother waving her magic wand in a pantomime: there's a bright flash and the pumpkin turns into a glittering coach with magnificent horses. But life isn't like that, and the deeper miracles can take an enormous amount of time, patience and sacrifice. I think there's hardly a love song that uses the word 'sacrifice' (except Elton John's famous hit, of course), but making sacrifices and learning to do things for the sake of others, including giving up our resentments, is crucial to any lifelong love story. I believe that Mike and I had to sacrifice some of our complex feelings and also some of our more self-centred motivations. The truth is that, after what seemed like a very confusing

period in Mike's life, thankfully, with God's grace and with sheer determination on the part of both of us, we made it through. I am delighted
to say that 20 years later we are in a wonderfully strong and totally loving
marriage that is as solid as a rock – but it took time.

Now I love the fact that we are growing older together, that we can
care for each other and simply love each other. We rarely talk about our
'wilderness years' and, if we do, it is without malice. Mike will sometimes
say, 'I treated you so appallingly back then. I am so sorry.' It was what it
was, and our underlying love for each other, thankfully, enabled us to
survive and fall in love again. But I hated it when people said at the time,
'One day you'll be glad it happened.' I disagree. I still remember it as the
most terrible four years of my life.

**

As Mike and I continued to rebuild our marriage, there were some rather
exciting moments and adventures which provided a real lift and gave
me enormous encouragement and confidence. First of all, I received an
invitation to Buckingham Palace. The event was a reception for Pioneers
of the Nation. I have no idea how I was chosen, and it was a bit scary as
partners were not invited so I was on my own. When I attended, it was
clearly an extraordinary gathering of about 200 celebrities of all kinds –
from stars such as Cliff Richard to sporting legends such as racing driver
Jackie Stewart! Richard Attenborough was there, so I went up to him
and introduced myself, saying that we had something in common having
both been given the Freedom of the City of Leicester. He was charming
and engaging, and made me smile when he said, 'Dave's here somewhere.
You must say hello to him too!' – referring to his equally famous brother,
David Attenborough.

The big surprise was that about 10 members of the Royal Family
were mingling among us, chatting happily with everyone there. It was
awesome to be in such company. By the time I met HM The Queen, I
had sipped my way through three glasses of wine, with no food, and felt
a bit squiffy. When Her Majesty asked what I did, I burbled out 'I'm into
diet and fitness' in a very casual and possibly slurry way! Perhaps not the
most eloquent response I intended when meeting our monarch for the
first time!

I kept going out of the rooms where everyone was gathering so that I could take a breath. I loved looking at the array of memorabilia of past generations of the Royal Family, all displayed in special cabinets within the grand gallery adorned with priceless masterpieces.

Then in November the same year, I received a letter from 10 Downing Street informing me that the Prime Minister was proposing that I be recommended to Her Majesty as a Commander of the Order of the British Empire (CBE) in the Queen's New Year's Honours List! I couldn't believe it, and I read and reread the letter 10 times before it actually started to sink in. I was flabbergasted. This was an extraordinary honour and I could hardly accept that it was being considered for *me*, a girl who left school a week before her 15th birthday, failed her shorthand exam and used to sell Tupperware!

I rang Dawn first and she was thrilled. I then rang Mike in Cardiff, and he was also very pleased for me. He said I deserved it because I had put up with him for 20 years! That made me smile.

Proposed recipients of New Year's Honours are given strict instructions to preserve total confidentiality until the Honours are formally announced. Having ticked the 'Accept' box on the form, I returned it to the Cabinet Office, where the Honours are administered. Just before Christmas, a smiling postman rang the doorbell and handed me what he realised was something very special because the large cream envelope carried the postmark of Buckingham Palace. Inside was a magnificent certificate confirming that, from the new year, I would be Rosemary Conley CBE!

The New Year's Honours are announced in the press just before the new year, and I was shocked that it was my photograph that appeared in the *Sunday Times* among so many other notable recipients listed.

Over the next few weeks, I received so many letters and cards of congratulations it was overwhelming! Included in them was a very kind handwritten letter from Dame Norma Major, and I also received a letter of congratulation signed by Tessa Jowell, Secretary of State for Culture, Media and Sport, and Richard Caborn, Minister for Sport and Tourism. They were all very kind and generous in their praise. It was so heart-warming and affirming.

It wasn't long before I received another communication with the Royal Postmark. This time it was my invitation to receive my Honour. So in

March, Dawn, Jeanne (Mike's mum), Mike and I went to Buckingham Palace. David drove us inside the grand gates and to the same entrance we often see on television where the Queen steps out of her coach and into the palace.

Standing on either side of the red carpet were soldiers from the Household Cavalry. The sight of them in their bright-red dress uniforms with silver and gold body armour, topped by shining helmets with pristine white plumes, was magical. It was such a privilege for us, along with many other Honour recipients, to know that these magnificent soldiers were here to make our special day even more memorable.

Having had a long drive from Leicester, the first thing to ask once inside the palace was 'Where's the loo?' We were told that the recipients were to go to the left and their guests were to go to the right, so off we went in our different directions. I was directed up one flight of stairs, then up another, and then told to turn left and along that corridor . . . I suddenly became worried and didn't want to run the risk of getting lost so, deciding to wait until later, I turned around to go back to find the others. Unfortunately, I tripped and fell down the stairs! My hat came off and unceremoniously went bump, bump, bump down the stairs. A very concerned footman in all his dress uniform rushed to my assistance. Thankfully, I hadn't hurt myself, hadn't ripped my posh suit or laddered my tights, and the hat was still in one piece and without dents! I reassembled myself, took a deep breath, thanked the footman profusely for his care and attention, and proceeded to join Mike, Dawn and Jeanne, who were just walking along towards me.

'Guess what?' I said.

'Oh, you didn't!' exclaimed Dawn and Mike in unison. 'You've fallen over!'

I have a history of falling over quite regularly – probably because I am always in high heels – so it is a bit of a family joke. In fact, in the car on the way to the palace, Mike had said, 'Now, whatever you do, *don't fall over!*'

Anyway, all was well and off we went, but again we were directed to our different destinations within the palace.

All the recipients were escorted to a room where we were offered a glass of water or juice. Everyone was very excited, and then a member of the Queen's Household came in to explain what was going to happen. It was announced that today the Honours would be presented by Prince Charles, and then he clarified what would happen when our name was called.

He explained: 'Your name and the reason for your Honour will be announced and only then should you walk into the room where all the guests are assembled. You are to walk up to Prince Charles and curtsey or bow. Prince Charles will speak to you, as he is briefed about every recipient, and when Prince Charles goes to shake your hand, that will be the sign that it is time for you to go. At that point, you walk backwards for three steps, turn to your right and walk out through the opposite door from the one through which you entered.'

Walk backwards! You have got to be kidding me. I have difficulty walking forwards without falling over, let alone stepping backwards in 3-in. (7.6-cm) heels!

We processed together in the designated order for the Honour we were receiving and then in alphabetical order with women first, which meant that I was at the front of the CBE group. It was like a dream! Was this really happening to me?

I know it is recognised that women find men in uniform attractive, but the military guy in front of me looked more handsome than James Bond in his dress uniform. I was *so* nervous, but Commander Gorgeous chatted with me and tried to calm my nerves. Soon it was my turn.

'Rosemary Conley, for services to the fitness and diet industries,' came the announcement.

I thought my heart was going to explode as it was beating so fast. Trying desperately to remember the instructions, I managed to curtsey to Prince Charles without tripping. *Phew.* Prince Charles was utterly charming and had a gift for making me feel as if I was the only person in the room. We chatted and he appeared genuinely interested in our efforts to help the nation to be fitter and healthier. I suggested that if everyone was as fit and active as he was, there wouldn't be a national obesity problem. He explained that he ate only one meal a day and that was how he stayed at a healthy weight. After what seemed like several minutes, he shook my hand (my sign to go) and I went to turn to walk away. *Oops!* Stop! Just in time, I remembered to walk backwards, which I managed to do without falling over. (*Phew*, again!) And off I went, leaving through the appropriate door.

I had hardly stepped out of the room when a journalist asked if he could interview me. He was alone so I naturally assumed he was the official press person.

'So, what did Prince Charles say to you?' he asked.

And so I told him.

Next day, in all the tabloids, there was a picture of me holding my CBE with the headline 'Prince Charles on Des O'Connor Diet'. But not only that; the press had contacted the palace to ask for more details! The spokesperson commented that it was really tough sometimes when Prince Charles carried on working throughout the day with no food when all his staff were really hungry. Oh, my goodness! Was I going to be sent to the Tower of London for being indiscreet?

Apparently, the entertainer Des O'Connor was well known for eating one meal a day, but I was so bothered about giving away Charles's eating habits that I wrote a personal letter of apology to His Royal Highness. I received a charming reply from his Private Secretary and it appeared all was well.

It was a day I will never forget, and it was on occasions such as this that I was so grateful that Mike and I were still together.

A month or so later, Mike was invited to join a team to trek to the North Pole with a view to raising money for the charity HOPE HIV, which supports children in Africa. He jumped at the chance. He trained for weeks, walking around our fields with a harness around his waist attached to a car tyre, as the team would be unassisted and would have to tow all their food and camping gear on their own sledges behind them. He also worked really hard on strength and endurance exercises so that he could cope with such a challenge. The trek was led by Alan Chambers, an ex-Royal Marine Commando, and over nine days they travelled across extremely challenging terrain, aiming to reach the North Pole – a journey of 60 nautical miles (111 km) as the crow flies.

Dawn was staying with me for the two weeks that Mike was gone. Almost at the end of his time away, the phone rang. An exhausted Mike breathlessly blurted out, 'We've done it! We're at the North Pole!'

Dawn and I were *so* relieved and also very proud, particularly as Mike had suffered with a leg injury for the last few days. It was an extraordinary achievement and the team raised almost £200,000 for the charity.

Apparently, to keep their energy up and their calorie consumption at a high enough level, the team members ate chopped-up chocolate, nuts and raisins as they trekked. During the trek, Mike consumed 20 bars of Cadbury's Dairy Milk, 20 Mars bars, 20 Snickers, 30 energy bars, 2 lb of peanuts, 2 lb of raisins and 2 lb of dried apricots, as well as a large packet of tropical fruit mix. Despite eating 6,000 calories a day, he lost 9 lb (4 kg) in the nine days. This was surely the ultimate 'Eat Yourself Slim' experience!

I was so excited to see Mike back safe and sound at the airport. He was exhausted, but it had been a great experience and he had certainly enjoyed the challenge. I was very proud of him and what he had achieved.

While we were still in the rebuilding stage of our marriage, Mike thought it would be a good idea for us to move from the Manor. I really, really loved that house and was reluctant to leave it but, if Mike wasn't happy there, then, in the interest of our marriage, I was prepared to move. We put our house on the market and found a plot of land in Hambleton in Rutland overlooking Rutland Water, a vast man-made reservoir. It was a magnificent spot and the existing basic farmhouse in the centre of the plot was ripe for redevelopment. We first bought the main plot with 4 acres (1.6 ha) of land, then two other fields, together totalling 27 acres (11 ha). An architect designed a fine house and we managed to get planning permission. We even invited the nearby neighbours over to the Manor so they could see the plans, and they were very kind and supportive.

This whole process took many months and, in the meantime, various people viewed the Manor.

By the summer of 2005 we had a buyer, but then Mike had a change of heart and decided that we shouldn't move after all. It was true: the new house would never be as beautiful as the Manor – not even close. Of course, I needed little persuading to take the Manor off the market, though the prospective buyer wasn't very happy.

Hambleton was a highly desirable village, so it didn't take long to sell the main plot with planning permission, and over the next few months

Mike negotiated a very lucrative sale of part of one of our fields to a neighbour who wanted to protect his view line. Overall, we managed to return our total investment in selling the main plot. With the proceeds of the sale of the additional field, we were able to fund a very exciting project at the Manor. The remaining 15 acres (6 ha) of land in Hambleton we still own to this day.

Our project at the Manor was to convert the formal dining room into a new kitchen with a sitting area. Over the following few months, we worked with Smallbone, a renowned kitchen designer, to create something very special. Work started at the end of January 2006 and the transformation took eight months. The most beautiful kitchen I had ever seen was created by a very talented designer, and a specialist plasterer designed and handmade a plaster frieze to replicate the style of the Manor. The plasterer stayed with us for two months in what had been our housekeeper's flat while he completed the job. He had designed and physically created the moulds and made the plasterwork using our stables as his workshop. His work was that of a true craftsman.

By September 2006 the kitchen was complete and looked magnificent. It transformed the dynamics of the house and took us nearer to the heart of this amazing building. Neither of us had anticipated what a difference it would make. Previously, we were using a kitchen which was on the colder, north side of the house where, in years gone by, the staff would have prepared the food for the household. Now we were facing south, overlooking the garden and open fields, and the sun shone into the kitchen from dawn till dusk. Having a project to work on together further helped our relationship. In fact, Mike admitted later that the main reason he had been looking to move was that he wanted a project to work on, but thankfully, when it came to this 'home-grown' enterprise, he acknowledged that he had made the right choice after all. I was more than happy with that.

***

At every Christmas, I would visit Aylsham and take Mabel to visit my father's and my mother's graves and her own parents' grave in the same cemetery. It was always such a poignant trip, because I knew that Mabel had come to a place in her life where she was only looking backwards and not forwards. We would go out for Christmas lunch locally, but it was hard for her to enjoy anything. There was no doubt she just missed looking after Oswald. When he died, she said she felt she no longer had a reason to live because while she had her husband to care for – and later to visit in a home – she had a purpose. That was it. Oswald was her only purpose. Although her devotion to her husband was touching, everyone needs other interests and friendships in life, especially in the hard times. It was very sad to see her so lost and so sad, but there was no simple solution. I wished there was. I would telephone Mabel every other day, just so that she could speak to someone in the midst of her great loneliness.

Despite our own problems (and we still had a long way to go), I knew that I still had a loving husband in Mike. I also had many other interests, excitements and joys in life, and the sadness of Mabel's loneliness made me realise how lucky I was.

16
Changes and challenges
2005–7

We all go through challenges, but we never know when something might happen that would dramatically change the way we view life.

Again, Mary and I were at one of our Clubs' Roadshows when I suddenly received a call. Miranda Menzies – one of our franchisees – had been out running when she suddenly collapsed. She had somehow managed to stagger home but was now in intensive care in hospital with a brain haemorrhage. Miranda was our franchisee in Northampton and was superfit and the loveliest, most enthusiastic young woman you could ever wish to meet. She was just 31 years old, and her husband had been told to expect the worst. Mary and I were in shock.

We obviously had to carry on with the Roadshow and our day of motivation and exercise but, at the back of our minds, this was a really tough thing to handle. All those words we say to ourselves in moments of shock and disbelief were going round in my head.

'Of all the people . . .'

'But she's so fit . . .'

Amazingly, incredibly, Miranda gradually recovered after two months in hospital. She was told that if she had not been so fit, she almost certainly would have died. Obviously, she had to forget her business. We managed to sell it for her easily and, would you believe it, five years later she bought it back! We were so pleased to welcome her return on so many levels because she was such an incredible ambassador for everything we stood for as a company – health, fitness and fighting spirit!

So often, we were approached by representatives of companies who simply saw Rosemary Conley Diet & Fitness Clubs as a perfect pathway to sell their goods. This wasn't surprising as we had 160 franchisees and around 50,000 members attending our classes every week. In addition, we had half a million readers of our magazine.

Towards the end of 2004 we had been approached by Fitness First, the gym chain. The company was looking to add a weight-loss programme to complement its fitness offering and saw our team of franchisees as the perfect potential partners. We invited Chris Ash, its Marketing Director, and his colleague to Quorn House to explain their ambitions. I usually attended such meetings personally as I was able to judge quite quickly if there was likely to be the makings of a working relationship. The meeting went well and, in this case, I was happy to take the discussions further.

A second meeting was arranged a few weeks later. Chris and I chatted through the challenge presented by the fact that our franchise network did not offer blanket coverage across the whole of the UK. Obviously, for Fitness First to be able to promote its new weight-loss service it would have to be nationwide, so we realised it wouldn't work. Chris went on to explain that he was now leaving Fitness First as the company had been taken over and, while he had been in line to be made the MD, this was now not the case and he thought it was time to move on.

I liked Chris and felt I could work with him. In some ways, we were at a crossroads in our own business. Simon Ford, our previous General Manager, had retired and things were ticking along within the business but not progressing. The franchisees were continuing to run superb classes, but attracting members was becoming harder. Inevitably, we lost a few every year for a variety of reasons, but we were successful in recruiting new ones so we were able to maintain our number of franchisees at around 160. The magazine was doing well, but the printed media publishing market was beginning to decline overall so it was a struggle to maintain the circulation figures we once had enjoyed. Also, Slimming World had now produced its own magazine, which inevitably diluted the market, and it was a very good publication.

My workload was still heavy despite no longer appearing on *This Morning*. In addition to all the usual responsibilities, we continued to hold presentation days for the recruitment of new franchisees, with Roadshows about every month, and every year I organised a special week at Ragdale Hall; Mary and I were also still running our annual activity holiday in Austria. All this was on top of writing a book every year and presenting a new fitness DVD, as well as dealing with the day-to-day demands of running a company – pressures that just kept on coming. In a perfect world we needed a Marketing Manager, but if, in addition, that person could help share some of my workload, that would be a massive help to me. And Chris appeared to tick all the boxes.

I told Mike, Brian and our accountant Stewart about Chris, and Brian suggested that we ask Chris to do an assessment of our business. We wanted to know what we could do better. What opportunities were we missing? A couple of weeks later, Chris came along to the Manor and presented his findings and opinions to the four of us. We were impressed by what he said and how he presented it.

So, in early 2005, Chris joined our team as Marketing Manager and I suddenly felt as though a huge weight had been lifted off my shoulders. We got along really well, Mike really liked him, and Chris appreciated our ethics and, I think, found us a breath of fresh air in the business world as we weren't a cut-throat, greedy company. Our overriding desire was to give a great service for a fair return. Our aim was to do our very best for our franchisees as well as our members and to offer the very best expert advice we could to our magazine readers. Mike and I were in a fortunate position financially where we earned sufficient royalties from the books and DVD sales to enable us to live very comfortably – so, providing the company made a profit, we were happy. It is because of this that I smile when people tell me what a great businesswoman I am. I disagree! I might have some good ideas, and sometimes some not-so-good ones, and I can be a bit soft and too trusting on occasion. The only time I am demanding financially is when I recognise my 'value' when people ask me to write, present or create something for them – something that I know is going to make their company a lot of money. In my own business, I am not hungry enough to be classed as a good businessperson.

Chris settled in with us in no time, and his arrival meant that I could get on with the work that only I could do. We worked really well together and his presence lifted a vast amount off my shoulders and gave me a huge sense of relief. Of course, throughout it all, I continued running my own classes, which I have taken on a Monday evening since 1972 and still take today. I think we may be calling them 'zimmaerobics' when I reach my 80s!

***

I always feel very grateful whenever I hear that one of my books or DVDs has made a difference to people. I have always believed that it is a real privilege to be invited into someone's living room or bedroom or kitchen via his or her TV and then to 'work out together'. I meet followers of my diet books and they tell me that when they go for a second helping or an extra treat, their husband or partner will comment, 'Rosemary wouldn't be happy with that, would she?' When I am out and about, it is not unusual for someone to come up to me and tell me that she still uses my DVDs today or that she is still slim from following my *Hip and Thigh Diet* 30 years ago. I love that.

One of the benefits of being in the public arena is that we can have some influence. Since 1994 I have been Patron of Steps Conductive Education Centre in Leicestershire for children with cerebral palsy, Down syndrome and other motor disorders. Steps was originally called the Charnwood School for Parents, in Loughborough.

We knew Canon George Crate, and his wife Heather, when George was our vicar at St Peter's Church in Mountsorrel. We lived in the Old Parsonage, directly opposite the church, and attended regularly when we became Christians in 1986. When George and Heather's grandson, Shaun, was born with cerebral palsy, the family were told that his condition was so severe that he wouldn't even be able to turn over in bed.

Friends, family and the congregation of St Peter's raised funds for Shaun to go to the Peto Institute in Hungary, which was renowned for its pioneering work, described as 'conductive education'. For three blocks of four weeks, over a period of a couple of years and at a cost of £10,000 each time, Shaun went to the Peto Institute. Thankfully, the effect of his conductive education was life-changing – not just for Shaun but also for his family.

Conductive education works by developing motor skills through repetitive specialist exercises combined with play. The results for Shaun were remarkable. Undergoing such treatment enabled him to be able to walk, talk, feed himself and ultimately go to college. Now in his 30s, while still very restricted, Shaun has a good quality of life and is a happy, outgoing young man who loves sport.

After witnessing the transformation in Shaun in those early years, four families in Leicestershire decided to create a facility similar to the Hungarian one – and the Charnwood School for Parents was launched as a charity.

Initially, the charity rented a room in a local school but soon was asked to leave because the space was needed for the school's own use. It then found another school which was again happy to accommodate the children and staff but, just as before, after a couple of years that school too needed the space for its own activities. By the time the charity was told it had to leave its fourth 'home', it had become clear that it had to find its own premises.

To be honest, up to this point I had had little involvement in the charity as Patron but, one day, something happened in my heart and I felt I should get involved and commit to making a difference. I arranged to meet George and Heather Crate and the Trustees of the charity at Quorn House to discuss the crisis. From that, we formed a building committee to help us find a permanent home for Steps, as the charity was now called.

At about the same time, I was asked to lead a masterclass for Young Enterprise in Leicester. I had just been appointed President of Young Enterprise Leicestershire, an initiative that I think is priceless in helping young people to develop their skills in entrepreneurship. On this occasion there were three speakers, all talking about their own life experiences of running their own business. Following my talk was a guy called John Montague who ran a not-for-profit building company, employing and training disaffected young people with a view to helping them become professional tradespeople.

When John sat down next to me following his inspirational talk, I whispered in his ear, 'I really need to talk to you.' After the event I explained our dilemma and pleaded, '*Please* will you come and join our building committee?'

John kindly came along to our next meeting, and the possibility of a purpose-built school was discussed. A kind-hearted local architect designed an ideal building with an estimated cost of around £2 million. And that was without the land. This seemed an impossible mountain to climb for such a small charity and we all went away somewhat crest-fallen. By the next meeting, one of the team, who was a churchwarden at St Botolph's Church in Shepshed, close to Loughborough, had spoken to the vicar and the Parochial Church Council (PCC). Apparently, since a brand-new school had been built in Shepshed, the old school, St Botolph's Church School, was now virtually derelict and the church was prepared to sell it to us for £235,000. This seemed like the perfect solution and much more achievable. The other great news was that the church authorities were happy to rent the school to us until we could raise all the funds to buy it. They were happy to wait. We were all so excited to hear this news and quickly set about raising funds. Steps moved into the one usable room within the old school as its new home. We were all thrilled and relieved, and the children and the staff loved it.

But the building funds would have to be raised *in addition* to the cash needed to pay the everyday staff costs of running Steps. Heather Crate worked tirelessly. She was very effective at writing bids for grants and managed to scrape together just enough to pay the salaries for the specialist staff. Steps was run on a shoestring. Nothing was wasted and maximum benefits to the children were miraculously achieved. Back then, Steps received a small grant each year from the local health authority but, apart from that, it was raw fundraising that kept the charity alive. And now, on top of *that*, we had to raise money to buy the building.

With a variety of fundraising initiatives organised within our network of classes, and through the kindness of local Rotary and Inner Wheel Clubs, gradually we managed to start saving. After two years we had raised £90,000. In desperation, an application was made to the National Lottery, and things were looking very hopeful after Heather had been interviewed twice and the lottery organisers had visited Steps. Then came the killer blow! They turned us down on the basis that they felt the building was larger than we needed. It was a massive disappointment, but we were determined to plough on.

A month later, in March 2006, the vicar of St Botolph's unexpectedly called to see me at Quorn House. She explained that she had heard we hadn't been successful in securing our lottery grant so she had decided that the church would withdraw its offer of the old school and would now sell it for building land instead.

'It would be more lucrative for the church, and you are unlikely to ever reach your target anyway,' she said.

I was utterly astonished and couldn't help bursting into tears. After all our efforts and determination, this was a cruel blow.

I pleaded with the vicar to give us until Christmas to raise the balance needed and, if we didn't reach it, we would pay double our rent for the year. She agreed but put the price up to £250,000. The Trustees were furious – partly because of her change of heart but also because she hadn't addressed them directly. After all, I was only the Patron. I had no legal standing on behalf of the charity.

Once we dusted ourselves off and came to terms with the reality, we launched a major fundraising drive, supported by the local media, particularly ITV Central. Gemma Binch was a news reporter for Central and had visited the Steps sports day at Quorn House. This was held as part of the publicity drive towards spreading awareness of Steps' plight and raising funds to buy the school. She filmed at the school and spoke to parents. Some time later, when we were working together on a TV series I was doing for Central, Gemma handed me a DVD. It was a brilliant six-minute film, all about Steps, that she had edited herself, in her own time, to help us raise funds for the charity. I was so touched and beyond impressed by her kindness. We used that film for years as we continued our fundraising efforts.

***

As the months went on, a Trust gave us a grant for £50,000, and other major donations were also made. We organised a sponsored walk in Abbey Park in Leicester, supported by many of our franchisees, who brought coachloads of their members to support us, and the local Rotary Club kindly marshalled the event. We raised £23,000. All types of fundraising activities were organised and, to boost the coffers further, I decided to raffle my Bentley. Tickets were offered at £1 each and were sold throughout our classes, and we managed to raise £26,000! The car was only worth a fraction of that, so I was delighted that my beloved Bentley would make such a difference to the overall total. Central TV asked me to go into the studio to draw the winning ticket live on air, and there was much excitement as we drew the ticket bought by a landlord of a pub in Peterborough. ITV Central filmed me handing over the keys to the very happy new owner a few days later.

But the best news of all was that by Christmas 2006 we had managed to raise a phenomenal £280,000! The relief was immense and, come the new year, the school officially belonged to Steps.

Gemma Binch and her team at ITV Central were well aware of the state of the old school and suggested we do a *Challenge Anneka*-style refurbishment, the equivalent of the current TV show *DIY SOS*, and they would film it. I put the idea to John Montague, who was the perfect person to know what needed doing. As I mentioned above, his not-for-profit building company (called Newlife) took troubled teenagers from difficult backgrounds and, through apprenticeships, taught them a trade. John is an extraordinary man, and his passion to help life's underdogs and the underprivileged knows no bounds. He felt that his team of young lads and his senior workforce, which covered all manner of trades, would be ideal to step up to the challenge. We also enlisted the help of another building company to create a new toilet block from pre-constructed framework units that had been promised to us by a firm whose director attended my own Monday night fitness classes. In situations like this, it's all about who you know!

It was decided that I would look after the refreshments for the workforce and also do the blagging for the goods and services from the many and varied companies which we were hoping would support us. The makeover had to be done in the Easter holiday fortnight while the school was closed, so the pressure was on. Mark Jermy, from architects Halsall Lloyd Partnership, created all the plans for the refurbishment, and so, three days before we were due to start, John, Mark and I sat down to establish what was needed and whom we should contact. We must have spent two days on the phone in preparation, as we were to start the renovation the following Monday when the ITV Central team would turn up with their cameras. The refurbishment was an extraordinary challenge to achieve in two weeks, but we were all set.

Then the other builder involved called to say his company couldn't help us after all.

I can remember sitting on a stool in my bathroom at home and answering the phone to John at 6.30 am as he offered expletives of frustration! Then he turned anxious: 'I don't think we can do it,' to which I responded, 'We have no choice but to go ahead at this stage. Central are all set. We *have* to do it.'

Half an hour later I got another call from John: 'I've called the builder and told them if they can't build a modular pre-made block of bogs for us it's a poor show' – or words to that effect. The builder agreed to proceed and we were *on*!

I contacted a catering equipment hire company which offered me a mobile kitchen unit and then asked me to select whatever equipment I wanted. It was like Christmas! This was so exciting as I had always wanted a deep-fat fryer but, being a low-fat advocate, there is no way I could ever have one of my own. But now I had the perfect excuse! I was going to cook for dozens of hard-working guys, and I was going to give them food to remember. With a three-oven range, a double basket deep-fat fryer (*yes!*), a fridge, a freezer, grills, cupboards and ample work surfaces, I had a fully fitted catering kitchen. I took the plates and cutlery from home and Quorn House, and collected as many mugs as I could lay my hands on.

Next it was time to blag the food. Samworth Brothers makes top-of-the-range ready meals for M&S, among others. I told its CEO what we were doing and asked if he could help. Early on the Monday morning, crates of ready meals were arriving: Tesco Finest lamb shanks, beef casserole in red wine, chicken chasseur . . . the range was vast. I also asked the Managers of local supermarkets if they could help and, when they knew what we were doing, they happily gave us vouchers for food valued at £300 to £500. Having successfully managed to persuade two supermarkets to help, I didn't find it difficult to get all the others to follow suit.

By the Saturday before the Monday start-date, we had installed ourselves. My mobile kitchen was up and running, and Shaun's dad had made a great sign that said 'Rosie's Larder' which we hung outside the serving hatch. John Montague, Mark Jermy the architect, Pete Tate the Project Manager, Shaun and I were there at lunchtime. I made cheese rolls for everyone and handed them around. We were all very excited.

Cerebral palsy is a condition where the brain is unable to, or has great difficulty in, communicating to the muscles of the body to move limbs or other body parts as it does in someone who is able-bodied. We think nothing of walking, going upstairs, eating with a knife and fork, or picking up a glass and drinking. We just do it. But it is very different for someone like Shaun.

As I held the plate out to Shaun, slowly, gradually, painstakingly – and with every fibre of his brain focusing on lifting and directing his hand toward the plate – very slowly but precisely, he put his hand on the soft bread roll and carefully bent his stiff, awkward fingers to pick it up, extremely carefully, and place it slowly on his plate. As he did so there was total silence. A silence that spoke a million words.

None of us said a word for several minutes as we realised how we all took for granted something as simple as picking up a sandwich. But for children like Shaun who had cerebral palsy, it was a major task, and it was because of children like Shaun that we were going to work our socks off over the next two weeks. We were all going to make a difference to the children who attended Steps – a charity which worked tirelessly and effectively to help those children develop their neuromuscular pathways and to become the very best they could be. It was a moment I will never forget.

By 8 am on Monday, the team of builders from John's company were on site along with Pete, his Project Manager. I was very relieved when the other building company arrived too, and when the articulated lorry delivered the modular toilet block there was a real sense of excitement. Soon the cameras were there to capture the demolition and recon-struction of areas of the school, and I set about making tea and bacon butties.

Peter Bearne was the reporter from ITV Central, and every other day he and his camera crew spent time with us, catching up on the progress. They filmed me calling various companies asking for anything from wall studding to a scissor-lift and, of course, they loved filming me cooking chips in a deep-fat fryer.

It was full-on cooking for the troops. There were often 60 workmen on site during the day and they all had bacon butties when they arrived, a proper cooked dinner for lunch, and then pizza, sandwiches and cake for their tea. I had help from Dawn, Mary and others from Quorn House and Steps, and somehow we managed to keep the tea and coffee flowing and the dishes washed in time for the next meal. In between it all, I was phoning companies asking for stuff. I had no idea what I was asking for most of the time, but John or Pete would hand me a piece of paper saying 'Ring *this* company' and 'We need *these* things'. I found the best way was to call and ask for the Managing Director's PA. When asked who was calling, I simply said, 'It's Rosemary Conley calling on behalf of Central Television.' These were like magic words because I got through to the MD every time. I always wanted to speak to the PA first because the chances were she would know who I was, whereas her boss, then usually male in the building trade, would not. 'Mrs PA' was always very interested and excited when I explained what we were doing, and she would then ask me to hold the line. There was often a few minutes' delay while I imagined she was explaining who I was, what we were doing and that her boss really should help us. Then came on the line a somewhat tentative male voice: 'Hello? Can I help you?' and I would explain what we were doing and what we needed. In almost every case the answer was yes, and within a couple of hours a lorry, a truck or a van would arrive with the goods. It was extraordinary.

How on earth John and Pete were able to decipher what was wanted and when we needed it is beyond me, but the whole project was gradually put together like a giant jigsaw puzzle. The young lads from John's company worked so hard, even through the night on a couple of occasions.

The people at BBC Radio Leicester were great too. On one day we needed a tiler to fix a load of tiles we had been given for the toilets, so I rang them in desperation. Within half an hour a tiler appeared on our doorstep. He had been working on a house two streets away, listening to Radio Leicester, and heard our cry for help. He downed tools and came straight round. He was inspiring to watch as he put those tiles on the wall like Smarties on a birthday cake. Then, on the last night, a decorating company worked through the night so that we would be ready for the big reveal, live on ITV Central the following evening.

We had 12 days to complete the transformation. We went from confident Wednesday to crisis Tuesday when we seemed a million miles away from being finished in time. All the windows needed to be reglazed, and some windows reinstalled after being bricked up years before. An old storeroom was made into a life-skills kitchen, and another store room into a breakout sitting room for the older children when they visited for 'After-School Club'.

On the Friday evening all the children and their parents gathered outside the building in readiness for the big reveal. I had not been allowed to go into the big room for several days as they wanted to film my surprised face when I saw the transformation for the first time.

Soon it was time for me and Shaun to be the first of the crowd to walk into what was now a stunning, modern, bright and beautiful conference room! It looked unbelievably different from the unattractive, old-fashioned pitched-roof room that it had been two weeks earlier. There was a new ceiling, new lighting, a mezzanine floor created for storage, a versatile collapsible stage, plus a fully fitted catering kitchen at the far end of the room where there used to be some very old toilets. We had a brand-new toilet block for the children, and the room where Steps had been operating was spruced up.

The guys who had worked on the project were beaming with pride. I gave the lads from John's company a Steps medal and, as they were presented, some of them said it was the best day of their lives. They realised how important they had been in making it happen. They had experienced, possibly for the first time, a feeling of appreciation and commendation. The families and the children were thrilled with the transformation. The workforce had, I think, all gained weight despite working so hard! They had eaten so well thanks to the generosity of the supermarkets and food suppliers.

(If you would like to see the entertaining ITV Central reports on the makeover, go to <www.rosemaryconley.com> and to the Rosemary's World section and click on My Favourite Charities.)

***

While we had achieved the near impossible over the Easter holiday, we realised there was more to be done. The main classroom for the children had only been cosmetically refreshed, the waste ground at the side of the school was completely overgrown and the car park was in poor condition, so I approached ITV Central to ask if we could do it all again in the autumn. Thankfully, the producers said yes, so John and Mark set about preparing for phase 2. I blagged the food, and Central were there filming on the first day to see what had to be done.

Mark's firm of architects designed a sensory garden to be created where the waste ground lay in front of the school. However, finding a landscaping company to take on the project was the most difficult task of all. We had been promised all the plants and the heavy plant machinery, but we needed experts to make it happen. I found a company in Nottingham and, after several phone calls and two 'no' decisions from the Manager stating that he was not able to help us, I called again. Apologising profusely for being so persistent and such a pain, I pleaded with the boss. I told him I had a team of workmen who would labour for us and we had all the materials (well, hopefully!). In the end, I think I had worn him down and he reluctantly agreed. I was *so* thankful. However, in my naivety, I hadn't realised how much work was involved. I now understood his reticence at agreeing to take on this major project. Truckload after truckload of topsoil was delivered, railway sleepers were dropped off to make benches, beautiful slabs were laid to create walkways and, of course, there was a water feature! We were also given a magnificent wrought-iron sculpture of a butterfly, made by students at Warwick University. Mounted on a plinth, the creation included small windows where stained glass would be inserted to reflect the children who had attended Steps over the years but who had sadly passed away.

When the garden was completed, it looked amazing, and everyone loved walking around touching, smelling, feeling, hearing and seeing the different sensory stimulations that had been created.

The Steps schoolroom was completely refurbished and transformed, and then, to top it all, a local company completely resurfaced the entire car park. Everything looked so smart and welcoming. Of course, with the help of Dawn and friends, we fed the workforce throughout the two-week project, but this time we had a fully fitted indoor kitchen. It was nowhere near as much fun cooking in there as it was in my mobile unit with the deep-fat fryer, but the guys were very appreciative.

On the final day, Peter Bearne and the cameras from ITV Central were there again to see the incredible transformation that had taken place. The children and their parents were stunned. It truly was an incredible feat when we realised that over the two two-week makeovers, 130 companies had given over £550,000 worth of goods and services absolutely free!

I am sometimes asked, 'What is the most exciting thing you have ever done in your life?' Without a doubt, the Steps makeover of 2007 was the most rewarding, exciting, challenging and hard-work project I had ever been involved in. The teamwork, the energy, and the goodwill of everyone who donated products and took part, made this the best ever. It was extraordinary to witness such creative dynamism and goodness being freely given by so many.

17

A stray dog and a contract with Universal

2007–9

It was a really cold day in January 2007. I was driving to the office, past Cossington Mill close to the River Soar, in Leicestershire. Suddenly, I saw an elderly dog-walker waving his walking stick high in the air, backwards and forwards. He was trying to flag down passing motorists. I wondered what drama or tragedy was unfolding; then I spotted a young sandy-coloured dog prancing around in the middle of the road.

I pulled over and shouted across to the guy, 'Is it yours?'

'No!' came the reply. 'Is it yours?'

I was worried the dog would be hit by a car and suggested that perhaps I should take it to the police station. So I called the lively creature over, and she immediately jumped in! And so began a rather special new 'dog chapter' in my life.

By now, you will have realised that dogs are often very significant characters in my story.

I had a brief chat with the dog-walker, who explained that the dog had been hanging around for over three hours; he wondered whether she might have leapt off one of the narrow boats passing through the locks and had run off and become lost.

I stepped back into the car but realised she had run over all the seats with muddy paws – and I was dressed head to toe in a plain cream suit in preparation for giving a talk to a large group at County Hall in an hour's time! I managed to find an old coat, which I placed over my car seat, and drove the three miles (about five km) to Quorn House where Dawn and my secretary, Melody, took care of the dog while I went off to my engagement. John the gardener gave her some food and, in the end, she had four bowlfuls as she was so hungry! Dawn then took her to the police station and we hoped someone would claim her.

***

Just before the previous Christmas, I had celebrated my 60th birthday – a birthday I felt very uncomfortable about. Turning 60 seemed officially 'old' and I politely asked people that if they planned on getting me a birthday card to please select one that did not have '60' on it! Looking back, that was so ridiculous! When I had my 65th and then my 70th and 75th, I didn't care a jot. So silly of me to be so vain.

For this momentous birthday, Mike and Dawn had really spoilt me. I had always been a massive fan of the film *The Sound of Music*, so when the TV show *How Do You Solve a Problem Like Maria?* appeared on our screens in 2007 I was glued. Over a number of weeks, potential Maria-hopefuls tried to win the starring role in the West End musical version of the film, and Andrew Lloyd Webber was head judge. Having watched the programme, for me there was only one young woman for the role, and that was Connie Fisher. When the winner was finally announced, Dawn and Mike breathed a massive sigh of relief. They had already booked to take me to London for a very special weekend which included tickets for the Royal Box at the London Palladium to see *The Sound of Music*, and they knew that if Connie Fisher hadn't won it, I wouldn't have been that bothered about going. But she did, and Mike's present to me was that we were all off for a fabulous weekend away.

So, Dawn, Mike and I drove down to London, and I felt like royalty as we watched the production from such privileged seats. We had a ride in a rickshaw, dined at Veeraswamy, attended a wine-tasting establishment and generally had a fabulous time. I felt utterly spoilt, but there was more to come.

Dawn is known for her super-thoughtful presents, and for this special birthday she excelled herself. She knew my utter love for *The Sound of Music*, the best film ever as far as I am concerned and the reason why I fell in love with Austria – a love that has remained with me all of my life since. On the day of my birthday Dawn presented me with a box of parcels. I wasn't allowed to open each one until I could remember the next line of the song 'My Favourite Things' from the film. I had obviously never let on to Dawn about the bit of my brain that was missing which prevented me from remembering words of songs or poetry. Nevertheless, this was the task. So, after unwrapping the bunch of 'roses with raindrops', then a toy kitten for 'whiskers on kittens', and a 'bright copper kettle and warm woollen mittens', it came to a 'brown paper package tied up with string'! Inside the brown paper package was a CD. Mike and I went on to my laptop to see what was on it, but the cover showed Julie Andrews singing on top of a mountain so we had a bit of a clue!

As the content of the CD unfolded, it appeared that Dawn had arranged for us to fly out to Salzburg to go on the official Sound of Music Tour! We were then to meet up with our Austrian friend Uli, and to stay with him and his wife Herta before they drove us all the way to Lech for a weekend at the Berghof Hotel – the wonderful place I visited every year with my activity holiday group, and where Mike, Dawn and I went skiing. Uli was head barman there.

We had the loveliest of times and a lot of fun. The Sound of Music Tour was brilliant. We saw the lake where the children fell into the river in their curtain clothes, the house where Maria arrived in the bus and knocked on the door of the Von Trapp residence, the church where Maria and Captain von Trapp were married and lots, lots more.

While enjoying our weekend at the Berghof, one evening at dinner, Dawn and I worked on Mike to try to persuade him to let us keep the stray dog if she wasn't claimed. Dawn and I had discussed the possibility on our own, but we hadn't mentioned it until now.

Mike wasn't keen. 'We already have Max and really don't need another dog', he said.

Rosie had been put to sleep the previous November after she had a seizure, having been so distressed by Bonfire Night. She had always been nervous whenever she heard fireworks and, when she reached such a grand old age, probably 16, it was just too much for her. It was really sad, but she had had a wonderful life with us for many years, following her very tough early years which ended with her being abandoned outside an RSPCA centre.

After Dawn put forward a very persuasive case that the stray dog might well be put to sleep if not claimed, Mike relented – but on one condition: that he would name her. We agreed in a heartbeat.

Mike called over the head waiter and asked him what 'orphan' was in Austrian German.

'I don't know,' he said, 'but a Waisenhaus is an orphanage.'

So the dog was to be called 'Waise' (pronounced 'Visor'). Unusual, for sure; in fact probably unique; but at least we had the green light. *Woohoo!*

I called the staff of the kennels where the dog was being kept and told them that we would be very happy to give her a home if no-one claimed her. When nobody did, Dawn and I were really excited. Mike less so.

We collected Waise and had her checked out by our vet. Apparently, she was between nine months and a year old, a whippet–lurcher cross, and was basically in good health.

After the first night, when we shut her in our carpeted and warm back kitchen, with a nice soft basket as a bed, we were shocked to discover she had just about demolished the wooden door! It turned out that Waise hated being shut in and insisted on staying in our bedroom. She had obviously been used to sleeping with her previous owner, so we gave in. She was no trouble but was a bit boisterous around Max initially. Over time, she settled and accompanied me everywhere that I could take her. Waise would always come to Quorn House with me and loved wandering around the various offices in search of strokes from the staff and a shaft of sunlight in which she could lie and sunbathe. As the sun moved around the building, so did Waise. On cold days she would come in and run at full speed up the elegant Georgian staircase and along the landings to warm up. To the staff sitting quietly working at their desks it sounded like thunder, so they would rush to their door to see what was going on, only to see Waise charging along the vast corridors, careering round the top into the accounts office, doing a U-turn and racing back to the far end of the building, and again and again! When she had warmed up, she panted like mad and collapsed on to the carpet. It was hilarious! (You can see a video of her doing just that at <www.rosemaryconley.com> if you click on Rosemary's World and then Dogs.)

As a lurcher, Waise was a natural wanderer. One day we even had a call from a woman in the village, a couple of streets away, explaining that she had gone up to her bedroom for something and found Waise fast asleep on her bed! Thankfully, Waise had a name tag so she was able to call us. It wasn't unusual for Waise to wander up the long drive and out of the front gate of Quorn House, which was a real worry – and that is exactly what she had done that day. On another occasion, our neighbour at Ashby Folville also enjoyed a visit from her in his bedroom. She just climbed on to the bed while he was still in it and settled down!

Over the years, Waise proved to be the most wonderful, faithful, adoring and loving dog I think I have ever known. The fact that sometimes she was naughty somehow made me love her even more. She was spoilt to death, and many of you will have seen her on the sofa with me during recordings when I was involved with our online Club.

***

The previous year, I had been invited to draw the raffle at a charity event in the next village entitled 'Music in the Meadow'. Kevin and Alison Ingram were holding the event for the last time on their land and were raising funds for Matt Hampson, the young Leicester Tigers rugby player who had been paralysed after an accident in training some years before.

Mike and I went along and thought what a great event it was. A fabulous music group from the USA seemed to be able to play anything from Andrea Bocelli to Dolly Parton, Coldplay to Abba. They were incredible.

But Kevin and Alison had decided this would be their last event, so we asked if we could take it over and run it from our grounds in Ashby Folville. They were delighted. The following year, we organised Music in the Meadow in the fields at the back of the Manor and invited everyone we could think of to come along. Kevin persuaded the American band to appear again as he ran an event company and was able to fit in their visit with other events to keep costs down. In addition, he had great contacts with a marquee company, a toilet provider, a staging and lighting supplier and, because of his significant worldwide corporate events, was able to persuade some of the five-star hotels he used to give us holidays for raffle prizes! We held the event in aid of Steps, Matt Hampson and our local village hall.

The lighting was amazing. The Manor looked like a scene from a Harry Potter film with its fabulous façade lit up in fluorescent pink and purple, green and blue. It was all very exciting! Lots of people brought their gazebos and champagne and everyone had a party. I organised a tombola and managed to blag loads of prizes, and we set it all up with the help of some friends.

One of our suppliers for our Diet & Fitness Clubs, Kevin Eastwood, ran a business where he supplied products for all kinds of companies. I called Kevin Eastwood to ask if he had any odd products or goods we could have for our tombola. Ideally, 10 smaller items rather than one big one. He said he had. In fact, he had a lot of china tea-sets left over from a promotion for a national newspaper. Did I want them all? 'Yes, please!' came my eager response, but when they arrived I was somewhat taken by surprise. The lorry was carrying 10 whole pallets of china tea-sets, cake stands, teapots, milk jugs and sugar bowls! The only stipulation was that they could not be sold and the name of the newspaper that had originally ordered them had to be obliterated from the packaging.

We offloaded the cartons into our now empty stables and, for the following five years that we held Music in the Meadow, the tea-sets appeared on the tombola, as well as at other charity events that we ran thereafter. We also gave many of them to local village halls, schools and also our franchisees who were organising their own charity events. It took years before they all were finally given away.

Music in the Meadow was a wonderful success and £26,000 was raised for the charities. This was a great result but, most of all, everyone had a great time, and we continued to run the event annually for the next five years.

The day before our first Music in the Meadow event, Jeanne, Mike's mum, called to say she wasn't feeling at all well. Jeanne was now living alone as her husband Philip had died some years earlier. We called the doctor and she was immediately admitted into hospital, where she stayed for 10 days. She had a bad infection and was very dehydrated, but thankfully it wasn't life-threatening.

Jeanne and I had become close friends over the years and I, along with everyone else she knew, always admired her elegance and poise. I would visit her most Saturday mornings when she would prepare a delicious and delicate lunch served on a tray with a starched lace tray cloth and pretty embroidered napkin. Everything was always perfect. But now she was 85 and I think that, having been eight years on her own, she hadn't taken as good care of herself as perhaps she should. She was always tiny, weighing 7½ st. (47.6 kg) at most. How she managed to bring up three strapping and strong young boys is beyond me, as her husband Philip was often away and she had to cope on her own. Now she was struggling, so Mike and I decided that she should come and stay with us. One of her sons, Steve, while local, was almost a recluse; even when Jeanne had had a car accident and was in hospital some years earlier, he didn't go to visit. Her other son, Mark, lived much further away, so it made sense for her to come to us.

Once Jeanne was well enough, we collected her from hospital and settled her into one of our bedrooms. As soon as she was in bed, Waise went upstairs and lay by her side – for a week!

Thankfully, we nursed Jeanne back to full health, but we decided that she should no longer live on her own. Our top-floor flat was empty and, if she was happy to, Jeanne could move in and still have her own space while having the security of knowing we were in the house.

Mike and I welcomed his mum into the Manor and made her feel comfortable. I brought all her clothes over from the family home, and stored them around the array of wardrobes on the top floor of the house. Jeanne was an avid dressmaker and had rails and rails of beautiful clothes. If she was to feel at home with us, the clothes had to come too. Her flat was very comfortable with a lounge, a good-sized bedroom, a fully fitted kitchen and a very nice bathroom, and we took up her meals if she wasn't dining with us.

Of course, I took Jeanne out with me to M&S to do the shopping or run any errands she needed to do, and gave her a lift if she wanted to visit her friends. In the evening when Jeanne would be in her flat, I often went upstairs and sat with her, or she came down to sit with me while I checked the magazine proofs. I enjoyed having Jeanne there. We were really good friends and we enjoyed each other's company.

***

Our mail-order business was growing year on year and, as well as food, we had developed our own Rosemary Conley range of electrical kitchen gadgets. This was a selection of high-quality and very effective and efficient woks and mini-grills, steamers and food processors. These items were also for sale in the shops, including John Lewis and Harrods. Later, we added non-stick pans and bakeware. Chris thought it would be a good idea to ask Dawn to explore some new merchandise as she was used to doing research for the magazine, so she visited a variety of exhibitions to see what was out there. Once she had researched a collection of products, I was invited to meet the supplier with Dawn to go through the possibilities and then I would make the final selection. Included in the array of products was a set of plastic measuring cups used in baking.

Every two years, we created a new diet for the members of our Clubs. It was always a big job because it was different from writing a normal book. It had to be smaller in size but contain a lot. It needed to be relatively simple and easy to follow. In a two-year period the classes would recruit around 200,000 new members, and each person would be given a 'New Member Pack' which contained the diet booklet and a variety of other items. Because of the quantities involved, we were able to keep the raw cost down and sold the New Member Packs to the franchisees at a small profit. This is common practice in franchising and was our only means of earning money from new members who joined the classes. This, of course, was in addition to the set weekly franchise service fee which they were contracted to pay for every class they ran. Anything they made above their weekly fee was theirs to keep, with the consequence that very good franchisees were able to earn a great deal of money.

We tried to improve the New Member Pack every couple of years to make it more exciting for a new member to join *us* rather than one of our competitors. As I sat at the boardroom table holding the set of five measuring cups, I suddenly had an idea.

I turned to the supplier and said, 'If I were to ask you to create a set of four, not five, cups, have them branded for us, and we gave you an order for 200,000, could you supply them for a small fraction of the normal price?'

He felt he could.

I explained that I thought they would make fantastic 'portion pots' to help our members control their portion sizes and therefore lose more weight. Instead of telling people to weigh 4 oz or 113 g of a certain food, we could say 'Use a blue [or red or yellow or green] portion potful' according to the food in question. It would make losing weight very much easier.

Within a few weeks we received the prototype and the price was agreed. Chris arranged for the name Rosemary Conley's Portion Pots® to be registered as a trademark. Dawn and I had great fun measuring out different portion-sizes of foods so that we could create a reference card to accompany the Portion Pots® to help our members, and anyone else who bought them from our website could buy them for £4.99.

Then we made some great discoveries. We found that a *blue* Portion Pot® of *uncooked* basmati rice equalled exactly the same number of calories as *cooked* basmati rice measured in a *red* Portion Pot®. This meant that if you were cooking only for yourself, you would just take a blue Portion Pot® of rice to put into your boiling water; but if you were cooking for the whole family, you would cook rice for everyone first and just take a red Portion Pot® full of ready-to-eat rice for you if you were trying to lose weight.

Whether it was wine, baked beans, peas, cereal, rice, pasta, Greek yogurt or porridge oats, with just a quick scoop, you could measure your portion and stay within your calorie allowance. We placed our order for 200,000.

***

Every autumn, we held our Annual Franchisee Convention. We always had an inspirational motivational speaker and among them was Richard Denny.

I had learned about Richard's motivational methods early on in the days when my *Hip and Thigh Diet* became so successful, and he very kindly sent me a copy of his set of audio cassettes entitled *Dare to Be Great*. I listened to these tapes so many times, and his words of wisdom and experience and enthusiasm totally resonated with me and helped to inspire me towards having a positive mental attitude. Now, I had the opportunity to invite Richard to be our keynote speaker at our Annual Convention. The franchisees lapped it up. They loved him.

And I will never forget this pearl of wisdom from Richard. He said: 'Success is not about making money; it is about these three things. One: having a goal. Two: having someone to share it with. Three: knowing that what you do makes a difference.'

Wise words indeed, and ones I have never forgotten.

Also at these events we would launch our marketing strategy for the following year and, at the end of the afternoon session, we would present service awards to our franchisees and our staff. For five years' service they were presented with an engraved glass award, which progressed to a Gucci or similar diamond-studded watch for 10 years' service. As time went on, for 15 years' service we presented them with a diamond necklace and, when they reached 20 years, diamond stud earrings. We were very happy to reward our long-serving and loyal staff as well as our franchisees. We loved giving them these gifts which I know they appreciated and treasured enormously.

Each year, we also gave awards for Newcomer, Most Improved and for the top-performing Franchisee of the Year – awards that were determined by a variety of criteria. In addition, I always gave a special award from me, personally, in recognition of a particular achievement; for example, showing courage while battling with illness, or devoting a great deal of time to raising funds for charity, or sometimes for supporting other franchisees. It was different every year. I was always so proud of our franchisees. They were really special women. As well as being fit, competent, confident and caring diet and fitness teachers, they were good people. When they came along to our Convention each year, they looked amazing, dressed in their business suits during the day and the most glamorous evening dresses for the gala dinner. And once the meal was over and the DJ played his first songtrack, every one of them was on the floor dancing. After all, these were physically fit women, they were dressed to the nines and they were ready to party! The DJ always loved doing our gig.

I remember one year we were in the large conference room in a hotel. In the next-door meeting room, an all-male contingent was having a tea break from their business meeting. When the doors from our Conference opened and out walked our fabulous franchisees, I wish I had had a camera to snap the looks on the faces of the guys! I think they thought they had died and gone to heaven! It was priceless.

We had occasionally accepted male franchisees but, for whatever reason, it never worked out particularly well for them. Most of our members were female, and I suppose people attending a weight-loss club are usually self-conscious about themselves and, when they step forward to be weighed, they would rather face a woman at the scales than a man.

At the next Convention, we launched my new *Gi Jeans Diet* together with our Portion Pots®, and they both went down a storm. Every new member who joined our classes from that January onwards would be given a set of Portion Pots® with a retail value of £4.99, plus a new diet, all packaged in a smart presentation bag. It was impressive and the franchisees loved it.

***

With Jeanne now living upstairs at home and life continuing to be busy, I kept up my regular phone calls to Mabel. By now the telephone calls had become somewhat predictable – to the point where Mike would be pre-empting how the call would go while I was dialling the number.

He would say, in 'my' voice, 'Hello, Mabel. How are things? . . . Oh no! . . . *Really!* . . . Oh my goodness! . . . You're *joking*! . . . Are you all right? . . . And what did the doctor say? . . .'

In a way, Mike's success in making me smile helped me get through these relentless conversations of disaster after disaster, peppered with Mabel's sweeping and extraordinary statements such as: 'They should close down the National Health Service and let people die naturally and that would solve the problems of overpopulation!' I would have loved to have seen her challenging the politicians on *Question Time*!

For all her foibles, Mabel had loved my father and tirelessly and patiently coped with him right up to his death in 2001, and I was grateful for her devotion to him. Often, she would say to me that she wished she had died at the same time as Oswald. Her remaining years continued to be very sad.

***

In the summer of 2007 my Agent, Liz Ayto, was contacted by ITV. Would I like to audition for the second series of the TV show *Dancing on Ice*? This was so unexpected and very exciting! I had never skated on ice in my life – only on the wooden floor of our conservatory in my socks when I was a little girl – but I *loved* watching ice skating!

Mike and I discussed this idea because of the large commitment involved and decided I should go for it. Beforehand, I went to Nottingham Ice Centre to have half a dozen private lessons. I needed to know that I could at least stand up on the ice before I went down to audition at Alexandra Palace where I would have to skate with one of the *Dancing on Ice* coaches. It turned out to be really scary as this professional skater tried to take me round the ice very fast. I didn't pass the audition process, but hoped that I might get through the next year.

Despite the disappointment, I was loving my skating even though progress was painfully slow. My coach, Karen Goodwin, was the most patient teacher and continued to encourage me. After I had learned to skate forwards and backwards, in a fashion, the next manoeuvre to learn is what is called a three-turn. This enables you to turn yourself from forward to backward in a single twist of the body and on one skate. Simple? I don't think so!

I must have practised the three-turn 500 times before I got it. Maybe this is another bit of my brain that doesn't work. I tripped; I scraped my toe pick (the rake at the toe end of the skate); I scratched the ice – all in an effort to turn. It seemed hopeless. I just could not do it! Karen loved the fact that I was so determined to learn and didn't mind how many times I tried and failed. With great perseverance, one day there was a Eureka moment and suddenly I could do it! Once I got the hang of it, I wanted to do it all the time! It is a fabulous move, and one probably appreciated and enjoyed more by me than any other skater!

Then, just as I was beginning to get the hang of ice skating, I was approached by the producers at Universal Studios to discuss making fitness DVDs for them. I was very happy working with Paul Hembury, who had continued to produce dozens of my previous titles, both when he was working for VCI and then when he moved over to the BBC, but the Universal bosses were persistent. They made me a very generous offer to entice me away from the BBC for three titles to be released in the following three to four years. I went to Paul and told him of my dilemma and, while he was delighted for me as a friend, he knew he would not be able to match what they were offering. It was a bittersweet situation as I loved working with Paul, but the team from Universal were very nice so I signed the deal. Thankfully, they agreed that I could still use Nick Patten, my long-standing Video and DVD Director, as the Director for these new titles, which was great. Looking back, it was rather extraordinary that a company would pay such a lot of money to sign up a woman in her 60s to present fitness videos.

Because of the sums involved and the risk that ice skating presented, I decided to put my skating on hold until all three programmes were recorded, which took three and a half years. The week after I recorded the third one, I was at the ice rink having another lesson. By now I was 63, but I was determined to learn to skate and one day, hopefully, to be selected to appear on *Dancing on Ice*. That was my ultimate dream.

18

A love story, a TV channel and a Fit2Win challenge

2006–9

My first DVD title for Universal was the *Gi Jeans Weight-Loss Workout* in 2006. This followed my *Gi Jeans Diet* book, which had been a highly successful *Sunday Times* No.1 bestseller. Around that time, there was a lot of talk about the benefits of eating foods with a low Gi (Glycaemic index) rating, so I had designed my own diet based on these principles. Susan Jebb, now Professor Susan Jebb, checked it for me, as she had for many of my previous diet books. The principle of eating foods with a low Gi rating is based on keeping our blood-sugar levels more consistent. Consuming foods which were of a lower Gi helped those who followed this form of eating avoid peaks and troughs in their blood-sugar levels, which was particularly important for anyone with diabetes. It also helped you to feel fuller for longer. With this new angle on how to lose weight, unsurprisingly, a plethora of low-Gi diet books inevitably followed, including several of my own, which thankfully did very well. There was no doubt that eating foods with a low Gi made sense so, from then on, I incorporated low-Gi foods into all future low-fat recipe and diet books that I wrote. At home, we continue to eat such foods today as a matter of course.

My second DVD for Universal was *Brand New You Workout* with Coleen Nolan which came out a year later. What a delightful and talented woman Coleen turned out to be! Together with my team of backing dancers (all members of our classes who had lost significant amounts of weight), and of course choreographer Mary, I loved working with Coleen. That particular title sold hundreds of thousands of copies, so that was exciting. For a variety of reasons, we didn't record one for January the following year, but my third title for Universal, my *Real Results Workout,* was recorded in March of that year, to be released in January 2009, and was to be my last DVD. I had recorded 30 videos and DVDs in my career. I had loved making every one of them and particularly the ones where Mary was involved, and enjoyed meeting and working with the inspirational backing dancers who had joined me on them. These men and women, all of whom had worked very hard, would patiently record take after take whenever any one of us went wrong, just enjoying the thrill of producing something that thousands of people would be working out to in their homes for many months and years to come. It was a special privilege for me and, I hope, for them. We had fun and we worked very hard, but now it really was time to call it a day. It was a lot of work for both Mary and for me. Selecting great music that could be approved to be licensed was always challenging, and it was particularly tough for Mary to keep creating even more variety in the choreography. We both agreed it was the right time to stop.

The day after *Real Results Workout* was recorded, I asked my TV Manager, Liz Ayto, to contact the producers of *Dancing on Ice* in the hope that I would be invited to audition again, and they agreed. However, yet again, sadly, I didn't make the line-up. Maybe next year?

***

There was much excitement when a new TV series was commissioned for ITV Central entitled *Slim to Win with Rosemary Conley.* We recruited seven volunteers to lose weight – two men and five women – who over six months would try to transform their weight. The programme was based at Quorn House, and most of them lost significant amounts of weight and improved their health. We recorded their monthly weigh-ins, filmed them at home and got to know them better.

But there was a problem. One young woman just wasn't achieving the results we hoped for, and at one weigh-in I got really cross with her. This went out on TV and I got a severe telling-off afterwards from Mike.

'I can't believe you did that!' he said.

It was very unusual for Mike to criticise my words or actions on TV, but he explained that for me to behave in this way was totally out of character and I really shouldn't do that again. He made it clear that he was just trying to protect me – but I *was* cross with her! I knew how many other people had wanted to be on the programme and I felt she wasted her opportunity. In the six months, she lost just 7 lb (3.17 kg), while the others lost several stone.

To accompany the TV series, I wrote my *Slim to Win* cookbook, helped by my TV chef, Dean Simpole-Clarke. It was great to be able to promote the hardback cookbook off the back of the TV series, which went out every Thursday evening for six weeks.

***

In our private lives, the very exciting news for our family was that Dawn had a new man in her life. She had been divorced some years earlier, but now she had met Laurie. They dated for a few months but soon realised that this relationship was very special and, just as Mike and I had done decades before, they became engaged in Austria! Her dad, Phil, and his wife Trish, and Mike and I were absolutely thrilled and there was great excitement as we looked forward to Dawn and Laurie's special day.

Their wedding was in early January 2010. There had been a significant snowfall the night before and it felt like the coldest day of the century. Dawn looked spectacularly beautiful in her golden-cream wedding gown, accompanied by three beautiful bridesmaids, including Laurie's daughter Harriet, aged nine.

The service was so full of love I had tears of joy in my eyes for most of the time! Dawn was such a special human being and deserved to find happiness, and today she was brimming with joy. Afterwards, at the reception, Laurie made the most heart-touching speech I had ever heard at any wedding. Dawn and Laurie were both Christians and he explained that when they had each married the first time, they intended that marriage to be for life, but they had found themselves on their own because their respective spouses had made other choices. He went on to describe how they felt God had brought them together and spoke of one beautiful and touching moment when they were some way along the journey of their friendship: Harriet (his nine-year-old daughter) had whispered confidentially to him, 'Dad . . . I think you should marry Dawn.'

At that, I think all the guests in the room had a tear in their eye too.

After the reception it was time for the first dance, which the bride and groom performed in spectacular fashion. Dawn had enjoyed ballroom dancing lessons before meeting Laurie, who had then joined her for their weekly sessions nearby. For this special occasion, they were determined to make the first dance at their wedding memorable. Having had to master endless choreography for my fitness videos over the years, I think that both Mary, who was also a guest at the wedding, and I probably appreciated more than anyone else in the room how intricate the dance was. At the end, Laurie spun Dawn around in a Cinderella lift as though they were on *Strictly Come Dancing*! It was amazing.

The following day, I was being interviewed by Aled Jones on *Good Morning Sunday* on BBC Radio 2. I was still buzzing after the wedding and Aled was asking all about it. He is such a lovely guy and I couldn't have wished for a nicer way to share the joy of the previous day.

Some months later, Dawn and Laurie enjoyed their honeymoon in Austria at the Berghof Hotel where Mike and I had enjoyed ours back in 1986. There is no doubt that the Berghof in Lech, and Austria as a country, hold a very special place in our hearts and in the memories of all four of us.

***

I have felt very fortunate in my life as I have loved my career. There was never a dull moment and I never ceased to be surprised or excited by the extraordinary weight-loss successes that were achieved by our members. I was also very interested in the next product or gadget that we might be able to include in our range. We were always extremely careful in our choices and only included products that would be genuinely helpful to the user. Some years before, we had launched our own range of dairy products, including the most delicious chocolate mousse. It was stocked in Asda and was the best chocolate mousse on the market. Also, it came in a large pot, which everybody loved because it was a really good-sized portion – unlike so many low-calorie products. It was imported from Belgium and was a massive hit with our members as it could be frozen too. Sadly, when Asda insisted that the price be brought down from £1.25

to 99p, which was impossible for the producers to achieve, this lovely product came to an end. We also had our own low-fat 5% hard cheese, which was similarly delicious and was produced by an award-winning cheesemaker.

In addition, we launched a low-fat ready-meal range called Solo Slim which, because it didn't need to be refrigerated and had a nine-month shelf-life, could be sold through our Clubs and by mail order. After the experience we had had with supermarkets, I decided that we should only sell this range through mail order. This added a new string to our bow and proved profitable for the franchisees and the company. It was a fantastic product and sold very well.

As with any company, we could never stand still, so we were always on the lookout for something special and a bit different. Our next initiative was to prove very exciting. We were forever looking for new ways we could support the Clubs. We had an outstanding network of franchisees and a vast number of loyal members. I was very much aware that what we offered was different from Weight Watchers and Slimming World. Both are great organisations that do a fantastic job and what they do works for their members. But we offered something different – diet *and* fitness – and our aim was to keep *our* franchisees and *our* members happy and staying loyal to *us*. I understood that not everybody liked either me or my diets. That was fine. But for those who did, it was important that we look after them in the very best way we could.

Around 18 months earlier, when the digital age had reached new heights, we came up with the idea of creating our own digital TV channel and decided to build a bespoke TV studio in our old warehouse building at Quorn House, which was now empty. Our mail-order business had grown significantly, so we had moved our warehouse to a new, much larger unit on an industrial estate nearby.

Chris and Mike took on the responsibility of organising the building work and the creation of the studio, together with all its equipment. Liz Ayto's husband, Rod Laverick, was experienced in such matters and guided us through the process.

With a significant investment and full of confidence that we would be able to make the enterprise cover its costs with advertising revenue, we proceeded to create RosemaryConley.TV (RC.TV). This would be an internet TV channel. We then advertised for our TV crew: a Producer/ Director, a Technical Manager, a Cameraman/Editor and a Production Assistant (PA).

Gemma Binch applied for the position of Producer/Director. I knew Gemma from working with her on my ITV Central TV series *Slim to Win*, which we had recorded previously. She had also really impressed me when she had so kindly made the DVD to help us raise funds for Steps. To me, she was the obvious choice for the job as she was naturally talented and I liked her. Lynn Douglas had worked with Gemma and took the post of PA. We found a very capable Cameraman and Editor in Brian Frith. The initial Technical Manager stayed with us for only a short time and was replaced by Susannah Goodwin, also from ITV Central – who proved to be an extraordinary talent in a TV studio.

Our TV studio was an impressive facility which took advantage of the new massive advances in technology, bringing the cost of our venture to a more practical level of investment compared with what had historically been the case in the realm of broadcast TV. We were already in the digital age, and broadcast was changing. It was no longer seen only on our TV screens but was now available on lots of different platforms, including laptops, as well as tablets and smartphones which had relatively recently arrived on the market.

The whole venture was revolutionary in the UK diet and fitness market, and it provided great excitement for the franchisees when we launched it at our Annual Convention prior to its national launch in January 2010. This was a very new concept and the franchisees loved the idea that they could be on the channel too. Their members also enjoyed coming to the studio for recording days. The look on their faces as they arrived said everything. Having their hair and make-up done by a professional make-up artist, and then cooking with our chef, Dean Simpole-Clarke, or chatting with me on the sofa, made their day memorable and exciting. We also filmed the photoshoots for the magazine, which meant that as the next issue of the magazine was published, readers could tune in to RC.TV to see the featured slimmers being interviewed. It added an extra, real-life dimension to their story and was highly motivating to any potential member.

We already had a notable team of experts who wrote for our magazine and they all had plenty of experience on TV, so it was a natural progression to invite them on to the channel. It worked brilliantly and the members and the franchisees loved it. As well as interviewing guests, we also created hundreds of films of chef Dean demonstrating how to cook our recipes. We recorded numerous interviews with Dr Hilary Jones on health issues, Professor Raj Persaud on psychology, Professor Susan Jebb on nutrition science and Mary Morris on exercise.

The franchisees would come to record workouts that viewers could follow at home in addition to attending their classes, and we were able to create specialist exercise programmes for individuals with specific needs, such as postnatal mothers or people with osteoporosis or back problems. We even included interviews with surgeons who performed gastric bypass operations, experts in breast cancer and many others. We were offering a free public service and we were delighted with how popular it turned out to be.

Originally, we had intended that RC.TV would be available on subscription, but the internet was developing so fast that everyone was expecting everything to be for free. We made the decision that we would rely on advertising revenue to cover our costs. Chris met up with representatives from Fox Media who said that if we were to attract 100,000 viewers, we would be able to earn a level of revenue that would make it all worthwhile. But by the time we reached the 100,000 target a year later, they told us it needed an audience of a million! We ended up only earning a tiny amount from advertising, but the benefit of the overall offering to the franchisees and their members made us feel that it was all worthwhile. We had something no-one else was offering.

We knew that RC.TV significantly extended our service to our Club members, and soon it was attracting vastly increased numbers of viewers for an internet channel. In addition, the franchisees benefited enormously because, through the work of our expert recording crew, we were able to film all of the presenters and training sessions created at our Annual Training Convention, held at Center Parcs in the spring. Our teachers were among the best in the land, and that was because of our care in selection and because our training, and continuing training and development, was superb.

Mary Morris had headed up our training department since 1994 but took a year out to do a Master's degree in Exercise and Nutrition Science some years later. In her absence Mary brought in Caroline Whiting, another highly respected Teacher Trainer, and Caroline took over as Head of Training. Now, with Mary as our Training Consultant, we provided an outstanding approach to the specialist training our franchisees needed. Our teachers weren't just fitness professionals; they were trained to cater for people with different degrees of fitness and abilities within the same class.

The TV team were great. They had a very different set of skills from the rest of our company and I loved learning from them. Gemma was an ace Producer, and Susannah a fantastic Technician and Editor, so between them they were a formidable force.

We now had the capacity to make films in our own right and I decided that I wanted to illustrate the drawbacks of being obese in a very personal way. First, the make-up department at Leicester College made me a prosthesis for my face to make me look fatter. Then I donned one of our 20-lb (9-kg) 'fat jackets' used by our franchisees for training, plus a whole-body fat suit which was taped around me to fit. I had purchased a size 18 top and a similar-sized skirt and some comfy flat shoes to complete the transformation.

Accompanied by our TV crew and Alan Olley, our photographer, we drove into Leicester city centre where I would be filmed. Getting into and out of the car was an uncomfortable challenge in itself, and as I walked into the lift in the shopping centre I was amazed that no-one even batted an eyelid at me. I then acknowledged the comment made by many of my successful slimmers when they came to our photoshoots: they exclaimed that when they were big, they felt invisible.

As I sat on a bench near the Clock Tower, a morbidly obese woman drove past in her mobility scooter and I found myself saying to myself, 'Well, she's fatter than me!' I was beginning to experience the feelings of a very overweight person. And that was how I wanted to feel. I wanted to remind myself why I don't overeat. Why I exercise regularly. I remembered only too well how I *hated* being overweight and I wanted to be able to 'step into the shoes' of someone who had a serious weight problem now. A weight that would adversely affect their health. At my heaviest I had only been 35 lb (about 16 kg) heavier than I am now – overweight, yes, but not obese.

I couldn't wait for five o'clock when I knew I could shed my uncomfortable, cumbersome, exhausting excesses. When we reached Quorn House and I was able to remove all the clobber, I felt unbelievably grateful. I didn't have to cope with those challenges, day in, day out. I was exhausted and I had only been carrying probably about 3 st. (19 kg) extra for seven hours. Imagine carrying 7 or 8 st. (44 or 51 kg) in excess weight – and I knew lots of people who did.

(You can watch this video at <www.rosemaryconley.com>.)

At the end of the experiment, I felt I wanted to suggest that every slimmer who had shed a significant amount of weight should dress up in all that cumbersome padding for a day to remind them of how far they had come. And when, just like me, at the end of the day, they could take it all off again, they would truly realise how wonderful it felt to be slim, and hopefully never be tempted to go back to their old eating habits.

Another fun bonus of having our own TV crew was that we could create special 'mini-movies' to show as the 'grand finale' at our Annual Conventions. Mike and Chris were the stars one year, when the plot involved rival Clubs 'Waist Watchers' and 'Slimming Universe' trying to steal our new diet, and it ended with Mike and Chris having a duel outside Quorn House. It was hilarious and involved every member of staff, including the dog belonging to John, our gardener! It was a masterful piece of film-making.

Another year, chef Dean and I re-enacted the infamous 'breakfast' sketch by the beloved comedy duo Morecambe and Wise. It was such fun to film, and it all ended with Dean wearing one of my Lycra catsuits from the 1990s and having a Portion Pot® attached as a fig leaf! On another occasion, we did a spoof of *Downton Abbey* called 'Downton Flabby' – which again was hilarious.

***

As the new decade dawned, there was a great deal going on, helped by the fact that Chris Ash had fitted in really well with the business and had taken a huge amount off my shoulders. Mike, and Angie who had worked with us since the beginning, got along with him famously, and he was also popular with the staff and the franchisees. One day, we asked Chris and Angie to join us in the boardroom at 5 pm. The staff finished work then, so we knew we would be on our own. They were very nervous wondering what we were going to say.

Mike and I had decided, with the blessing of our Non-Executive Director, Brian, that we should give directorships to both of them. Chris became our Marketing Director and Angie our Franchise Director. Angie had become such a valuable member of the team, having worked in almost all areas of the business during her 20 or so years with Mike and me. They were both thrilled.

We had a great team of staff throughout the business, and we had a lot of fun with everyone. One year, we decided to treat all our employees to a trip to London, but there was an extra surprise in store. Once they were all on the coach, Chris, Mike, Angie and I arrived – but dressed as waiters and waitresses so that we could serve *them* with food and champagne on the coach! We travelled down to London and went to see *Dirty Dancing* together; then we piled back into the coach to return home. They absolutely loved it and we felt it was a very special celebration.

***

Every year, I had the pressure of writing a new book, and in 2010 I decided it would be my *Amazing Inch Loss Plan* which would be a day-by-day diet and progressive fitness plan over 28 days. While I had devised similar programmes before, this was going to be different.

The Atkins Diet had become very popular, and eating a high-protein diet had become the new fashion. I decided that I would do a trial with 50 volunteers to see which diet was more effective – high protein or high carbohydrate. I offered my trialists the option of a 'high protein' or 'high carb' diet of 1,200 calories for the first two weeks and 1,400 calories for the following two weeks. In addition, I wanted to see if it was possible for my trial to lose an average of 14 lb (6.35 kg) during the month. I had done several trials before where we had conclusively proven that dieters could lose 7 lb (3.17 kg) in 14 days. Now it was time to push the bound-aries. I consulted with Professor Susan Jebb and discussed my plan, and she was happy for me to go ahead and had no issue with my trying to prove that a dieter could lose a stone in a month.

My 50 volunteers came to Quorn House and, coincidentally, there was a 25–25 split for choosing high protein or high carb. With ages ranging between 18 and 70, they were all weighed and monitored by my team at Quorn House over the following 28 days and, at the end, yes, they had lost between them a remarkable 50 st. (317.5 kg)! Some trialists had lost more than a stone and others had lost less, but the average, amazingly, was 14 lb (6.35 kg). With that result, I could put on the cover of my book 'Lose a stone in a month!' and we had all the evidence to back it up. The trialists were thrilled and I was delighted with the results, and I could now complete the book with every confidence it would work, irrespective of whether people followed the high-protein or high-carb options. It was exciting.

***

Also in 2010, I came up with the idea of a community project called Fit2Win. We were a couple of years away from the 2012 London Olympics, and I felt we could build on the impetus of such a momentous event and create an initiative in Leicester and Leicestershire that would make a real difference to the health and fitness of the local population.

My aim was to attract 100,000 people to enrol in the initiative. The plan was to create a healthy bespoke website (similar to what was now Rosemary Conley Online) where they could register, record their progress and download further information. Everyone would also be given a 'Fit2Win Pack' that included a booklet offering key healthy eating and exercise information, a fitness DVD and a set of Fit2Win-branded Portion Pots®. The programme would run for six months with rewards for achieving certain health milestones – for example stopping smoking, losing weight, exercising more – with the 50 top achievers each winning £1,000.

There would be a separate programme for schools with the children earning stickers for healthy eating and activity, and medals awarded to participants at the end. Initially, I talked through the idea with Mary Morris, and she was excited and happy to help me with the creation of the programme. Everything would be written and produced in cooperation with the departments of education and public health at the local level.

This was a not-for-profit voluntary project and I needed like-minded people to come on board. Before I set the wheels in motion, I decided to create my expert panel, so I went to see the CEO of Leicestershire County Council to see what he thought. He was very enthusiastic. I then went to see the CEO of Leicester City Council; she was similarly excited and commented, 'I love the fact that you're aiming for such a big number.' Subject to all the funding being put in place, each agreed to put £250,000 into the funding pot, but first we needed to test the reaction of the people by carrying out a research project and holding focus groups. I knew of a company that I was sure would do a great job, and in fact its bosses agreed to do it for a fraction of their normal fee. I was confident that if the local councils provided half the funding, we would be able to get the UK Government to match it. I estimated the average cost of each participant to be in the region of £10, based on £9 per person for the materials (the Fit2Win Packs), plus £100,000 for promotional activity and prizes – so a total of £1 million.

I approached Loughborough University and had a breakfast meeting with its Vice Chancellor. She was very keen and agreed to give us a PhD student to analyse the results of the initiative and help us design the website. We needed to see evidence of lifestyle change to justify the cost.

Next stop: our local newspaper – the *Leicester Mercury*. The Managing Director, without hesitation, was delighted to support the initiative.

I felt confident we would enlist the interest of some of Leicestershire's biggest employers – our four hospitals, the police force and fire service, plus our local councils – and their workers would be in addition to the public in general. I was very confident we would get our 100,000 participants.

My next step was to put together a team to enable us to drive the project forward. I approached someone I knew at the National Audit Office, James Robertson, and Professor Raj Persaud whose degrees in psychology and psychiatry I felt would prove invaluable. Both James and Raj were enthusiastic about the project and were prepared to travel up to Quorn House from London for every meeting. Along with representatives from the city and county councils and the others, I also included Mary and Chris from my end. In total, there were about a dozen of us.

Everything was moving along at a pace, and Mary and I were working on the content of the two packs – one for children and one for adults. A graphic designer, Richard Pyne, whose company, Pyneapple, had worked with us since the inception of our Diet & Fitness Clubs, agreed to give his time. He produced some terrific creatives, and everyone was getting very excited.

With the proposed branding, together with the principles of the project all prepared, the focus groups were held. Some of us went along to watch the reaction of the people being interviewed. We were behind a one-way glass so they didn't know we were there. It was very encouraging to hear their responses. From what we could observe, it appeared there was real enthusiasm for the Fit2Win project.

A few weeks later, the research project had been completed and the results analysed, so I called a meeting of the whole team, including the CEO of Leicestershire County Council, who had paid for the research.

The results were thorough and interesting, offering some further suggestions and observations, but the overriding view was that this was a project that could work.

In May 2010 there had been a General Election in the UK. A new Government had been formed, and with it came well-publicised budget cuts which would directly affect local councils. At the end of the presentation of the results of the research project, the Chief Executive of the county council explained that, very unfortunately, because of these cuts and the impact on local authority spending on physical activity, the county council would no longer be able to offer its grant of £250,000. Within 24 hours, the city council announced it was in a similar position and also withdrew its offer. With such significant budget cuts, it became obvious that the new Government would not be disposed to making any grants either; so, suddenly, that was the end of Fit2Win.

It was a total shock to us all and we were bitterly disappointed as we had all invested lots of time and energy in the project. We were so confident that it would have been life-transforming for so many people in and around Leicestershire, but it would only have worked if the local government agencies could have been party to it. Sadly, therefore, we had to abandon the project. There really was no other option.

After I had offered my grateful thanks to everyone involved, the meeting dispersed. I wrote to everyone I had involved in the project to express my sadness and regret that we would no longer be proceeding with Fit2Win 2012. It was incredibly disappointing, but it was out of our control. I am a firm believer that sometimes our best-laid plans can just fall through the floor and, when they do, we have to let them go. This was one such occasion.

***

It was while Mike and I were away in Portugal in the summer of 2010 that I was invited to audition for a third time for *Dancing on Ice*. Without hesitation I flew back specially, but sadly, yet again, it was not to be. This was my third failed attempt, so I was now convinced that I would never get on. Then I saw that Dr Hilary was included in the line-up for 2011! I was really happy for him but *so* envious!

After the series had finished in 2011, Dr Hilary was due to come to Quorn House to record the next batch of interviews for RC.TV. I couldn't wait to talk to him about *Dancing on Ice*. Hilary is such a lovely guy. We have always got along well and had been friends since we first met when I started writing my column for *News of the World* back in the mid-1990s. I am always so impressed that Dr Hilary can answer any medical question off the top of his head. You only need to listen to him on TV or on Steve Wright's programme on BBC Radio 2 to appreciate his vast and instant knowledge.

Having explained to him how envious I was that he had got on to *Dancing on Ice*, and that I hadn't, I showered him with questions about the show and he happily answered them all. I told him I had auditioned three times without success and felt it was hopeless now, but I loved skating and really, really wanted to do it.

Hilary watched a short DVD that showed me skating on the ice rink; this was a little film that Gemma and Susannah had kindly recorded for me. He made a few helpful comments and then suggested I write to Jayne Torvill and Christopher Dean to say how much I wanted to do *Dancing on Ice*. I should send them a DVD and see if that helped. I was also to send Hilary a copy of the letter and the DVD. And I did.

It wasn't long before Hilary told me that he happened to see the *Dancing on Ice* Producer in the corridor at the ITV studios while he was there doing his regular slot on the early morning show, and that he had handed the disc to him and said, 'You must watch this. I think she'd be great on the show.'

19

Never give up on your dreams
2010–11

My *Amazing Inch Loss Plan* book was published in January 2011 and was very successful. While I didn't want to do any more fitness DVDs, I was contracted to write two more books, including one that was quite different from my normal 'diet' programmes.

Over the years, I had learned so much from make-up artists and hair artists, fashion stylists and photographers, that I felt I could put all that knowledge into a book that would help other women of a similar age to me. After all, there were lots of us – we were the 'baby boomer' generation! I was doing everything I could to hold back the years, and I felt my approach could resonate with other women. In addition, I had been using a facial toning device since I was in my early 50s and knew that it worked. Facial-Flex® had been invented by a plastic surgeon in the USA to help facial burns patients, who needed something to help exercise their facial muscles after skin grafts. This device had a somewhat surprising side-effect on his patients. All their muscles around their face, neck, chin and chest began to lift, and in a few weeks they looked much younger! He then decided to promote the product for the anti-ageing market. I was sent one in the early 1990s to try. I started using it a few years later when the signs of ageing were escalating and I was keen to hold back the effect of loose skin, droopy jowls and a double chin.

I realised the beneficial effect of exercising our body to tone it up and keep it in shape, so why not do the same for our face? It is exactly the same principle, and soon I could see a difference. By placing the Facial-Flex® device into the corners of your mouth, and by squeezing the two ends of the device towards the centre against the resistance of a tiny band attached to the centre, you activate 30 muscle groups. As you squeeze against the dynamic resistance provided by the tiny orthodontic band looped over the centre of the gadget, the band expands, and your muscles begin to work much harder. In turn, this helps your face to lift and tone. By using it for just two minutes morning and evening, over a period of a few weeks, you can give yourself a natural face lift. If you continue to use it every day, and progress the strength of the bands so that your muscles become even stronger, it will continue to keep your facial muscles strong so that you don't appear to age so fast. I have used it now for over 20 years and I never go a day without using it.

All this experience encouraged me to put it into a book. I loved writing *The Secrets of Staying Young* and happily sat at our dining table in our kitchen at the Manor, tapping away on my laptop telling everything I had learned over the last 40 years. Within it I also told my woeful story of auditioning for *Dancing on Ice* and how I had resigned myself to the fact that they probably considered me too old at 64 and that it was not to be, even though, secretly, I never gave up hope. In fact, I had put my hope on my prayer list – a list of people and things I pray for every day. After three unsuccessful auditions, I told Mike I had decided to stop praying to be on *Dancing on Ice* as it obviously was not going to happen, but he said, 'No! Don't stop. Keep praying. You really want to do it.' So I did.

I had been asked on various occasions if I would be interviewed and photographed for *Hello!* and *OK!* magazines, but I had always resisted. Then in the summer, Liz, my Media Agent, called me and said that *Hello!* was really keen to do a big feature on Mike and me 'at home'. After discussing it with Mike, and based on the agreement that my fee would be paid to the charity Steps, in September 2011 we agreed.

The journalist came to the Manor and we chatted away as she asked lots of questions about my life and career. Mike joined in and was happy to be part of it.

When she left, Mike turned to me and said, 'Now! I have some good news and some bad news.'

'Oh no!' I responded, worried that something awful had happened. 'Tell me the bad news first.'

Then, with a smile on his face, he said, 'The bad news is that you're going to be very busy. The good news is that *you've been accepted for Dancing on Ice!*' and then he gave me the biggest hug!

He went on to explain: 'That was the phone call that came in while you were being interviewed.' Liz had tried to call my mobile without success, so had called Mike.

I was exploding with excitement and disbelief. I was ecstatic! And I hadn't even been auditioned this time. I could hardly believe it!

I immediately phoned Dawn. Her response was not quite as enthusiastic, but there was a reason for that, as we discovered later. I ran upstairs to tell Jeanne and she was thrilled because she knew how much I wanted to do it. My ambition was to learn to skate, and where better than within a concentrated, highly professional programme with Torvill and Dean inspiring us! I knew it would be the adventure of a lifetime.

Of course, I couldn't tell anyone outside my close family and friends, and they were sworn to secrecy. So when I went to the office the next day, I closed the door where Chris, Angie, Diana (my new PA, as Louise had left to run her own business) and Chris's PA Anja and I worked together.

'Guess what!' I said excitedly.

'What? What? What?' they asked, looking very puzzled.

There were hugs all around as I told them, and they too were so excited for me. This was the answer to my prayers and felt like the fulfilment of a dream.

A couple of weeks later, I went to Alexandra Palace where the whole process of the show was explained. I would be provided with 30 hours of private ice-skating lessons with a coach in Nottingham throughout October, plus I would have a private lesson with Jayne Torvill and Christopher Dean! *Really?* I was incredibly excited at the prospect of meeting these icons of the ice-skating world. Then, in early November, I would meet my professional skating partner. The show's producers didn't say who that would be and, frankly, I didn't care. I was sure all the professionals would be great.

I couldn't wait to get started, and booked my coaching times with Nottingham Ice Centre straight away. I loved going every weekday for lessons and progressed much more quickly than I had previously with my fortnightly one-hour lessons. After each session, I went back into my office but, in my head, I was having to move away from the business and concentrate on learning a whole new sport – fast! My colleagues, who were in the know, understood only too well that my being on prime-time national TV every Sunday evening would be great exposure for the brand, so everyone was very happy to accommodate my impending absence.

One of the benefits of being part of the show was that the *Dancing on Ice* producers were happy to pay for my driver. Sadly, David, who had been my driver for years, had suffered a medical episode which prevented him from driving for a while, so we offered him a job at Quorn House as our receptionist. We knew David very well, as he had lived in our cottage at the Manor after our horse-eventing friends, Gary and Gemma, had left and when David and his wife had separated. We were happy to offer him a roof over his head and he had stayed for five years. David took to the role of receptionist as if he had been born for it, and we really loved having him as part of the team at Quorn House. Also, by then, he had met one of our franchisees, Pauline, at our Annual Convention. They fell in love and later married. When Pauline moved to Leicestershire, she too was working for us at Quorn House, though by then they had a home of their own.

Over the years, whenever David was not available to drive me, he suggested I hire Peter Legg, another chauffeur he knew. Now that David was no longer able to drive me, Peter stepped in and drove me from then on. When David was fully fit again, he was offered a full-time chauffeuring job, and we were sorry when he left his role as our wonderful receptionist.

So here we were, with Peter driving me all over the UK to attend skating lessons at different rinks wherever 'ice time' was available. First, however, I was invited to meet Christopher Dean and Jayne Torvill at Lee Valley Ice Centre so they could see how I skated. There was also the opportunity to meet the press team and to be interviewed on film. It was all so surreal and I was on cloud nine and couldn't wait to meet Chris and Jayne. The singer Chesney Hawkes was just leaving the rink as I arrived, and other celebrities were going through their induction process.

As I was called to the rink, Jayne was there with her clipboard. Having said hello, she explained that unfortunately Chris couldn't be there at the moment, but would I like to skate around the rink? Off I went – slowly – and doing my very best, when suddenly Christopher Dean leapt on to the ice, grabbed me and whisked me around the rink! *Wow!* Was this really happening?

Chris and Jayne then put me through a variety of fitness challenges to see what I could do. Next, they played Abba's 'Dancing Queen' and I was asked to skate freestyle to the music. I loved Abba and I loved skating so I was in heaven. Afterwards, I was fairly happy at how it had all gone.

What I hadn't realised was that, as I had arrived at Lee Valley, there was a member of the paparazzi hiding behind a hedge, photographing me as I got out of my car. On the following Sunday, I was inundated with texts from franchisees.

'You're in *The People*!'

'You're on *Dancing on Ice*!'

'Fantastic!'

The franchisees went mad with excitement – as did the rest of our staff. To see the news leaking out was such a shock but also, to be honest, a massive relief! Now that it was out in the open, we could all relax.

The following week, I was to have a private skating lesson with Chris and Jayne. *A private lesson!* Can you believe it? What an utter privilege! I had to keep pinching myself. To be honest, I can't remember very much about that as I was in such a daze. While there, I was also asked to fill in some details of my measurements for the costume department and to list my favourite music tracks by female artists. Then, renowned dress- and costume-designer Stephen Adnitt (who had designed costumes for contestants on *Gladiators*, among many other shows) measured me up in what seemed like a hundred places and asked me for my colour prefer- ences for the costumes. Another very exciting prospect!

Soon the day arrived for me to meet my professional skating partner – Monday, 7 November 2011. A date now etched in my memory. I had been speaking at a church event in the Wirral the evening before, and then stayed with my brother Robert and his wife Jane in Cheshire, which was a treat. They were so excited about coming to see me with the rest of the family on *Dancing on Ice* in the new year.

The following morning my driver, Peter, drove me to Blackburn where I was met by a producer and an assistant, together with a TV camera. Everything was all very carefully planned for the big reveal when I would meet my skating partner for the first time. When I was all togged up in my skating gear, I had to stand with my back to the rink (I was being filmed throughout); then I was to turn around, and there on the ice I could see a stunningly good-looking, superfit young guy who was skating like a ballet dancer. He was Mark Hanretty. My eyes immediately welled up with tears of joy as I realised that this was the person who was going to teach me to skate over the next few months and with whom I would go on the most exciting journey of my life.

As Mark came over to meet me, I said, 'You are so beautiful' – quickly adding, 'such a beautiful skater!' And it was, for me, love at first sight! Not in an inappropriate way, I hasten to add, but I just knew this adventure was going to be magical.

I stepped on to the ice and we chatted for a short while – Mark in his delightful Scottish accent – and then he put his arm around my waist and we skated off together. At that, with great surprise he said, 'You can skate!'

'Only a little,' I explained.

Later in the lesson he picked me up and spun me round with the words, 'And you're so light!' Isn't that something any woman wants to hear? And then he said, 'I just want to make you look beautiful on the ice.' By this time I was melting.

Afterwards, when the lesson was over, we sat talking and found out a bit about each other. Mark was 27 years old, newly married to the very beautiful Kathy, and both Mark and Kathy were professional ice-skating coaches. Mark had represented Great Britain at international champion-ships, having been British Ice Dance Champion. He had fallen in love with skating at the age of nine after watching Torvill and Dean at the 1994 Olympics. From that moment on, Mark's goal was to become a professional ice skater, something he had achieved with huge success – both as a skater, and later as a choreographer and as a coach.

Later that day he texted me: 'Hi Rosemary, lovely to meet you today. ☺ I look forward to skating with you again tomorrow and the fabulous journey we have together ahead. Hope you have a good evening. Mark x'.

Mark and I would now skate together on five days a week throughout December wherever *Dancing on Ice* (*DOI*) could find us ice to skate on. Unlike *Strictly Come Dancing* where the competing pairs can hire a village hall or studio in a gym to practise dancing for hours on end, ice time is hard to come by. Ice hockey, public skating sessions, private lessons for youngsters aiming to be the next Torvill and Dean – they all had to be accommodated, and there is usually only one ice rink in a whole city! *DOI* booked blocks of available ice wherever they could get it, and over the coming weeks Mark and I travelled all over the country for our sessions: Coventry, Slough, Sheffield, Blackburn, Bradford, Brixton, Elstree Studios near London where there was a practice rink, and also the studio rink from where the show was transmitted live on Sundays.

Every week, Mark and I spent additional time training off the ice, practising the moves, the lifts, the skills, flexibility and posture, and we would scrounge a studio room whenever possible. The management team at Nottingham Ice Centre were brilliant. They were happy to have us there and did everything they could to accommodate us. I really loved those practice times. I loved being in Mark's company as he had such a positive attitude and was brimming with enthusiasm and encouragement.

The golden rules of an ice dancer are *posture, knee bend* and *extension,* and Mark was a perfectionist. He was determined that I would achieve my very best. I was determined to learn and didn't mind how many times I had to try – I would keep on persevering. Mark liked that. He was *so* patient! It was a whole new experience for me, but very exciting, and I loved every second of it.

At many of the training sessions, we would also have another *DOI* coach join us on the ice. Mark was a professional coach already, which really helped me, but having an extra pair of eyes was very useful to me and all the other celebrity skaters. It was also a safety precaution, as it was good to have someone alongside with an extra pair of hands for those moments when we were learning a tricky lift and there was a potential danger of falling head first on to the ice.

There was no question: I needed to learn the basic skills to a reasonable level to even stand a chance of getting past Week 1 of the show! Now, in Series 7, the expectation placed on the celebrities had risen hugely, compared with the earlier series. We both knew we could not be as adventurous with our manoeuvres as some of the younger competitors, added to which was the fact that I wasn't a dancer or an actor, so my only chance of success was to skate well, technically, within my limitations. My other problem was that as soon as he spun me around more than one spin, I felt sick!

Sometimes, Mark and I were able to skate on our own at Nottingham. There are two ice rinks there, both with beautiful ice (yes, the ice quality does vary a lot from rink to rink), and on one occasion we had the whole ice arena to ourselves. We played Josh Groban's *Closer* CD on the sound system as we skated together. It was the nearest thing to heaven on earth I have ever experienced! The whole training process was pure bliss. We got along amazingly well and laughed a lot. I loved being taught to skate by Mark – he was the consummate professional.

Mark and I had a real laugh the first time we had a training session on our own as we chatted about personal matters. When you ice dance with someone, you get very close, and each person's hands are all over the place. It goes with the territory and you just have to get on with it, but one also worries about other things. 'You must tell me if my breath smells or if I've got lettuce in my teeth!' I told him.

Thankfully, Mark was very protective and caring and, if we had the cameras there, he would remind me to retouch my lipstick or adjust my hair. And I was very happy to make Mark some lunch while I was packing my own. All in all, we created a wonderful partnership.

The following week, Mike came along to one of our practice sessions at Nottingham. He wanted to see who was going to be looking after his wife on the ice and with whom I was going to spend most of my life for the next few months. Mark and I felt quite nervous, as though we were getting approval from a very protective 'dad' after we'd been seeing each other for a week! It was very funny. But after everything Mike and I had been through, it was really lovely.

The good news was that Mike thought Mark was great. He felt confident that I was in safe hands so he could relax, which was a relief.

Next, Dawn wanted to meet Mark. This time it was in Coventry. She enjoyed watching us skate and really liked Mark, but she told me off later: 'You really will have to stop looking at him with those doe eyes!'

I felt I was being told off by my mother.

Earlier, I mentioned that there had been a slight hesitation in Dawn's voice when I called to tell her that I was to be on *Dancing on Ice*. She had only just learned that she was pregnant. The baby would be due the following May but, back then, she hadn't yet told anyone. After she had had her first scan, Dawn and Laurie had come over to show us the photograph of the scan. We were ecstatic for them both, and were thrilled that we were going to be grandparents! And apparently Laurie's daughter, Harriet, was also over the moon as she had been badgering them to have a baby ever since the wedding! I did feel very guilty, though, that I would now be putting them both through the stress of seeing me appearing on live TV every Sunday evening in the new year. Also, if they wanted to come down to the show, their weekends would be significantly affected over several weeks – providing I didn't get knocked out in Week 1.

So that I could be focused on the challenges that *Dancing on Ice* presented, I didn't go into the office and I didn't take my Monday evening classes. Mike and I knew we had a very able team at Quorn House, and our Directors, Chris and Angie, were totally capable of running the business. Then one day Chris, whose role was Marketing Director, called me and asked if he could be made Managing Director of our Clubs business. We had worked very well together and he had done a good job in marketing and, since I was going to be out of the picture for a while and was trying to reduce my workload anyway, Mike and I agreed. Angie would stay as Franchise Director.

***

About three weeks into our training, Mark and I were invited down to Elstree Studios to be given our choreography by Chris and Jayne. I hadn't realised that Chris was a world-renowned choreographer, and what I hadn't appreciated was that, back then, he designed *all* of the skating programmes for every couple, every week of the show. Plus, he selected the music, which would be edited down to 90 seconds for each performance. A minute and a half may not sound long for a piece of music, but when you are skating to it and you have to fit in so many skating manoeuvres as well as dance, I promise you, 90 seconds seems like half an hour and, because you are extending every sinew of every muscle in your body with every move, you are utterly exhausted at the end of it!

The track we were given for our first live skate was to be 'Fernando' by Abba and it was beautiful. Chris and Jayne demonstrated the routine and made it look so simple – and then we had to have a go. It all seemed so daunting, but I was still loving every second of the experience.

Then came 'Show and Tell Day' when all the celebrities and professionals would meet up at Elstree Studios and do their routine in front of one another. I felt quite confident and was hopeful we would look good. What I hadn't realised was how incredibly good some of the others were! It didn't help that, when we skated, I slipped and fell, but I immediately got up and carried on, with Mark smiling throughout. Thankfully, I was just one of many who fell, so maybe it was just nerves getting the better of us.

After our next training session at Nottingham, Mark said, 'Right. We need to be realistic here. Expect to get to about Week 3 or 4 at best.'

I accepted that, but was determined to do my absolute best.

As part of the publicity for the show, I was to appear on *This Morning* with all the other skating celebrities. That was a bit stressful, but I was comfortable to be there, having spent a day a week on the show for seven years back in the late 1990s. It was still as lovely to be there this time. Of course, Richard and Judy had moved on, and now the presenters were Phillip Schofield and Holly Willoughby.

Soon it was time for Mark and me to go to London to Elstree Studios for the celebrity photoshoot. This was very exciting as Elstree is an interesting studio complex. The *Big Brother* house was on our right and the *Who Wants to Be a Millionaire?* studio was on the left. The training ice-rink was in a separate building from the *Dancing on Ice* studio and we were ferried in a golf buggy between them. It was all very glamorous and exciting.

The first thing we did was to walk into a makeshift wardrobe room full of sparkly ice-skating dresses and matching tops for the male skating partners. It was like a little girl's fairy-tale cave of sparkles! Hundreds of bright pretty dresses encrusted with Swarovski crystals glittering like magical diamonds. We were invited to just choose whichever costume we wished. Heaven!

I selected a dayglow-pink, long-sleeved dress which looked so pretty on the hanger. Mark thankfully was happy with the bright-pink men's shirt, together with black skating trousers. Then it was into make-up and to have my hair styled. The make-up artist and hair artist were amazing; I had never had sparkly turquoise eyeliner applied before.

Dressed in our new costumes, it was time for the official photographic session. From a ceiling that was about 50 ft (15 m) high, strobes of light shone down on to a Perspex sheet where Mark and I posed in our skates. It was like being in a Hollywood film. But there was more to come.

With the photos finished, we were invited into what I can only describe as a mirrored cubicle. The door was closed and Mark and I had to place ourselves in all kinds of positions as different shots were taken magically through one of the mirrored walls. It was all such fun!

After all that excitement, I then went down to Mitchum in Surrey to the costume-makers for my first fitting. Costume designer Stephen Adnitt was there, and he had prepared for me a beautiful champagne-coloured dress which was really pretty. The female costume is basically a leotard made to fit one's individual body shape, and then the skirt is sewn on afterwards. Next, the Swarovski crystals are stuck on with special adhesive; they are a work of art and cost a fortune to make. Once I had slipped into the skating costume, a fitter then came in to stretch the fabric over my arms to make it tight like a second skin. It was fascinating.

We had two weeks off over Christmas and were told not to skate. Unfortunately for Chesney Hawkes, he didn't heed that advice and sadly broke his ankle very badly while skating on his own. He was now out of the show and I really felt for him.

At home I practised my routine in front of the big mirror we had in our home gym on the top floor of the Manor (I don't know why we had a gym because neither Mike nor I ever used it, but we had accumulated some kit over the years). I practised most days to help me memorise the routine and to increase my flexibility and strength. One of the moves within the 'Fernando' routine is what is called a 'spiral', which is a position where a skater stands on one leg, leans forward and lifts the free leg as high as possible behind, while keeping it poker straight. Very, very sadly, in trying to stretch my leg to its limits I suddenly felt a twang. Disaster had struck. I had pulled a muscle in my groin. I was devastated.

Despite the fact that it was New Year's Day, I immediately called my physiotherapist, who lived in the next village, and pleaded for an urgent appointment. He said he could see me first thing the next day. I called Mark and explained what I'd done. He was really worried, but supportive, and told me not to worry and to rest. I was so cross with myself. Would I now be substituted for another skater waiting in the wings, desperate to take my place?

My physio saw me early that Monday, thankfully, and then Peter drove me down to Elstree where I would stay for a week prior to the first show the following Sunday. I felt a mixture of excitement and dread. I knew *DOI* had a great physio in Sharon Morrison, who appeared to perform miracles on injured skaters in previous programmes, but I also knew the show had reserve celebrities ready to step into our skates at any time. I had met Sharon in the run-up to the training for a brief medical, just to check there weren't any serious issues. There weren't then, but there was now. The Celebrity Liaison Manager looked after all our arrangements, and thankfully she booked me in to see Sharon immediately. While I had done some pretty serious damage to the top of my hamstring, Sharon was confident that it wasn't beyond repair. This was the most fantastic news and I trusted her completely.

I was shown to my personal dressing room, which was spacious and comfortable, and would be mine for as long as I was on the show. Franchisees, staff, friends and family had been so kind and had sent me teddies with skates on, cards and flowers, so I soon made the room my own and enjoyed pinning up my many 'good luck' cards and messages on the noticeboards on the walls.

Because there were 15 celebrities in this series, we were divided into two teams. Team 1 would skate the first week, and Team 2 would skate in Week 2. We didn't know which team we would be in until the Friday morning before the first show on Sunday, 8 January.

The week was full of skating practice (I could still skate despite my injury as long as I didn't lift my right leg too high), as well as daily physio sessions, costume fittings, group rehearsals and full rehearsals for the show itself. Mark was included in the show's grand opening sequence, which would be performed by all the skating professionals, so he was practising for that too.

***

A week before Christmas, I received some shocking family news. My stepmother, Mabel, who was now living in a residential home, had suffered a fall and then had a severe stroke. A few hours later, she died. Her cousin John called to tell me and he kept me informed of all the arrangements. The funeral was arranged for the Thursday in the week before the first live show when I was staying down in London for the rehearsals. I explained to the *DOI* producers that I *had* to attend the funeral but that I would return to Elstree immediately afterwards and would be happy to have my practice session at midnight if need be. They, and Mark of course, were very kind and accommodated my situation.

Mabel had suffered meningitis as a small child, which had left her very unstable on her feet. As she became older, falls were commonplace and so, in the end, she had to go into residential care. She had a wonderful cousin, John, and his wife Julie, who were kind and caring and ensured that she was well looked after. We couldn't help feeling that because Mabel had married my father, Oswald, she had had a significantly more interesting life than perhaps she had imagined, but she had missed him terribly in the later years. Now she was at peace.

The funeral was sad, but lovely at the same time, with many people from Aylsham in Norfolk attending. Mabel had lived in the town all her life and knew most of the townsfolk. I told the congregation the story of how Father had proposed to Mabel out of the blue after he felt God had told him to marry her. People had no idea that that was how their 18-year marriage had come about. Robert and Jane stayed for the wake but, as soon as the service was over, I asked Peter to drive me back to London for rehearsals.

***

Mark and I had our training session that evening, and the following day we found out that we would not be skating our routine till the second week because of my groin injury. I was hugely relieved. It gave us an extra week to perfect our programme, but one week less to practise the next one – if we got through. Even though we were not performing on Sunday's show, everyone still had to skate on to the ice so that we could be officially announced and 'presented' as participants.

As I knocked on the door of Sharon's treatment room, I was invited in, only to find Chris (Dean) on the treatment table. This was reassuring, and he made me feel very relaxed.

'Come in, Rosemary,' he said, and we chatted while Sharon completed his treatment. He knew about my groin injury and told me that it would probably be a year before it was completely back to normal but not to worry at all about trying to lift my leg too high in our routine. He said it really wouldn't matter. This was such a relief!

Chris Dean's care and interest in my welfare and his supremely calm professional manner made all the difference. His kindness and encouragement set me up perfectly. I was ready to roll – although hopefully not to roll over.

20
Having the time of my life!
2012

There was to be a full dress-rehearsal in front of a live audience on Friday evening in preparation for Sunday's opening show, so it was 'all systems go'. The excitement was growing and everyone was getting nervous. We all had a rehearsal of everything personal to us, including our spray tan, make-up, hair, nails and costume, and then we all had extensive briefings for timings. I really don't know how the production team put a show like that together. I have done lots of live TV in my time, but this was utterly different. There were so many variables. So many things could go wrong. They had back-up video in case of an accident and there was even a rehearsal in case someone died! They had to be prepared for anything and everything.

Thankfully, the producers were really nice all the time and we could not have been looked after better. I felt utterly spoilt. These people were at the top of their game – so competent and so unfazed. For our part, Mark and I shared a mutual desire to make everyone who helped us feel special and we both, simultaneously, found that we naturally wanted to learn everyone's name. It was fun for us to do that, and it was clear that the staff members really appreciated the fact that we took the time to call them by their individual names.

I mentioned 'timings'. One of the things we all had to learn was the exact timing of our entrance on to the ice through the 'tunnel', which was the entrance to the studio's ice rink. This was timed to the second. Each pair of participants was to skate on to the ice precisely on the final beat of the fourth bar of the introductory music. The Assistant Floor Manager was there to count us in: '1-2-3-one, 1-2-3-two, 1-2-3-three, 1-2-3-four – go!' and off we would skate into the middle of the rink, perform a fancy lift and then strike a pose, smile the biggest smile we could muster into the camera lens and hold it for five seconds, and then skate off to join the rest of the Team of 2012 who were collecting at the back of the rink. Such a simple task, but pretty scary when you come to do it live for the first time!

With the introductions out of the way, the competing contestants performed their routine, with the judges giving their verdict and their marks. These marks would account for half of the total, with the public vote creating the remainder. The judges in 2012 were different from previous years. Jason Gardner had been replaced by dancer and choreographer Louie Spence; Katarina Witt, a two-time Olympic ice-dance Gold Medallist in the 1980s, had taken the place of Karen Barber; while Robin Cousins, also an Olympic champion, was Head Judge. I felt fortunate that Jason wasn't on the panel, as he could be quite harsh with his comments and, because I am very sensitive, I could see myself in tears if he was too brutal about my skating. I did, however, meet him on another occasion, only to discover he was actually a really nice guy.

The Friday night dress-rehearsal went well and every one of the Team 1 skaters was given the same marks. Obviously, there was no public vote as we weren't transmitting on TV. It was a really great experience, and Mark and I couldn't wait for Sunday to arrive.

We had Saturday off because we were in Team 2, and that night Mark and I met up with Professor Raj Persaud for a drink. Raj had been a friend of mine ever since we first met on *This Morning* back in the 1990s when he was the show's resident expert psychologist. He and his wife came to my 50th birthday party and had stayed at the Manor with Mike and me.

Raj wanted to support me on my journey into this jungle of extreme physical and mental pressure of live, prime-time television, performing in front of millions of viewers while learning a very challenging and potentially dangerous new skill. He also realised it would be tough for me to be competing with very well-known celebrities, many of whom were less than half my age. We had a lovely evening together and both Mark and I found his words of wisdom to be golden. He said: 'Ice skating is really difficult and dangerous and the public love adversity. See the camera as a person you fancy madly and want to impress, and also understand that there are folk at home watching who are having a really tough time and that *Dancing on Ice* is a way to, hopefully, bring them some light entertainment on a Sunday evening. Enjoy it!'

From that day on, Raj texted or called me every day to see how I was doing. He was such a great friend and support, and I will for ever be in his debt for his wisdom, kindness and concern.

***

Waking up on Sunday morning was like waking up on Christmas Day as a child. This was the day I would skate on to the ice with Mark in front of a live audience and millions watching at home! It was the full works all over again with spray tan, hair, make-up, nails, and there was such a buzz of excitement around the studio.

Mike, Dawn, Laurie, Karen Goodwin (my first ever ice-skating coach) and her mum, plus Angie from the office came to watch. I knew there would be some franchisees in the audience because they had tried for weeks beforehand to get tickets, and many others would be watching at home, as would thousands of our members. I couldn't wait to see those who had managed to get tickets. There was such a sense of anticipation in the air!

The members of the audience were asked to take their seats at 4 pm and had a long night ahead of them. The show went live at 6 pm and came off air for an hour at 7.30 pm. Then there was an hour's break while the viewers' votes were calculated alongside the judges' scores. At 8.30 it was time for the results show when the two couples with the lowest combined scores would be in the skate-off.

Waiting in my dressing room to be called to go down, I looked at all the texts that were flooding in, wishing me well – including messages from Raj, of course! Everyone was so kind.

It was beyond exciting to skate on to the ice that first time, live on TV. Then, and only then, did I truly believe that I was actually on the show. I know that may sound ridiculous, but any one of us could have had an accident and broken something any time up to that moment. Now, I was actually, definitely, really on *Dancing on Ice* and I was ecstatic!

At the very beginning of the show, Mark and his co-professionals skated their opening routine to Lady Gaga's song 'The Edge of Glory'.

We couldn't see it, but apparently it was incredible. Mike said it was the best live performance of anything he had ever watched in his life! High praise indeed.

It was after this that, along with the other celebrities, we made our grand entrances. Mark and I then went to a small skaters' sitting area near the judges, from where we enjoyed watching the celebrities and their professional partners skate their routines. A warm-up guy had entertained the live audience prior to the start of the show, so everyone was revved up to be enthusiastic and encouraging to all the skaters – and they certainly were. It was amazing.

At the results show, the two with the lowest combined scores competed in the skate-off. Andy Akinwolere, a presenter of the children's TV show *Blue Peter*, was eliminated, which must have been heartbreaking for him as he had skated so well. It also left the rest of us in shock! Andy had skated to a very high standard and had come third on the leader board after the judges' scores. It was a sudden wake-up call that the public vote was crucial. This presented me with a problem. While I potentially had support from the 40,000–50,000 members attending our classes and from the many people who had followed one of my diets or fitness videos, I wasn't like the other celebrities. I was up against actors and stars, some of whom had *millions* of fans who watched them every week on one of the big national soaps – *Coronation Street, EastEnders, Hollyoaks* and *Emmerdale*. I would have to pray for a miracle to get me through when I skated next week!

After the show was over, we all went to The Bar, which was the name of the in-house pub, for the after-show party. We and our guests were all invited, which was exciting for them as they were able to meet some of their TV idols in person. It was a joy to see Mike, Dawn and Laurie after my week away, and then we all went back to the Holiday Inn, Elstree, where I and many of the celebs and professional skaters were staying, and rolled into bed at around midnight.

The following day, the skaters on Team 1 were given their choreography for two weeks' time by Chris and Jayne, while the rest of us carried on practising for the following Sunday. Mark and I skated on the practice rink at Elstree, after I had a physio session with Sharon, then I went home – which was great, having been away for over a week. It was lovely to see Jeanne and tell her all about it, and to see the dogs and to be back with Mike. I so appreciated the fact that he was accommodating my ice-skating dream, which he said he was very glad to do because he had never seen me so happy.

Each week, I was given Tuesday as my day off, when I did the washing and shopping, and caught up with myself.

Mark and I skated in Nottingham for four hours the next day – bliss! Then, on another day, our RosemaryConley.TV crew, Gemma and Susannah, came along to interview us for our internet TV channel. These were the first of our weekly interviews that they recorded – and the ITV bosses loved the fact that we did it, and watched it on our channel. Everyone at Nottingham Ice Centre was so kind to us and wished us well for Sunday. I was even presented with a montage of pictures made into a card by the pupils of a local school who took lessons there. It was really touching. Later that afternoon, Peter drove me and Mark to the Holiday Inn in Elstree, ready for rehearsals the next day. Along with many of the other celebs and professionals, Mark was also staying in the Holiday Inn, which was great for me as he could set up my laptop on the internet and be there if I needed any help with anything. One of the best tips I learned was to ask for a mini fridge in my room. This meant that I could keep a carton of milk for multiple cups of tea and also some yogurt in case I needed it.

The following day, Mark and I were rehearsing on the studio practice rink when Chris Dean came to see our routine and commented, 'Well, that's one routine we don't have to worry about on Sunday.' This was really encouraging.

That night, I went with Mark to the home of Raj and his wife Francesca for dinner and to meet their children. Their house is magnificent. It is situated in an exclusive part of London not far from the centre, with great views. We felt privileged to be invited. It was a joy to spend quality time with Raj and his family. Mark showed the children how to do some ice-skating lifts, which they loved and, with a beautiful meal that Francesca had created plus some sports psychology from Raj, it was a truly fabulous evening.

Saturday was a full dress-rehearsal day, which meant that we had to do our entire routine and be filmed. It provided the opportunity for the camera operators to familiarise themselves with our routine and to road-test the costume and check that my hair didn't move when I was upside down. We were also measured up for our costume for the following week. I thought, *Let's hope I get to wear it!*

That evening, several of us who were staying at the Holiday Inn met up and had a meal together, which gave us the opportunity to get to know one another. The other skaters were all so nice to me. It helped that I didn't present a threat to them, as obviously I wasn't going to win. But they respected me for my career and were very supportive of my efforts.

Sunday, 15 January 2012 finally arrived! I was so excited but also nervous. This was it. Our 'Fernando' routine would finally be skated on TV. Mike, Dawn, Laurie, Chris (our new MD) and Mary Morris were in the audience. I thought my heart was going to explode with emotion and nerves.

Mark and I joined all the other Team 2 skaters gathering in the 'tunnel', waiting until it was our turn to skate on to the ice. And now it was. My name was announced, and then a two-minute film about Mark and me was shown. Then came the countdown: '1-2-3-one, 1-2-3-two, 1-2-3-three' – Mark and I looked at each other, smiled, and he gave me a quick squeeze around my waist – '1-2-3-four – *go!*' and we skated on and took our starting position.

Wearing my very pretty champagne sparkly skating dress, I performed the first part of the routine well, and then, just as we skated in front of the judges, I tripped on my toe pick! I looked at Mark and he just beamed the most loving and forgiving smile and we carried on for the rest of the routine. The audience went mad and the applause was deafening. It was amazing and I felt such relief that it was over!

TV co-host Christine Bleakley asked the judges for their comments and their scores. Robin Cousins described the skate as 'exquisite', and Louie Spence said he was glad I had the little 'trip' as after that I seemed to relax and wore a beaming smile from then on. Katarina said that I had 'poise' and was an 'inspiration'. I was thrilled. However, the marks were just 12.5 out of 30. This was not so good and I was in real danger of being in the skate-off. It turned out that if a skater tripped or fell, he or she was severely punished with a significant drop in marks. Nothing like extra pressure, then!

The others skated their routines, including Jorgie Porter from *Hollyoaks* who skated like a ballet dancer! She was exquisite in her performance with her professional partner, Matt Evers. We ended up being third from the bottom before the lines were opened for the public vote.

In the interval, when all the people in the audience were given a doughnut to keep them going, Mark and I went to see our family and friends, along with our franchisees and their members who had managed to get tickets. It was lovely to see them and we so appreciated their support.

Then it was crunch time. The results show. We all skated into our rehearsed positions under a spotlight on the ice, waiting for our names to be called out. Co-host Phillip Schofield announced the names: 'Our first skating pair, through to next week, are . . . [long pause and scary music] . . . *Rosemary and Mark*!'

We just about exploded with joy, flinging our arms in the air and then around each other for the biggest hug of celebration! The previous year, on Mark's first appearance on *DOI*, he and his partner had been eliminated in Week 1. At least this year we had managed it through, and I was *so* pleased to have got this far. Also, somehow, the psychological boost of having our names called out first was enormous. Even though the presenters say, 'and in no particular order', for a moment we felt as though we had the most votes. Crazy, but that's how it felt and we were euphoric! It was a massive boost to my confidence.

***

The choreography for the following week was given to us the next day by Chris and Jayne. How Chris created so many routines each week is beyond my comprehension. He is an extraordinary talent and Jayne works so well with him. The ultimate partnership!

This next routine was much more complicated. I only had a week in which to learn it, so we went straight from the choreography lesson with Chris and Jayne on the show rink to the practice rink round the corner. The cameras came too.

For some reason, Mark seemed very short with me. He was giving me strongly worded and almost aggressive instructions and was really pushing me. This was so out of character for him, but I just took it and thought, *OK, if this is how it's going to be, I'll handle it – but it will be so much harder!*

Peter, my driver, drove me home and as I walked in the door I said to Mike, 'The honeymoon's over! Mark was really tough on me today. It was very hard.'

Unbeknown to me, Mike subsequently contacted Mark and explained to him that if he wanted to get the best out of me he should be nice to me. 'Being tough on Rosemary won't work,' he told him, 'but being kind and encouraging will.' Mike only admitted this to me later.

The new routine also involved two challenging lifts. For one of them, Mark would lift me up to sit on his shoulder; then I would slowly go backwards down his back, head first, and he would suddenly grab me round my waist and put me back on my feet. As you can imagine, I was finding it very tricky. Somehow, I couldn't get up far enough to sit on his shoulder. In the end, with the help of one of the other professionals, Lukasz Rozycki, we found that if Mark put his hand right through my legs and put his hand in front of my right hip, he could get more traction and I should get high enough. While the rehearsals were really tough, we did manage it – just. I so hoped it would be all right on the night.

A few months later, Mark confessed that he had been told by the *DOI* producers to give me a hard time that day. They saw me as having too fabulous a time, as if I was treating the whole experience as a fun day out, and they wanted to create a bit of drama and discourse between Mark and me. Of course, it didn't work and all was back to normal on the next practice day!

I would be wearing a baby-blue dress encrusted with crystals for this movie-themed week, and we were to skate to Bette Midler's 'Wind beneath My Wings' from the film *Beaches*. It was a beautiful song and I loved skating to it.

I was very excited this week because almost my entire family would be in the audience. As well as Dawn and Mike, my brother Robert had brought a large party of relatives from Cheshire, including my sister-in-law Jane, my two lovely nieces Nicky and Suzy, Suzy's husband Tim, and their two young children, Ella and James. Unfortunately, children under the age of three were not allowed to attend, so Nicky's husband Chris valiantly stayed back at the hotel to look after their baby, Ben. He watched everything on television. Meanwhile, all the members of my live family audience were wearing black T-shirts printed with 'Vote for Rosemary' in bright pink and carrying a huge banner!

Sadly, when I was skating in the live show, not only did I trip again but also I didn't quite reach Mark's shoulder in the big lift so it all looked a bit messy. Despite the fantastic family support, I was really upset. Thankfully, we did get through to the next week, but I felt very despondent and worried that I would never be able to perform a clean skating programme.

When I went shopping to M&S on the Tuesday, I was just about to walk into the store when a guy saw me and held the door open.

'Rosemary Conley,' he said, 'please may I shake your hand? You are an inspiration on *Dancing on Ice*! Well done!'

I could have kissed him! And then, as I walked around getting the week's groceries, lots of shoppers came up to me and said some very nice things too. It really gave me a boost. I have no idea who the guy was who spoke to me at the door, but I want to thank him from the bottom of my heart because he, together with the other shoppers, made me change my attitude. I decided to look at it this way: maybe I would trip *every* week. So what? I was doing my best and everybody seemed to be impressed with my efforts, despite my mistakes. I cheered up fast, picked myself up and looked forward to next Sunday.

***

It was now Week 4 (my third skate) of the series and the *DOI* bosses decided to do something different. We were all paired up with skaters of a similar level of ability, and each pair had to go head to head, skating to the same song in a kind of 'duel'. One pair would skate half of the routine and then the other pair were to come forward and skate the other half; then both pairs skated the last few bars of the music together. I was paired up with Andy Whyment from *Coronation Street* and we skated to 'Baby, It's Cold Outside'. The music was faster than I was used to, and our choreography included some serious lifts which really tested my strength and flexibility, but I was determined to master it.

Thankfully, we skated on the night without any trips or stumbles (helped by half a glass of wine which I disguised and sipped from a water bottle I had filled beforehand!) and when it came to the judges' decision to 'save' one of the pairs and give them a free pass into next week, they saved Mark and me. I was ecstatic and so relieved that we didn't have to go through the agony of the potential skate-off. Raj, who was still texting me encouragement and asking if I was OK on a daily basis, and chatting to me regularly, told me that my goal was to *not* get into the skate-off. And this week, there was no danger of that. *Phew!*

Week 5 was looming, and Mark and I were skating to 'Perfect' by Fairground Attraction. In an attempt to attract extra votes, Mark suggested we include a really difficult lift that he had designed himself. It worked as follows: Mark would put the back of his head between my legs as I was skating backwards; I would then lean back and put my arms round the back of his shoulders and through to the front to hold on; simultaneously, Mark would stand up (with all of my weight on the back of his neck!) and lift me upside down, with my head pointing down towards the ice, several feet up. Since this was a new lift that Mark himself had devised, on the choreography day Chris and Jayne were fascinated, as was Mark Naylor, one of the *DOI* coaches. So much so that while I was upside down in position, they all had a chat! After a couple of minutes, I asked if I could be lowered to the ice and then I very nearly threw up! Thankfully, Mark rushed to me with a waste bin just in case, and of course this was all on camera!

The following Sunday it was showtime and we performed our routine, including what we now termed as the 'Sick Lift'. Phillip Schofield chatted to us after we finished our performance and said, 'So, you managed to keep your dinner down!'

I think everyone was amazed at what we did and Katarina Witt gave us our first score of 7! She said, 'For me, it's amazing the challenges you take on and the guts you have to go out there and do those tricks. The way you connect with each other – it's really beautiful pair-skating.'

Mark and I were so happy. The votes came flooding in and thankfully we managed to get through to the next week.

***

Outside the door of the practice rink for the duration of the whole of *DOI* there were pallets of Müller Corner yogurts stacked up, ready for us all to help ourselves. Mark and I lived on these throughout our time on *DOI* and ate two or more every day. They were delicious, healthy, cold (it was now February) and nutritious. We loved them. However, now six weeks into the show, we were gaining a few pounds and, when it came to the costumes for the Week 6 show, mine was too tight and Mark couldn't wear the velvet waistcoat they had made for him because it was stretching too much across his front! *Oops!*

It was a Valentine's theme for Week 6 – halfway through the series. I was now, at age 65, the oldest contestant to get this far in the history of the show. This week, Mark and I were to skate to 'I'll Stand by You' by The Pretenders and, to help me to increase my speed across the ice, *DOI* sent me along to an ice rink in Slough to play ice hockey with a male hockey team. But when Mark arrived at the rink, he looked ashen.

'What's the matter?' I asked anxiously. 'Are you OK? What's happened?'

He went on to explain that he'd just come back from the Elstree practice rink and had seen what the celebrity skaters were going to have to do the following week, and he knew it was beyond my capability. The producers were setting a challenge in which each celebrity would have to skate a routine that involved performing 23 different skating skills in sequence – on his or her own! Mark knew that I would struggle to complete some of the moves anyway, and I knew I would not be able to remember the sequence due to the memorising flaw in my brain. I would struggle to remember six moves, let alone 23! We both knew this was going to be the end of the road for us.

Nevertheless, ice hockey was now my new challenge, so I was dressed in men's ice hockey gear, which was huge on me, massive gloves, helmet and heaven knows what else, and then skated on to the rink! It was hilarious! Of course, it would make for a great film to show on Sunday evening before Mark and I came on to the ice.

We had no idea what any of the other celebrities' routines would be like until the dress rehearsal on the Saturday. It was then that I realised they were leaping ahead in their competence and I was only nudging forward.

So it came as no surprise that I found myself in the skate-off, where I was to compete against Chemmy Alcott, an Olympic skier and competent skater. Needless to say, it was my time to say goodbye. The judges made some lovely comments. For me, it had been the most thrilling experience of my life. The whole team – the make-up, hair and nail artists, the people in the costume department – had been a joy. Presenters Phillip Schofield and Christine Bleakley, Tony Gubba the commentator for the show, and the judges – including, of course, Chris and Jayne – could not have been more charming or supportive. The entire *DOI* team were exceptionally lovely. Everyone. I couldn't fault a single thing.

Mark had been so kind, unbelievably patient and always encouraging (well, almost always!), and we developed a friendship that I honestly believe will last a lifetime. When you have entrusted your life into the hands of someone to such an extreme extent, inevitably you develop a special bond. Sometimes such relationships don't work but, with us, it really did.

Throughout my time on *DOI*, I had been filming a blog around the *DOI* studio and from my dressing room. It had been fun to do. That night, I filmed myself tearfully explaining how I felt at the end of this extraordinary experience. It was the hardest 'piece to camera' I have ever recorded.

Finally, I went to bed and just cried. My dream had come to an end. I think I only slept for about four hours.

The next morning, I had to be up for 5.30 to be taken to ITV's breakfast show *Daybreak* at 6.20. I looked dreadful. With hardly any sleep and so many tears shed, and suffering from monumental disappointment, I would rather have been anywhere else in the world that morning. Then followed press interviews with journalists from *The Star* and *The Sun* newspapers, and after that we were both off to *This Morning*. Thankfully, the programme's presenters, Eamonn Holmes and Ruth Langsford, were fantastic, and so was Mark.

We went back to the studio and the hotel to collect all our things, and then Mark drove me home. It was a quieter journey than we would have had normally – we usually chatted all the time. Today there was an air of sadness, and we were both very tired too.

***

In the days that followed I felt as though I had had a psychological car crash. Suddenly the adrenalin stopped flowing and exhaustion overtook me. I was so appreciative of Mike and Dawn who had been so unself-ishly supporting me every weekend, cheering me on. The Quorn House staff, our own RC.TV team, our franchisees and our members, who had managed to get tickets and travel endless miles to support me, were just amazing. Everyone had been truly wonderful, but now I was utterly drained.

However, what followed was quite beautiful. I was sent the loveliest texts, emails, cards and messages from many people congratulating me on getting so far and for doing so well. It's funny, but when you are in the middle of that show you just do it and don't think anything of it. On reflection, making it to Week 6 was quite creditable, I suppose. I hadn't disgraced myself and I had progressed in the quality of my skating. Robin Cousins had been complimentary. Katarina had described my skating as 'beautifully quiet across the ice'. People stopped me in the street for months afterwards, saying how much they had enjoyed seeing me on the show. It was lovely of everyone to be so kind.

A week after I had left *DOI*, Mike and I went to our house in Portugal for a couple of weeks. Mike had been so loving and supportive that I felt I owed him some quality time with his wife, and I was more than happy to go. I was very tired and for the first seven days I slept for 12 hours every night, but after a week I felt fine. I picked myself up and returned to normal life – though of course I missed Mark. We had worked as a brilliant team aiming for a united goal, and that had provided the perfect foundation for any partnership to flourish. Ours certainly did.

Mike and I decided that we would offer our villa in Portugal to Mark and Kathy for a free holiday because Mark had looked after me so well and Kathy had been hugely supportive too over the last few months. They were very grateful and we were delighted to be able to do it.

On Mothering Sunday, Dawn gave me an amazingly thoughtful gift: a CD compilation of all the tracks of music Mark and I had skated to and all the tracks of music featured or performed by stars who had appeared on the show during my time there – Lady Gaga, One Direction, Pixie Lott, Christina Perri, among many others. It was wonderful and I used it to choreograph a workout routine for my own classes; we all exercised to it for months afterwards! I suppose I didn't want the memory of such an exciting experience to fade, and working out to those tracks certainly helped to keep the memories alive.

Mark and I met up again for the final show and we decided to create some 'Skate into Shape' days around the country, which we did over the following few months. These were skating workshops where Mark coached skating and we shared our experiences from *Dancing on Ice*. The events gave us the opportunity to work together again, and also to perform a couple of our favourite *DOI* routines.

As I write this, 10 years on, Mark and I still maintain a genuine friendship, meeting up and keeping in touch throughout the year, and I love hearing how his career, which now includes commentating on Eurosport, goes from strength to strength. He is an inspiration. Happy days!

21

Tightening our belts

2012–13

I soon settled back to normal life at the office after the excitement of *Dancing on Ice* – but it was different. Chris had taken over the reins of the business and the dynamics had changed. I told myself that maybe that was a good thing. Up until the day I went on *DOI*, I was very much in control and all the decisions were run past me. In my absence, understandably, decisions were made without me, and many initiatives and ideas had been implemented while I was away. The organisation within the office had changed too, with different departments being shaken up a bit. I didn't mind this as I was ready to step back to some degree and just be involved in the things that only I could do, which included any significant decision-making.

Every year, we would look forward to our Annual Training Convention which we held at Center Parcs in Nottinghamshire in April. Motivating and teaching our franchisees and their employees to stay up to date with the latest fitness trends was important to us. It was also an opportunity for them to enhance their skills and capability. We always invested in professional fitness presenters to inspire and teach them by running masterclasses held over the two-day event. There was a constant buzz and I was so proud to see 'our girls' working out with such enthusiasm and talent. I loved it. And so did they.

One year, someone special presented one of the sessions – Kardy Laguda. Kardy was a showman and he was incredibly fit – in the truest sense of the word – and the franchisees adored him! I saw him present his session and could instantly recognise that he was not a 'show-off' as some professional presenters can be. He had charisma and was genuine, and I could see he was a 'humble' showman. In fact he was delightful, and we decided to work with Kardy on a whole new fitness regime called

Kardy-O-Fun. Kardy ran training sessions for the franchisees and their employees, and they subsequently took their learnings into their classes. The members loved it too. Later, Kardy and I worked together on a DVD. It was a progressive fitness programme and I enjoyed working with him on Levels 1 and 2, while a couple of our franchisees, Cherie Ford and Sedge Gooding, who had been professional dancers before working with the company, performed Level 3 with Kardy. That was too fast and complicated for me!

We launched the Kardy-O-Fun branding, and the franchisees started running Kardy-O-Fun classes, which the members loved. It was our answer to Zumba, the aerobic Latin American dance programme that was becoming so popular at the time. Our TV crew would follow Kardy around the country, and suddenly Kardy would arrive at a class in progress; our crew would then film him working out together with the members. It was all part of the fun that we were trying to achieve – fun through fitness. It helped boost the classes and we could do it because we had our own TV crew.

Our greatest source of excitement that year, however, came in May. Dawn and Laurie presented us with the glorious gift of a grandson, Isaac. He was beautiful and healthy and the most joyful blessing to us all. It was a whole new experience for Mike as well as me, making us thrilled to the core. We were overflowing with happiness. My maternal instincts came flooding back but, of course, it was totally new for Mike and it didn't take long before he and our new member of the family became best pals. Mike turned out to be a natural superstar 'Gramps'. He and Isaac have such enormous fun together and I love it when Isaac comes to stay with us. I cannot remember any time in my life when I have so enjoyed just sitting on the sofa, doing nothing except simply listening to the two of them together with a great big smile on my face. Our treasured grandson has also helped us to realise what is most important in life.

Shortly afterwards, Diana, my PA for the last couple of years, handed in her notice. Di lived in Nottinghamshire and spent a lot of time travelling to and from Quorn House, and her husband wasn't happy with her long days away from home. I understood Di's decision to leave, but I was sad because we worked well together.

Having spent so many hours in the car with Peter as he drove me to various ice rinks over the previous six months, I had got to know him well. He had spent 12 years working for the local council, looking after the Mayor of Loughborough and organising the diary, events and foreign trips, before going freelance to run his own chauffeuring business. Who better then, I thought, to organise me? I asked Peter if he would be interested, and we agreed on a trial period to see whether he would enjoy being deskbound compared with driving his clients. Thankfully, he slotted in remarkably easily. However, he stipulated one condition: he would only take the job if he could still be my driver, as and when I needed one. And that suited me too.

After we decided to stop running Music in the Meadow, we chose to organise a fundraising event for Steps that would be a bit different. Kevin (creator of Music in the Meadow) and I, with Mike's blessing, decided to host a corporate dinner combined with a quiz between the courses. We would call it 'A Question of Brains' and, just as we had done with Music in the Meadow, every penny we raised would go to the charity. It took some doing to find the sponsors to cover all the costs, but I was introduced to a contact at Next by Rugby legend Peter Wheeler, whom I had known for some years but more so since he became a Deputy Lieutenant like me. Peter had played rugby for Leicester Tigers for years, had captained the England team and toured with the illustrious British Lions, and he was a man of influence! Fashion retailer Next, the Tigers' sponsor, soon agreed to pay for the food for our event. Peter also introduced me to Hughie Murphy of Charles Street Buildings, a very successful businessman in Leicester, who kindly agreed to provide the wine on the tables.

We were all set, but we needed a venue. Peter (who in 2020 became the President of the Rugby Football Union (RFU)) at that time was CEO of Leicester Tigers, and he very kindly allowed us to use the Club's Premiership Suite, which meant that soon we were able to put the event together. He also introduced us to representatives of another Tigers sponsor, the luxury jeweller Goldsmiths, who gave us a fabulous raffle prize – a diamond necklace! Kevin's friend Phil Whetter ran an audio-visual presentation company which had produced Music in the Meadow, and Phil was happy to support us again. We were all set.

Kevin is in the event management business and was able to acquire some cracking holiday prizes, as well as direct the event on the night. And, to top it all, Mike donated his Harley-Davidson motorbike as an auction lot.

The entertainment for the evening was a bit different from the norm. You may remember that breathtaking chase at the beginning of the James Bond movie *Casino Royale* where the villain leaps across the rooftops in an attempt to escape James Bond. That was freerunner Sébastien Foucan, and he agreed to come along and give us a demonstration.

Sébastien was a fellow celebrity competitor on *Dancing on Ice* that year with me, and we became friends. He didn't usually accept this kind of gig but, on the night that I was eliminated, I asked him if he would do this for me and he very kindly said yes. On the night of our event, we constructed a scaffolding rig which he leapt over, swung from, dipped under and flung himself around. It was spectacular! The audience loved it, and his performance is still spoken about in awe even today!

We had 280 guests attend that first A Question of Brains event, and every table was hosted by a celebrity guest. Almost £100,000 was raised, with every penny going directly to Steps. Over the following years, the same event went on to raise well over £500,000 for Steps Conductive Education Centre, a sum which has proven to be a lifeline for the charity.

***

Back in the business, while Chris was running the company, Mary and I continued to enjoy running the Roadshows and, this year, it was decided that we would take them to bigger venues. So, instead of having 300 people join us, we found ourselves with an audience of 800! It was amazing to meet so many of our followers and particularly to see in person so many women, and some men, who had lost phenomenal amounts of weight. It was thrilling to mingle with this throng of advocates of my diets and our classes, and to see the results in the flesh – and they all looked amazing because they had toned up with our exercise classes as well as slimmed down on the diet.

Our Roadshows gave the franchisees an enormous boost because, after each one, members would go back to their class the next week with renewed motivation and determination. It was wonderful. And

Mary and I loved doing them, even if they were exhausting. We would sign hundreds of books and DVDs and chat to almost everyone, and hundreds of photos were taken. I felt it was such a privilege that, through our business and the expertise of our franchisees, we were making a huge difference to so many lives.

Of course, 2012 was the year of the London Olympics. I was delighted to be asked to skate at a special event at Nottingham Ice Arena when Torvill and Dean would be carrying the Olympic torch on its journey around the UK before the Games started. I was invited to be part of the ensemble and, in the absence of Mark, was partnered by Tristan Cousins, the nephew of Robin Cousins. It was a great thrill to skate at such a prestigious event. Then, later in the year, I was invited to perform in a pantomime in Hull. *Cinderella on Ice* was being produced under the direction of Karen Goodwin, my first ice-skating coach. I only had a small role to play, but I loved being part of a 'pantomime family', and by the end of the year I totally understood why many are attracted to amateur dramatics. I know of nothing else that draws people together to be their best and be supported by one another.

***

Back home, Mike's mother, Jeanne, was becoming frail. It was rather strange but it seemed as though, after Jeanne had celebrated her 90th birthday, she suddenly realised she was getting old. As an example, one time a few months before her birthday, she had an acute pain in her foot and found it difficult to walk, so I took her to the doctor. He remarked that he thought it was probably gout, to which she sharply replied, 'But I thought only old people got that!' The doctor and I looked at each other and burst out laughing!

After getting Jeanne washed and dressed every morning, I always filled her kettle before I left for the office so that it would be easier for her to make herself cups of tea. But soon it became obvious that she wasn't drinking enough. The problem with elderly people is that getting up out of the chair, walking to the bathroom, going to the loo and walking back again takes so much effort they unconsciously drink less. The consequence of this is an inevitable urinary infection, and with that their mind can start playing tricks. At one point, Jeanne was admitted to hospital with a severe infection, and it was only then that we realised she needed some additional support because she couldn't be left for too long on her own.

Gwen, who has helped me in my classes for over 45 years and who house-sat and dog-sat for us whenever we went away, had always been a true friend and was happy to help whenever we needed extra support. Gwen was wonderful with Jeanne and treated her as her own mother. Nothing was too much trouble. She was patient and kind, so it was ideal for her to sit with Jeanne and look after her when she could. And another good friend, Jennie, was a great help too. Millie, who delivered the meals that she cooked for us each week, would always go up to Jeanne's flat and sit for a while with her and make her a cup of tea. Everyone was so kind.

At the same time as Jeanne's needs changed and became more demanding, we were aware that the diet and fitness market was changing and class attendances were not as they used to be. Franchisees were growing restless. Then in early 2013 the 'horse meat scandal' came to light and seriously affected our sales of Solo Slim. The horse meat scandal occurred throughout Europe when it became known that some ready meals advertised as containing beef were found to contain undeclared horse meat. While our Solo Slim products were completely 'clean' and had unquestionable provenance, the news devastated the ready-meal market and our sales dropped significantly – not only in our mail-order business but also for the franchisees who sold the products through their classes. Naturally, this affected their income and soon some franchisees decided to leave.

In our business we were so stringent in our selection of franchisees and we only accepted people who we were convinced would have the personality and drive to make their business a success. Ours was a personality-led enterprise – it was not just about me as a figurehead and the brand but, more importantly, about the franchisees themselves. *They* were the personality in *their* Club. My name might get a person through the door on the first week, but members would continue to attend a class because they liked the instructor. Our franchisees needed to be caring, interested in their members, and able to make their classes fun and entertaining, inspiring and educational, as well as desiring to help their members become slimmer and fitter. As the years went by, attracting new members became more and more difficult for some franchisees, as different fashions in exercise emerged in their locality.

While Chris was running the business, I worked on creating my next diet and began to write my next book. I also spent time promoting the Clubs by doing press and radio interviews. For the large number of franchisees who were very successful, it was wonderful. I loved meeting their members when they came to take part in our photoshoots for the magazine, and they were delighted to visit Quorn House to be recorded for our online TV channel. And while it was something of an endless job, I still enjoyed proofreading everything that went into our magazine. So I was still busy, although not as frantic as I had been.

We were very much aware that I wasn't getting any younger and we needed to give the business a new look. We exhibited each year at the Vitality Show and, the previous year, Chris and I had been approached by an exciting marketing company, Red Shoe, run by two very charismatic and impressive women, Sam and Emma. They felt they could re-energise our branding, so we decided to work with them to rebrand the Clubs and the magazine. With focus groups and a huge amount of design work done in-house to keep the costs down, we were excited about the ideas that were emerging and the prospects for the future. We knew we needed to do something as there was a sense of discontent growing within the franchisees and several were leaving. It was disappointing, but we were aware that room-hire fees were increasing and attendances were falling due to the many alternative options popping up in their localities, with the consequence that their income was declining.

***

As the year progressed, life at home became even more demanding as Jeanne needed extra care and attention. Thankfully, Mike and I were getting along and enjoyed our evenings and weekends together. He was really grateful that I was prepared to care for his mum, and I was very happy to do so. I loved Jeanne and I was perfectly content to get up at 5.30 am, give her some breakfast, wash or bathe her, and get her dressed and do her hair; but Jeanne was fast reaching the point where she needed more care.

Over Easter, Mike and I went on holiday to our house in Portugal. When we returned, our friends Gwen and Jennie, whom we employed to help look after Jeanne while we were away, were both in agreement that they were no longer able to manage when we went away. Jeanne's behaviour was becoming challenging at times and her ability to cope in the bathroom was presenting problems. I remember her once saying to me, 'I bet when you married Michael you didn't think that one day you'd be wiping his mother's bottom!' and we would have a laugh about it.

Then one day, Jeanne had a fall in the corridor of her flat. She lay there for hours before we found her. Unfortunately, she had forgotten that she had a small alarm hung on a lanyard around her neck; one press of the button would have sent an alert to tell us she was in trouble. As she had also hurt her arm and her hip and was badly bruised, we realised that we had reached the point where we had to bring in professional care immediately.

Despite all this, right up until she was 92, Jeanne still put on her make-up every day, took time to have her hair put into a beautiful chignon and wanted to dress elegantly. She always looked beautiful.

***

The summer is always a quiet time for slimming clubs and we feared that we might lose more franchisees. And indeed we did. As more classes closed, so the sales of our magazine and Solo Slim dropped too. It was then that we knew we had to make the horrible decision to cut back on staff. Making people redundant is the worst part of being a boss.

An essential aspect of being in business is ensuring you are keeping an eye on the housekeeping and making tough choices when you have to. While we cut back and made further staff redundant, we were totally confident that things would improve in the new year as they always did.

It is not unusual in franchising for discontented franchisees to try to create a breakaway group. In 2013, as attendances continued to decline, very sadly several of our franchisees attempted to do just that. Within the terms of the Franchise Agreement, former franchisees were not allowed, for a period of 12 months, to take classes within a 9-mile (15-km) radius of the place where their classes were held when they were part of our company. A Franchise Agreement is sacrosanct and it is something that has to be protected, both for the franchisor and for the other franchisees. The consequence of this was that legal action had to be taken if anyone broke the agreement. If franchisors do not protect their boundaries, the entire credibility of the franchise network breaks down; so now we had no choice but to protect our boundaries from the franchisees who were challenging us. This was the last thing we needed – emotionally and financially. We won, of course, but at a significant cost.

Despite the challenges, we were very much looking forward to our Annual Franchise Convention, which we held at the England football team's training facility at St George's Park, Burton upon Trent, in the autumn.

We were excited and very optimistic about January. The new branding looked fabulous and we were confident that this would give our franchisees the boost they needed to lift and energise the class attendances, as well as boost all our ancillary activities. We had dropped the word 'Diet' from our Club's name, and part of the rebranding process involved renaming the classes and the magazine as 'Rosemary Conley Food & Fitness'. So, when we launched the new brand at our Annual Convention in the October, all the franchisees were buzzing. I had written a new diet, the Fat Attack Booster Diet (published as *The FAB Diet*), and we had a new 'Starter Pack' full of great products which all the members would be given upon joining classes. It looked amazing.

We had introduced 'FitSteps' classes to our franchisees, and many had qualified to teach this exciting dance-cum-fitness programme inspired by the *Strictly Come Dancing* professionals Ian Waite and Natalie Lowe, along with *Strictly* contestant and Olympic swimming star, Mark Foster.

As December approached every year, our cash flow was always tight. This was particularly true in the run-up to the new year if we were launching a new diet, as we had to buy in a lot of new stock. And this year, because we had lost so many franchisees, cash was tighter than usual. The bank agreed to give us a loan, and Mike and I cashed in some ISAs to tide us over, but the reality was that by the end of the year we had lost 40 franchisees. That was 25% of our entire network.

However, despite this, we were excited about the year ahead and the whole new look for our company in January. We broke up for Christmas and couldn't wait for 2014 to arrive when we would launch our Slimmers of the Year, our new branding and my new diet.

Sadly, as so often with New Year hopes and expectations, the reality turned out to be very different.

22

A perfect storm
2014

The new-look magazine went on sale just after Christmas and had a fresh and modern appearance. The franchisees were excited at their newly branded kit for their classes, as well as the fabulous New Member Pack that they knew their members would love. Their leaflets and press advertising looked bright and attractive and we were all so optimistic that there would be a significant uplift in sales of our magazine. We anticipated new members joining classes, and these would be in addition to lots of 're-joins', which usually happened in January.

For the creation of all the rebranding, considerable investment was needed. But, as I have mentioned, money was tight as our income from the franchisees had fallen by 25% in the last 12 months because so many had left. Also, it was the peak time when banks were being ultra-cautious and not wanting to offer loans or overdrafts to businesses.

We thought this was only a temporary situation, so Mike and I put in all the cash we could muster at the time, which was £100,000, to help bridge the gap. In the light of this, the bank agreed to extend our borrowing and added a further £200,000 to the total that was put into the business.

We were all excited about January 2014. As well as seeing my new book, *The FAB Diet*, being published, I was going on Ideal World shopping channel on 1 January to sell our food, Solo Slim. It was superb food and I would be appearing on and off air for 24 hours (yes, I slept at the Ideal World offices), which was a great opportunity to sell a significant amount of product. Unfortunately, while lots of orders were taken, the sales didn't reach anywhere near our expectations or the figures suggested to us by Ideal World.

***

On 3 January I was in London on TV when Mike received a phone call from the police. His older brother had been found dead in his house. Mike had to go and identify him. Steve was just 57 and had died of a suspected heart attack. He lived alone and was a reclusive character who really didn't want any contact with friends or family. The last time we had seen him was at his father's funeral some 14 years earlier, though Mike did keep an eye on him from a distance, as did our very kind GP.

It was an awful shock. How were we to tell Jeanne, in her very frail state, that her eldest son had died? Immediately, I rang our doctor's surgery and spoke to a different GP, who had recently visited Jeanne at home, to ask if she felt Jeanne was strong enough to take the shock of the news. Should we tell her or not? The doctor was confident that she was strong enough and was adamant that, in her opinion, she should be told.

Mike and I waited a few days, then sat down with Jeanne and told her about Steve. She went very quiet for a few moments, but then said she was glad he was now at peace.

'I've thought of him every single day and wondered how he was. Now I know – and that's a relief,' she said.

Jeanne always sent Steve a birthday and Christmas card, together with a cheque, but she never received a response in return. That must have been so hard for her. But now she too could find a sense of peace.

As there had to be a post-mortem, the funeral was held a few weeks later, and Jeanne managed to walk across to the natural burial ground where Steve was to be buried. He had been a groundsman for most of his working life but hadn't had a job for many years because of his mental health problems. After the graveside service, we invited all Steve's neighbours, who knew him as 'Rimm', back to the Manor. It was good to hear their thoughts and memories of Steve. They had kept an eye out for him, and occasionally took him a meal. They knew he had issues, but they were kind and accepted him for who he was. It was comforting for us to know that.

***

All of this was happening alongside a worrying and disappointing start to the year for the business. We were aware that the magazine sector was in decline, but we hoped our new branding would buck the trend.

Sadly, the new-look magazine didn't fly off the shelves as we had hoped and, after two weeks, sales were down by 50% year on year. Then the franchisees started reporting poor attendances at their classes too, with fewer new members than usual. With the disappointing sales of Solo Slim on the Ideal World channel, as well as on our website and at our classes, things were looking really worrying. It was a shock and desperately disappointing.

Then the crunch came. It was time to send the next issue of the magazine to the printers. Chris came to me and told me that we hadn't enough money in the account to pay the printers for the previous issue, due to its low sales figures, and he wasn't comfortable, and rightly so, about placing another order.

This was the moment I remembered again the profound lesson we had learned from Dr Brian Smith, our now retired Non-Executive Director. He said: 'Turnover is vanity, profit is sanity and cash is reality.' It was a phrase Brian always taught people at our franchisee presentation days. A company can have a turnover of £10 million and be making a profit of £200,000, but if it doesn't have the cash in the bank to pay the bills, it's in trouble – and that is exactly what had happened to us.

There was no other option but to make one of the most difficult decisions of our lives. I felt sick. This was the moment when I realised we had come to the end of the road. We couldn't borrow any more money. Mike and I had invested all our available cash and had nothing left to give.

I rang Mike, who was at home, and told him. I said, 'It's all over. We've got to close the business. I'm going to call Stewart [our accountant] and set the wheels in motion.'

Mike was really shocked too. Of course, he had attended all our Board meetings and we were both aware that trading conditions were difficult, but we were both shocked to learn that it was *that* bad!

Mike was very supportive when I told him the news, as were Dawn and Dr Brian Smith when I called them. I dreaded telling Angie, our Franchising Director, who had been with us since the beginning. It was an incredibly sad day. We had achieved so much over the previous 21 years since setting up the company, and our franchisees, our classes, our magazine, our online Club and our TV channel were the best. This was a dreadful waste, a terrible shame, but we knew that we had to act responsibly. We could see so easily how companies could just dig themselves further and further into debt. It was a really tough decision but it was one we had to take, and quickly. Of course, we couldn't tell anyone – not yet.

The following Thursday, Chris, Mike and I met at our accountant's offices. Stewart had brought in a firm of administrators to handle our case. There was also a representative from the bank, which was very anxious to retrieve its loan. And so, we were introduced to the world of 'administration'. I sat there feeling numb.

A company goes into administration when it has found itself in financial difficulties but there is still potentially a viable business that could be rescued. Going into administration is very different from a company going into liquidation, when there is no hope of any rescue. In that case the business is closed down immediately. If a sole trader or partnership (not a limited company) finds itself in significant debt, the person or partners may be declared bankrupt, in which case assets are seized and their credit rating is affected. We were going into administration because we still had 120 franchisees running weekly classes, we had an online Club that was profitable and we had a magazine with a huge archive of material that was valuable. We just needed to find an investor, or a number of investors, to help rescue it.

Only someone who has gone through the demise of a business can really appreciate the heartache, the sense of loss – emotional, financial and practical – and also the hurt that inevitably comes with it. It is devastatingly sad. Our wonderful business, which had provided such happiness and help to so many over the previous 21 years, was coming to the end of its time and there was nothing more we could do to save it.

When so many of our franchisees left in 2013 and sales of Solo Slim dropped significantly because of the 'horse meat scandal', cash had been tight but we knew we had acted responsibly; we had made some staff redundant and Mike and I hadn't taken any salary for months. We had been so excited and optimistic about the new branding which was to launch in January 2014 and we were certain that this could give the business the boost it needed to thrive. If we hadn't been completely confident, Mike and I would not have put in our own money nor borrowed extra from the bank.

Once the decision is made for a company to go into administration, what follows is a very strict legal process determined by the administrators. Rosemary Conley Food & Fitness Clubs Ltd, as it was now called, was a limited company and should not be confused with Rosemary Conley the person. I was a totally separate entity from the company. What happened next was not what I would have done or wanted to do. But this was no longer *our* company, even though the company name included the name 'Rosemary Conley' in its title.

When you create a company with your own name in the title, you never think of the potential consequences in later years. I was now realising how painful and complex this could be. We were also finding that one of the hardest things was that we had no control over the destiny of the company. It was now governed by different laws and economic realities, as well as legal requirements. Once a company goes into administration, the administrators have all the power. They make all the decisions from that point on, and the previous owners are legally obliged to do whatever they instruct.

Thankfully, the proposed Administrators in our case, Mark Hopkins and David Watchorn of Elwell Watchorn & Saxton, were very helpful and constructive. They went through our accounts and looked at the facts of the business and what had gone wrong. One major problem was that Ideal World, the TV shopping channel, insisted that the packs of food we sold, which had potentially a nine-month shelf life, should have at least six months still to go. We had lots of food in our warehouse with four or five months' shelf life remaining, but Ideal World demanded six months. Because of that, and unbeknown to me, a huge order of new packs of food had been placed in anticipation of a big upturn in January from sales on Ideal World and from new members joining the classes. It also didn't help that we had 25% fewer franchisees to sell both the food and the magazine. Suddenly, there was the realisation that this was 'a perfect storm'.

I dreaded the following day as the proposed Administrators were due to move into Quorn House. However, the staff were unaware who they were and assumed they were simply part of our team of accountants who had come to carry out normal accountancy work. The administrative process meant that there were formalities to be completed through the court, and we learned that this would take two weeks and that during that time we were to carry on as normal. This wasn't easy as all our assets were frozen, we couldn't pay any cheques and we had no access to our limited company funds. It was incredibly stressful for the few who were aware of what was happening because we had to act and respond normally to the rest of the staff, the franchisees and the outside world.

I had a quiet word with Peter, my PA, in the boardroom and said, 'This is going to be an unbelievably tough time and I need you to be my friend and look after me, because everybody in this building is going to hate me.' And look after me he truly did. I couldn't have asked for a better friend and protector from that day on.

Mel, our in-house Head of Accounts, Angie our other Director, Peter my PA, Chris our Managing Director and I had to behave as though it was business as usual. This went against every fibre of my body because we had always believed in a culture of openness and honesty, but the process of administration demanded that we follow the rules, and the rules were that we must carry on as normal. Fortunately, we all shared an office; this was helpful, but we still had to be extremely careful and think about every conversation, every decision and the implications of any of our actions. It was really hard. The thought of everyone losing their jobs was heartbreaking and difficult to comprehend. Our staff were like a family, as were our franchisees. They were our friends. It felt as though we could see a tsunami in the distance but there was nowhere we could run to escape.

The next worry was that in two weeks' time, after the court process which follows the decision to go into administration, the news would be in the public domain so we needed to be ready for the press. Dan Baker is a Crisis Communications Public Relations (PR) expert who runs a company called PLC Media, and we knew him as he had hired our TV studio for some of his TV training days with corporate clients. We had no money to pay him, but Peter suggested I call him anyway. Fortunately, he was happy to help us for free.

Dan and I met the week before the announcement to decide how we would address the press and to find the most appropriate words for the press release. Dan was kind and understanding, and he helped me so much to clarify the messages we wanted to convey about what had happened and why the business had gone down.

It was decided that the press release would go out at 9 am on the Monday morning and, simultaneously, we would release a pre-recorded video message to all the franchisees and also address our staff in the library at Quorn House. I was dreading it.

On the Friday before Monday's public announcement, I arranged to meet Mary Morris at Dawn's house as she lived nearby. Mary was now a close friend, having been our Head of Training for the Clubs and having worked so closely with me for 18 years. Over the previous 16 years, she had joined me on the Austrian activity holiday trips that we ran together. When I told her the news, she was totally shocked and felt so sorry for us. She realised more than most how hard we had worked over the years to make the company the best it could be, and she had seen the investment we had made to give the franchisees the best chance possible to succeed.

Mary told me about a couple who were close friends of hers, and recalled how awful the whole process had been for them as their business went down. 'But the worst bit', she said, 'is how horrible people were to them. I feel *so* sorry for you – it's going to be awful.' Little did I know how true her words would turn out to be.

That weekend, Mike and I went shopping for enough food to last two weeks as I knew I would feel uncomfortable to be seen in public after the news had hit the press. It was a strange weekend. Not surprisingly, I hardly slept, and I kept going hot and cold with fear and trepidation as I came to terms with the devastating news that I was going to announce on Monday. News that would drastically change so many people's lives.

I realised also that I needed to make arrangements for my classes on the Monday evening, so I called my three helpers: Gwen Cherry, my long-term friend and cashier; Marion, who helped demonstrate the high-impact version of my exercise routines; and Chris, my hostess, who welcomed new members when they joined. I told them that I needed them to go to the class as normal to just weigh the members, that I would give Gwen a letter for everyone explaining what was going on, and that next week I would be there as usual.

Keeping to my routine, I woke up on the Monday morning at 5.30 to wash and dress Mike's mum, Jeanne. As I sat and ate my breakfast with her as I always did, I told her what was about to happen. Maybe – hopefully – she didn't fully understand the gravity of the situation.

Chris, Angie, Mel and I arrived at Quorn House early, as did Dan. He sat at Peter's desk with his finger poised over the 'send' button to release the press statement.

As we assembled in the library, which was not unusual if we wanted to tell any news to the staff, everyone was cheerful and fresh after their relaxing weekend.

As I stood in front of them, with Chris looking ashen, I explained the situation and that we had no alternative but to go into administration. Mark Hopkins, our Administrator, then spoke to the team explaining what happened next – that *he* would now be running the company, that the franchisees would continue to run their classes, but that there would be staff redundancies which he would decide upon at the appropriate time. He explained that he would try very hard to find a buyer for the business, or part of the business; so everyone was to keep working as normal for now. He also stated that, in the meantime, Mike and I would pay people's salaries out of our own pocket, which he described as highly unusual and a really generous gesture, but I don't think anyone registered the information. Everybody walked out of the library in stunned silence. I felt sick. It was such a horrible moment.

Not surprisingly, everyone was shell-shocked. The phones were ringing from franchisees, inevitably asking questions. Dan was receiving calls from the local and national press and regional TV stations. It was bedlam. Back-to-back interviews for radio and press with reporters asking, 'So what went wrong?' Thankfully, they seemed genuinely shocked too and were kind and sympathetic.

In Leicestershire our company was seen as a homegrown success story, so it was no surprise when the Business Editor from the local paper, the *Leicester Mercury*, called to speak to me. I rang him straight back and we talked through the situation. It made headlines the next day. He later wrote how surprised he was that I had called him personally, and that I had called immediately, as most business owners in our situation apparently would just hide away and put a spokesperson on the phone or in front of the camera. To me, that was never an option. We had found ourselves in this situation; we had nothing to hide. Like so many companies, we had simply discovered that trading conditions had changed and were now too difficult.

The producers of BBC Midlands Today wanted me to go on live TV that evening, but they also wanted an interview for their lunchtime bulletin so they sent a crew to Quorn House. This was followed swiftly by the team at ITV Central News, who came to Quorn to film for their evening news. It seemed so strange that we were making headlines. We were the lead story on both channels in the Midlands. Even Steve Wright mentioned it on his afternoon show on BBC Radio 2. I was shocked that we were that significant!

The overriding message we were determined to give was that our Clubs were continuing as usual. This was a crucial point as we needed an investor to take them over. Thankfully, and somewhat amazingly, everyone in the media was really kind and supportive; people were genuinely sad for me.

Walking around Quorn House the next day was very strange. It was no longer our company. I had no authority. I was no longer the boss. Now we had to find someone else to take on the challenges we had faced to see if the business could be salvaged.

In the middle of all this happening, I received a phone call from Les, the partner of Jan Bowmer, the long-term Editor of all my books and a really close friend. Les explained that Jan had become critically ill and was now in intensive care where she had been put into an induced coma for her own safety. Les just wanted to let me know.

This was truly awful news. Jan was such a wise and lovely friend and I couldn't believe she was so poorly. It was so sad, but at the same time it made me put our own problems into perspective. All I could do was to pray for her recovery.

In the meantime, we invited all the franchisees to a meeting the following Friday – 7 February. They came from all over the country and we met in a school hall nearby. Chris our MD, Mark the Administrator, Mel (Accounts Manager) and I prepared ourselves for the inevitable disappointment, anxiety and questions that would be directed at us. I dreaded it.

After I had welcomed everyone and explained how sad it was that we had found ourselves in this situation, Mark spoke to the franchisees to explain what would happen now. He advised them that the classes would continue to run and that, as franchisees, they would be obliged to continue to pay their weekly franchise service charge (the set fee payable to the company for every class that ran), and that he would do everything in his power to find a solution to the situation.

I knew they would be upset and even angry, but what happened next was a shock. When Mark had finished speaking, understandably there was a barrage of questions but I wasn't expecting the personal attacks and accusations that came at me like bullets from a firing squad. What hurt most were the personal attacks from franchisees whom I considered to be my friends. I underwent a character assassination and spent three and a half hours fighting back the tears, trying to answer their questions and explaining the circumstances surrounding the situation in which we all now found ourselves. Chris sat in the front with his head in his hands. Mark said afterwards it was the most vitriolic meeting he had ever experienced in his long career as an Administrator. I was physically shocked at how some of the franchisees had verbally attacked my ethics, my character and my credibility. It was heartbreaking. I could never have imagined, after all the years of working with these wonderful people, that it would end like this.

Human nature, understandably, puts people on a pedestal and we like having someone to look up to. In our business, that person was me. I was the brand – the solid, dependable, backbone of the business – and now they felt I had let them down. I knew that I was not the cause of the downfall, and that we were where we were because of circumstances beyond our control; but, in these situations, everybody wants to blame somebody and, if it's your name above the door, you are the obvious target. I understood that, but it didn't make it any easier.

While I was driving home, I rang Dawn.

'How did it go?' she asked.

'It was horrific!' I explained.

I deliberately didn't call Mike. I wanted to tell him face to face so that he could give me a hug as I explained the annihilation I had just experienced. I was shattered by the whole experience and he was shocked. And yes, he gave me the biggest hug.

We had launched our new branding in October with such confidence and optimism, and the franchisees must have felt we knew this downfall was going to happen. But of course we didn't. If we had known in advance, Mike and I wouldn't have invested our own personal money into the business to keep the company afloat and, believe me, nor would the bank have given us a loan. We were *so* sure that our trading position would improve.

That weekend, I just rested and looked after Jeanne. Mike was loving and very supportive, and Dawn kept calling to check I was all right. I felt as though I'd gone 10 rounds with Mike Tyson.

23
The aftermath
2014–15

The following Monday I went to my classes, as I had done for the previous 42 years. My members were so kind and caring and, as I read out their weight losses, one of the women came forward and gave me the biggest bouquet of flowers. She said, 'We're really sorry for what's happened and, after you didn't charge us for last week, we decided to put the money together for these flowers.' Tears filled my eyes. After so many people had been so horrible to me, being given such support, love and kindness was overwhelming and I found it difficult to hold it together. As I write these memories now, tears are streaming down my face as I remember how lovely they were to me. And that's why I still take my classes today. My members are my friends and I will always love them.

About two weeks later Stewart, our accountant, called me as I was driving home. He said, 'You need to know you only have £200 in your Enterprises account.'

Rosemary Conley Enterprises was separate from the business and was set up as a partnership between Mike and me to receive all my book and DVD royalties, and there had always been ample funds available for us to live on. It was from these funds that we drew the money to cover all our household bills and expenses. But, of course, we had poured so much into the business to keep it afloat that, alas, the cupboard was now bare.

In the mid-1990s, when we were earning a lot of money from my books, videos, serialisations and columns in Sunday magazines, Mike and I had invested in property. We lived in a very large house and we had a house abroad and, while they were worth a lot of money, they also cost a lot to run and we now had virtually no funds. Our office, Quorn House, was owned by our personal pension fund, and the property was rented to the company. But it hadn't received any rent for months because of the cash-flow issues, so that too had been bled dry. Our villa in Portugal was already on the market because we felt we didn't use it enough to justify the expense of maintaining it. However, up until now, no buyer had been found as the house market over there was in the doldrums. We were facing a difficult dilemma: we were asset rich but cash poor.

I called Mike immediately, dreading his response because he always left the family finances to me. But Mike is amazing in a crisis. If ever there was a real emergency, such as a fire or an accident, there is no-one else on this earth I would rather have to control the situation. This situation was no different and, by the time I arrived home, he had a plan.

'We'll ask my mum if we can borrow some money and I'll sell my car.'

He was so supportive, giving me a massive hug and speaking comforting words.

Mike's mum, Jeanne, who had now been living with us for six years, had been well provided for by her husband, who had died 14 years earlier. She gladly and very kindly gave us enough money to tide us over. It was a lifeline.

***

It wasn't long after the announcement in the media that Mark, the Administrator, was receiving enquiries from speculators interested in the business, varying from venture capitalists to private individuals. There were three elements to the company that were potentially viable businesses: the Clubs, the magazine and the online weight-loss Club.

Sadly, it wasn't long before the redundancies were being made. Angie, our Franchising Director, was one of the first. She had worked with Mike and me for over 25 years and had seen us grow from a tiny business in our attic at the Old Parsonage to a thriving and profitable enterprise. Angie accepted her redundancy with true grace. Her Christian faith meant that she felt it was God's plan. This was despite the fact that she wouldn't get the substantial redundancy package that she would have been due had the circumstances been different, but instead would just receive what is paid by the Government in these situations. She knew so much about the company and how hard we had worked, and she knew and respected us in making the decision we did. We were very proud of her.

At the same time, Peter, my PA, was made redundant, but he continued to come into the office anyway, unpaid, for which I was so grateful.

Over the coming weeks, one by one, others were given notice, including Chris who was the highest-paid staff member and had a company car. I was made redundant too but, like Peter, I continued to come in every day. It was terribly sad saying goodbye to people I considered were friends as well as colleagues, particularly Chris as we had worked so well together. Many took it very badly and were quite hostile. It was a natural human response to a situation that was inevitably going to change their lives and the lives of their loved ones.

I hated the fact that there was so much bad feeling. It was heart-wrenching. My only comfort was the knowledge that over the previous 20 years we had provided our staff with good jobs, had rewarded them well and looked after them, and paid millions and millions of pounds in salaries. The experience they had achieved in that time would stand them in good stead for the future. Franchisees had earned a very good income, some of them an exceptional income of around £100,000 a year, and they had all been trained to be the very best they could be. On top of that, hundreds of thousands of their members had been helped to lose weight and become fitter and healthier. Yes, it was desperately sad it had all come to this, but a lot of what we had done in those 21 years since we launched the Clubs was truly wonderful. I had to keep telling myself that we should never forget that.

Over the coming weeks, Mark and I met a variety of interested parties in the hope that we could find a company or individual with whom I could work to salvage parts of the business and pay off the creditors. Tanfield, the producers of Solo Slim, had a vested interest in finding a future for the company. Tanfield was also interested in buying the Clubs, and a price was agreed by Mark on behalf of the administration.

Another part of the business that was creating interest was our online weight-loss Club. Chris had shown some interest in this himself but later withdrew. Another interested party was one of our franchisees, Sarah Skelton, who had run her franchise very successfully in Norwich for 15 years and was also the only franchisee who was employed by the company, part-time, as a Consultant. As well as being a Franchisee of the Year, Sarah had also been a finalist for the British Franchise Association's national Franchisee of the Year Awards. She was an exceptional business-woman and I really rated her, and now she was interested in buying Rosemary Conley Online.

Mark also received an offer from an unknown party via a firm of accountants. This prospective buyer asked for no information regarding how the online business ran, how profitable it was or how many members we had. Nothing. Despite that, Mark took the offer seriously.

However, it was a large company from London that showed the most interest and offered significantly more than the anonymous bidder. Mark and I had several meetings with Andrew Gardner, MD of Appello, a venture capital company in London which was keen on encouraging a sense of health and well-being among its clients; Andrew felt their company could make a beneficial connection with our online Club and our health and well-being editorial archive. He was very interested in involving Sarah as he could recognise her expertise and experience – and knew I rated her very highly. After some serious negotiation, of which I had no part, of course, Appello made a significant offer and Mark, on behalf of the administration, accepted it. The offer included the online business, the TV and magazine archive, and the right to use my name. In addition, Appello wanted me to be involved to endorse the deal. It was a very strange feeling to acknowledge that I no longer owned my name as far as this company was concerned. But I was thankful to be involved, and to the purchaser my involvement was crucial.

With the negotiations completed, I was to be employed by Appello to oversee the business under the supervision of Andrew Gardner, a very charismatic businessman, who had done all the negotiations; assisted by Tom Barclay, a whizz-kid IT expert; plus a Financial Manager, Simon Derrick; and with Sarah Skelton running operations. It felt strange as I hadn't been employed for over 30 years since my IPC days, but I was very grateful that I was still involved in part of the company that carried my name.

Discussions had also been held with the owners of Kelsey Publishing, who were interested in taking over the magazine, and they in fact did take the edition that was all ready for the printers when we decided to call in the Administrators. Bless them; Kelsey paid for the printing, sent copies to our subscribers and would have collected any revenue if it had proved profitable. Sadly, it didn't.

Mark, the Administrator, was controlling a balancing act of all the interested parties, and he had to decide where he would make the most money in the negotiations.

A few weeks after the announcement that the business was going into administration, Jan Bowmer, my Book Editor, who had been in intensive care and an induced coma, suddenly telephoned me. It was such a relief, a joy and a wonderful surprise to hear her voice and to know that she was out of her coma and alive! In a gentle and quite frail voice she told me she was getting better and on the road to recovery but breathing was difficult so she couldn't speak for long. Then she said, 'I'm so sorry to hear about the business. Of all people you *so* don't deserve this. Keep your head down and your pecker up! You'll get over this.'

It was the most humbling moment. I could hardly respond as my eyes filled with tears of relief that she was getting better, combined with such appreciation of her kind words. It was those generous and positive words and comments from a variety of people, just like Jan, that kept me going and enabled me to continue to believe in myself.

***

At the beginning of April, the Administrator, Mark, issued a statement to all the franchisees to explain that they now had two options going forward. They could (1) go with Tanfield and continue running the classes as before under new ownership, or (2) break away and operate under their own name immediately and pay no further monies to us, or anyone else, and understand that all contractual obligations as a franchisee with our old company, Rosemary Conley Food & Fitness Ltd, would now cease. Under option 2 they would not be able to use the Rosemary Conley name in their business.

Sarah, who was seen as something of a natural leader within the franchisee network, had already put together a plan for go-it-alone franchisees which they could follow to give them a head start if they wanted to become sole traders. Many of the franchisees were unsure what to do. Very interestingly, three of the franchisees who had verbally attacked me in their anger on that 'Black Friday' in February called me for my advice. One of them said she had spoken to her husband and he had said, 'Look, call Rosemary. You know you can trust her.'

It was only a small thing, but it made all the difference to how I felt. My recommendation was that they should go on their own. Our now ex-franchisees were immensely capable teachers with good classes. Their members attended every week because of *them*, not me. They could be infinitely better off because they would not be paying any fees to us or anyone else, and they knew how to market their business because we had taught them how to do that. Many of them did go out on their own and benefited financially from being sole traders. One franchisee, an ex-dancer, who was amazingly successful and running lots of classes every week, admitted to me later that going it alone was the best break she could have had. It saved her £20,000 a year!

Mark Hopkins was astute in his negotiations and would say to me, 'I may be moving in mysterious ways, but trust me. I know what I'm doing.' He worked in the same office as Peter and me, and he became very aware of how we ran our business and what the ethos of our business was, and quickly learned about the franchisees. He also knew that I really cared about our staff.

The following Thursday, Mark held a 'creditors' meeting' at Quorn House. This is an opportunity for people who are owed money by a company that goes into administration to come together and to hear from the Administrator the facts of the situation and to learn the proposed plans going forward. Anyone who was owed money was entitled to be there, from the largest to the smallest creditor (including one member of staff who was owed £30 expenses), and so the creditors' committee was formed.

When the company went down, many of our suppliers told us how sad they were. They said that, as a small company, they had really appreciated over the years how they could always rely on our paying them every month, on time; for some of them, we were the only business that ever did. This was a fundamental rule that we had in our company: pay all the invoices on the 20th day of each month.

Mark Hopkins, our original Administrator, sadly left, and the remaining Administrator, David Watchorn, continued the work with another colleague. David was shocked at the attitude of the creditors' committee, as he soon realised they were out for blood. Then, just before Christmas, we received a letter from the Insolvency Service to tell us that we were going to be investigated. Someone had triggered such an inquiry, but our Administrator was not concerned. He knew that there had been no wrongdoing.

Under this inquiry, we had to answer lots of questions and I had to consult Chris to fill in some of the detail. This was good as we had hardly spoken since he left, which saddened me. We had worked so well together and no-one was apportioning any blame in the downfall of the company. It was just one of those things; a 'perfect storm', in fact.

Earlier in the year I called my friend and motivational guru, Richard Denny, to explain the demise of the company, only to learn from him that he was battling with cancer. I was so shocked and sad. But in true Richard character, he was only concerned with our ailing company, not himself. We kept in touch throughout the year and he seemed to be optimistic about his health, which was a relief. Then in December he called to say he would like to visit us at Ashby Folville. He came specifically to give me advice and support through this really tough time, an experience which he had gone through himself some years before but in a slightly different way. It was so lovely to see him looking well and to just be in the presence of this man who exuded an aura of positivity and optimism. I couldn't help but be uplifted by his words of wisdom, encouragement, strength and love.

As Christmas approached, I wrote, as usual, a short résumé of our life over the previous year to include with our personal Christmas cards. I am conscious of not producing a tome of the year's activities – just the headlines so that our friends are kept up to date. For 2014, I decided to write something a little different:

GREETINGS FROM ROSEMARY AND MIKE
After what has been a challenging year for us, after our business went into administration in February, I am pleased to be able to say that we have experienced many unexpected blessings throughout this year for which we are extremely grateful. I thought I would like to share them with you.

My 12 blessings of 2014:

1. The unfailing and devoted love and support of Mike. He has been my rock and my best friend throughout the year. He has been such a blessing.

2. The support, love and wisdom of Dawn who has been extraordinarily wonderful. And her wonderful husband Laurie.

3. The unexpected care and support of the general public and friends who have sent flowers, letters, cards, emails and messages of support. So very, very kind.

4. The media who were really nice to me.

5. Appello, who bought Rosemary Conley Online from the Administrators and gave me a job! And our Administrators who were kind and understanding.

6. My PA, Peter, who has been there throughout and who still enjoys working with me – but at home.

7. Good health in our family including Mike's 92-year-old mother, Jeanne, who lives with us and is still mentally bright and physically mobile.

8. Total adaptation to our new life – and loving it.

9. The enjoyment of organising a very successful A Question of Brains charity event in November which raised £50,000 for Steps Conductive Education Centre.

10. The amazing support and prayers of our fellow members of Meadows Community Church.

11. The unbelievable joy of our grandson, now 2½ years old, and the realisation that this is what life is about!

12. And lastly, but most importantly, the immense love and incredible blessings of our gracious God who has blessed us this year beyond words.

Many of our friends had been unaware of our changing circumstances and wrote beautiful letters of support. It was lovely to know that we still had some genuine friends after all the hostility.

In the new year we received good news from the Insolvency Service. Apparently, our company had been thoroughly investigated and we were given the all-clear and confirmation that there had been no wrongdoing.

While we were sure we hadn't done anything improper or unlawful, it was good to receive that letter of confirmation.

In the spring of 2015, a year after we had first gone into administration, everything was brought to a conclusion. I discussed with the Administrators the fact that, while we knew we had no legal duty to do so, we wanted to pay some of the creditors from our personal cash as we were now on a better financial footing. I was told that what we did was entirely up to us and that we had no obligation to do anything because all of this was the legal process of winding up a limited company. It was not our personal responsibility. But when I explained that there were some people we felt we wanted to pay, the Administrator was adamant about one thing. He told me we were *not* to pay certain people who had been vitriolic and vindictive.

The first person we did pay was a newly recruited franchisee who was the only franchisee to have paid for her franchise licence, her training, her accommodation, her kit and her marketing without ever receiving anything back for it. I was so glad we could do that for her.

***

Quorn House was becoming emptier and emptier and there was now just a handful of staff helping to clear out all the old records and paperwork. Can you imagine the filing cabinets and desks of 50 staff? Everything had to be examined and processed appropriately. What should we keep? With the rest we had to decide what category of waste it fell into. We had created an area which was dedicated to huge waste bins. There were receptacles for recycling, bins for confidential papers that would be taken away and shredded, general waste, and a huge skip for all those odds and ends – broken chairs and so on that had found their way into the cellar. It was a mammoth job, which in the end was left to just Peter and me.

Martin and Dolores were still living in The Lodge at the end of the drive of Quorn House and they were wonderful. So kind and supportive, helping us to clear stuff and carry it down the huge flight of stairs and to clean everywhere. My long-standing friend, Gwen, who had worked part-time at Quorn House, also helped us to clean throughout this vast building ready for an anticipated new buyer.

Peter and I moved our office into the Manor, and we had boxes and boxes of 'stuff' in the various downstairs rooms waiting to be sorted. It was a daunting task, but we just worked our way through it over the coming weeks. There was so much of it that had to be carefully filed and logged.

By September, Quorn House was empty and, on the final day, I was on my own as I closed the beautiful big oak front door behind me.

As I locked the door for the last time, I turned to look at this beautiful Georgian house and said out loud, 'Goodbye, Quorn House. Thank you for so many happy memories and for the fun we had. It's been a blast.' And then I drove away. No tears. Just the end of a remarkable chapter.

Later, I considered the incredible effect that Quorn House had had. If it hadn't been for that property, over the previous 21 years we would not have created the business in the first place. But that business had provided jobs for over 200 people and created over 500 franchised businesses. More than 800 people had become qualified Diet and Fitness Instructors, who in turn welcomed over two million members to join their classes, learning how to eat more healthily and to exercise safely and effectively, for the benefit of their long-term health. Since 1996 we had also published 136 issues of our magazine, each of which had been read by almost half a million people. Hundreds of thousands of viewers had enjoyed our internet TV channel, and tens of thousands of people had lost weight with us online. Also, during that time, the franchisees had raised well over £2 million for cancer research through Race for Life, and lots more for many other charity initiatives, including Children in Need.

Then I thought of the benefits to the Treasury. The tax that had been paid; the National Health Insurance that had been invested into the economy.

'Yes, thank you, Quorn House. You have made a massive difference to so many people's lives. Without you, we would not have done this!'

I remembered my determination to buy the property in the first place and how that had triggered the idea of starting the franchised business. There would undoubtedly be a legacy from all of this, so all was not lost. Quorn House, and everyone who had worked inside it, had been a force for great good.

24

Sadness and surprises

2015

Once the various transactions had been completed, everything seemed a lot calmer. Some of the franchisees had decided to join the guys from Tanfield (the makers of Solo Slim) to create a new organisation called 'Glow'. This was a perfect solution for those franchisees who wanted to be part of a group. However, most of the franchisees had decided to go it alone, which was no surprise. They were very capable and had built up successful businesses and had learned so much from their experience with us. The online business and the archive from the magazine and the TV channel were sold to Appello; and Sarah Skelton and I were invited to be part of the team to take Rosemary Conley Online forward. The administration process was now completed and it was time for new beginnings.

Several staff members kept in touch and let us know about their new jobs, and I occasionally bumped into others while shopping who had also moved on to new employment or businesses. Others were there with their new babies, which was wonderful to see, and some had even started new lives abroad.

***

It was a very strange feeling to step out of one environment, a business that I had enjoyed leading for two decades, only to find myself being employed by a whole other company. I was now part of a new team and we were all working from home. Thankfully, we all wanted to be part of that team and we gelled very quickly. It was a fresh challenge. A different challenge. But it was 'something', and for that I was grateful.

So, the new team – Sarah, Tom, Simon and I – did everything we could to reorganise the new business of Rosemary Conley Online, and we enjoyed the task. We held our Board meetings at the Manor, where everyone stayed over, and these became very sociable occasions. Sarah was a brilliant cook and Simon loved turning his hand in the kitchen too, so we always ate very well. The Manor was a great house for entertaining, and the whole ambience of the place was warm and welcoming despite its size. We all got on really well as a team, each one of us bringing our unique experiences to the table. We all got paid the same – there was no hierarchy – and we all had the same goal: to make Rosemary Conley Online the best internet-based weight-loss club in the UK. With our extensive archive of film from RosemaryConley.TV, we had thousands of videos to include on the site and thousands of recipes, and we knew no other online weight-loss club would have that.

Our only problem was the website itself. It had been designed years before and been developed and added to so many times – rather like a four-bedroomed detached house now with a dozen extensions making it impractical and inefficient. Thankfully, Appello decided to invest in a brand-new website, which Tom designed.

It was exciting to still be involved in a team working together, which included our online coaches, plus Dan Baker who handled our PR and Susannah Goodwin who produced my films for the site. Together we were helping our members to become slimmer, fitter and healthier. We all worked from our individual homes dotted around the country, which suited me very well. Peter and I had settled into our new office in what at one time had been Mike's study.

It was only a few months later that we realised there were some changes being made at Appello, and after Christmas I was invited to have lunch with its Chairman, Paul Lester.

I had met Paul a couple of times before, when Appello had first taken over part of the business, and I liked him. We got along well and I respected him massively for his entrepreneurial flair and the ability to spin so many heavy-duty plates at once, managing to be Chairman of numerous different companies all at the same time. Paul doesn't beat around the bush and I knew he wasn't inviting me to lunch just for fun. Sarah, Simon and Tom knew that too.

After we had ordered our starter, Paul asked how Rosemary Conley Online was going. I was able to say that things were going well and that the team worked very happily together. The new website was taking shape and would be launched in May.

Then he said, 'We have decided to change the direction of our company and your business doesn't really fit in with where we are going. We will be happy with a minority shareholding if you want to organise a management buy-out. We will continue to honour the rebuild of the website, but you sort it all out between you.'

We were all excited by the prospect of such a development but didn't have much money to invest in the business, so we decided to earn shares by 'salary sacrifice' with some investment from those who could afford it. Since we four Directors were investing, we invited other members of the team to do the same; so Peter (my PA), Susannah (our Film Editor), Dan (our PR guy) and a couple of the coaches for Rosemary Conley Online, Amanda Scott and Sue Menzies, and also the Directors of the IT company in Poland that was building the new site, all decided to invest. The legal documents were created and in just a few weeks we were all shareholders. This brought a whole new dimension and level of excitement and motivation to the team, and we worked hard to drive the business forward. We were grateful to Appello for giving us this chance and completing the build of the new, very complex website.

***

While all this was going on, Jeanne was becoming increasingly frail, so my working from home was proving really valuable, though by now we were having round-the-clock, live-in care for four days each week. When the carer wasn't there, I took over, which I was happy to do with some additional help from friends Gwen and Jennie.

Meanwhile, I decided to write a new diet book, greatly encouraged by the rest of the online management team. We decided it would be a very positive move to create something that would give the Rosemary Conley brand some much-needed publicity and at the same time enable us to add a new diet to the online members' website. In addition, Sarah, now our Chief Operating Officer, was an ace cook, so I commissioned her to create some appropriate recipes to include in the book.

I wanted to try a new way of dieting along the principles of the 5:2 diet but making it quite different. Usually, a 5:2 diet involves eating normally for five days a week and then drastically restricting one's calorie intake for the other two days. My diet would be 'low-fat based' and, instead of having 'fasting' days allowing only 600 calories, I would offer 'light' days of 800 calories. On the remaining days, I would create eating plans suggesting around 1,400 calories, while offering some leeway with fruit and vegetables and even alcohol. I have been in this business too long to believe that people who are overweight are going to be 'sensible' on the normal days. I believe they would be thinking, *Yes! I can eat whatever I want today because today is a normal day! Woohoo!* Which isn't the spirit of such a diet. From my experience, I believe dieters like boundaries, so I set out to give them just that – but with soft edges.

My idea was to suggest that dieters had three 'light' days in the first week, two 'light' days each week until they reached their goal, and finally one 'light' day a week for maintenance. I named it the 3-2-1 Diet. But before I started, I called Professor Susan Jebb to ask for her opinion. As well as working together over many years, Susan had educated and advised me when I wrote some of my previous books. Thankfully, she was very encouraging of my plan, as was my publisher. My only problem was that this was going to be a complicated book to write, and I was going to struggle to do it with all my other commitments to Jeanne, Rosemary Conley Online and life in general. I then had a brainwave: I needed an intern to help me.

I contacted someone I knew at Loughborough University and asked how I might go about getting an assistant, explaining that I was happy to pay the right person. We worded a brief description of the task in hand, and an email was then sent around to the appropriate department, with my phone number. Within a couple of hours, I had a call from John Bolton. He had seen the email, and rang me immediately. He sounded great, and within a couple of weeks John moved into the office I shared with Peter and we began work on my new book, *The 3-2-1 Diet*. Sarah produced the recipes, which were fabulous. John was only with me for nine weeks, so we had a deadline. He had to catch two buses to get to Ashby Folville, but he made it each day and we worked really well together. However, I don't think he will ever want to type out another recipe for the rest of his life!

One day, I told John that Peter and I wouldn't be in on Thursday as I was going down to Elstree Studios to appear on a celebrity edition of the BBC1 quiz show *Pointless*.

'You're kidding me!' he exclaimed. 'I *love Pointless*!'

So, two days later, we all drove down together. Peter and John were in the audience while I was introduced to my *Pointless* partner, the ice-skating superstar champion Robin Cousins. I was thrilled to be partnered with such a legend, particularly as my only experience of Robin was as one of the judges when I was on *Dancing on Ice* three years previously.

After make-up we went into the studio, where Robin and I were asked to stand on stage in the centre of the back row. The co-hosts, Alexander Armstrong and Richard Osman, were very welcoming and the show was about to begin. As the screen came up for us to read the questions, I realised I couldn't read them! I used long-distance glasses for driving but never thought to bring them with me. I was horrified and went into panic mode.

The first challenge was to think of *any* word 'that ends in "-act"' – let alone the least likely one to have been selected by the audience!

'*Pact*', I thought instantly, but then dismissed this as being much too easy and something that would score far too many points. *Ah*, I thought, '*react*'. *That's better.* Not a brilliant answer, I realised, but my brain had frozen and I decided to just go with it. I kept saying it to myself: *React. React. React. Remember, R for Rosemary. React!* Yes, it was locked into my brain.

'Rosemary, you have been working in the health and fitness . . .' suggested Alexander Armstrong and, while I was responding to his various questions, a bit of my brain was holding on to the word 'react'.

'So, Rosemary, what is your *Pointless* answer for something ending in "-act"?'

'PACT!' I blurted out.

What an idiot! I thought. I was so embarrassed. It scored a massive 69 points and I felt so cross with myself. Thankfully, by some miracle, one of the other celebrities gave an answer to a question which caused him to be eliminated. I can remember praising God under my breath that I hadn't gone out in the first round!

Round 2 involved cookery books and their authors. On the distant screen were what looked like a dozen titles and the initials of their authors. I struggled to read them, let alone remember a single celebrity chef's name. One of them was written by 'A. H.' Then I remembered a well-respected chef called Angela Hartnett, so I gave that as my answer. Alexander looked at me quizzically, obviously not recognising the name, but Richard Osman, thankfully, had heard of Angela, which made me feel slightly better. But it was the wrong answer. The correct answer was, of course, Ainsley Harriott, and I was knocked out, feeling extremely guilty that I had let Robin Cousins down. From that day on, I vowed never to participate in another TV quiz show!

However, there was a silver lining to the day. As Peter went to collect the car and John and I walked to meet him, John remarked that he had just seen Bradley Walsh standing outside the studio where the popular quiz show *The Chase* was filmed.

'You are joking!' I exclaimed to him. 'I love that guy!' I immediately dropped everything on the spot and ran back to see him.

'Bradley Walsh!' I blurted out. 'I'm such a massive fan of yours. You are amazing in *Law & Order UK* and my husband and I watch it all the time!' Then I continued, 'I'm so sorry! You must think I'm a madwoman. I'm Rosemary Conley and I've just been doing something next door.'

To this he replied, 'I know who you are, Rosemary, and it's so lovely to meet you!'

We chatted for quite a long time and then I asked Peter to take a photo. It was such a thrill, because Mike and I watched the long-running *Law & Order* series almost every weekend until we'd seen all the episodes at least twice. They are so well produced and directed that we never tire of them. *Law & Order UK* is the British version of the US-based long-running series and Bradley Walsh plays a middle-aged, highly capable detective – a role Bradley totally commanded. He *was* that detective. To be able to tell Bradley to his face how brilliant he was in the series was a joy. I was so happy and so was he!

Some weeks later I was invited on to *The Chase*, which Bradley hosts. After my disastrous appearance on *Pointless*, it will come as no surprise that I graciously declined.

With just two days to go before John reached the end of his nine-week internship, we completed the book. Peter, John, Mike and I sat in the garden drinking champagne to celebrate the completion of a challenging task. Having John as my full-time assistant had made a massive difference to me. It had meant that Peter could get on with everything else, so there was no need for me to worry about the day-to-day stuff. The following Monday, I sent the manuscript off to my publishers.

***

Quorn House proved to be a challenging property to sell. It had been used as offices for over 20 years so needed significant investment to convert it into a domestic dwelling again. It wasn't until the following spring, some seven months later, that we managed to find a buyer: Lafarge Tarmac, the company that owned the quarry close to Quorn Park. There had been another potential buyer – a family – but Quorn House was complicated. We didn't own the mineral rights under the ground and, while *we* had been prepared to accept that risk when we purchased it in 1993, not surprisingly others were not.

The owners of Lafarge Tarmac were only too aware of the significant dust their company created locally due to the constant blasting of granite from the quarry, and they were often subject to complaints from local residents. By buying Quorn House they were able to be in control, in effect, of a barrier of 147 acres (59 ha) of parkland belonging to the property. As far as we were concerned, they were the perfect buyer as they obviously weren't worried about the mineral rights; if anyone was going to quarry the land, it would be them! They bought Quorn House to create a training centre for the staff of their group of companies, and I am sure they will enjoy it as much as we did.

It was a massive relief once the sale went through, but such concerns were soon put into a new perspective.

***

It turned out that 2015 was a year of highs and lows. In June of that year my first husband, Phil, was suddenly diagnosed with acute myeloid leukaemia. Extraordinarily, he had been playing tennis on the morning of the diagnosis. It was the bruising that was appearing around his eye which had prompted Dawn and Phil's wife, Trish, to insist that he see his doctor. Thankfully, his GP recognised the signs and ordered a blood test instantly, and within 12 hours he was seen by a haematologist. It was such a shock to all of us when he was given the diagnosis.

Phil had always been a sportsman ever since I first knew him at the age of 16. He was a great cricketer and a talented badminton player, and later played for the County Seniors team; more recently he had taken up tennis, which he also loved. After the shock of the diagnosis, Phil decided that he wouldn't go for any treatment. He felt that if he could have a couple of 'quality' years before he lost his battle, he would be happy with that. You can imagine his shock when the consultant told him that, if he didn't have any treatment, he would only have two to three weeks to live. Everyone was in shock. Dawn was beside herself. Trish was distraught. I was devastated. This seemed so unbelievably unfair and came as an incredible blow. We all felt so helpless.

Thankfully, Phil agreed to chemotherapy and soon was undergoing treatment. But because of the severity of his leukaemia, the medication was brutal, and it had to be administered to him as an inpatient. Apparently, had it not been for his incredible level of fitness, he would not have survived this extremely severe treatment or been as resilient to its cruel side-effects. What made it even harder for Phil was that he had an innate fear of hospitals. He couldn't help it. It was just the way he was. All of us were very aware of that, and it made us feel doubly sorry for him. Everyone was devastated.

From the very start, Dawn was by his bedside for at least four hours a day, which must have been such a comfort to Phil. They had always been close but this was different. Phil remained in hospital for weeks and occasionally was allowed home, but he had to be very careful not to catch any germs or eat anything that potentially contained bacteria that could affect him adversely.

Only months before, we had said goodbye to our very close friend, John Blackburn, to the same brutal cancer. John had been Phil's best man at our wedding in 1968. When I told Annette, John's widow, of Phil's diagnosis, it was clear from the initial silence and then from her voice that her heart had sunk. She knew only too well that this was a desperately sad situation.

***

In the meantime, caring for Jeanne was becoming increasingly challenging, and now we had to make the decision to have live-in, round-the-clock care *seven* days a week. I still had my breakfast with her, helped her select her clothes each morning and styled her hair, and I would plan or prepare the meals for us all. Everything else was taken care of by the carers, but Jeanne wasn't happy. She was accepting of the help from Gloria, who had been her main carer for over a year, but she really didn't like the additional help when we had to introduce it. All the carers were brilliant, but I understood that when you are 93, and very proud, it must be extremely difficult to accept that you are unable to look after yourself.

By mid-July 2015, Jeanne was really unhappy and said she wanted to move. 'The quality of this place has gone downhill,' she complained, 'and the Matron [that was me!] doesn't even wear a uniform!'

I asked her if she wanted to go somewhere else and she said she did. Mike and I were really at our wits' end trying to work out what to do for the best.

We then set about that awful task of finding the best possible residential nursing home nearby where we all felt confident that Jeanne would be comfortable. A couple of weeks later, after consulting with our doctor, we moved her to a nursing home. She hated it. Three days later we moved her to another nursing home where she felt more comfortable and where the Matron wore a uniform (!). She seemed to settle there but, four weeks after she moved in, we received a phone call.

I answered the phone.

'Is somebody with you?' asked the caller from the nursing home.

When I said there was, she told me that Jeanne had passed away. Despite knowing that her life was nearing its end, we were still shocked. Mike and I went very quiet and didn't know what emotion to feel. We knew her passing was a blessing, but we loved Jeanne. Really loved her.

That afternoon, we were looking after our grandson. He was three years old and picked up on the fact that our mood had suddenly changed.

So we told him we had just had some sad news and that was why we were a bit quiet.

He paused for a moment and then said, in a hushed tone, 'I know! Why don't we play hide-and-seek and that will make you happy again!' It was a precious moment.

Jeanne's funeral was held a couple of weeks later and, at Mike's request, Dawn took the service. By now, Dawn was joint-leader of her local church, and Mike knew how much Dawn cared for Jeanne and how much Jeanne had loved her. He felt it would be the loveliest way to say goodbye to his mum.

Dawn did a wonderful job of leading the service, the first funeral she had ever taken, and we were all so glad that she had done it. From the time when she was eight years old, Dawn had grown up knowing Jeanne and was able to speak about her fondly, with genuine respect and admiration for this very special woman whom we all loved. It was a beautiful service, and afterwards we all celebrated Jeanne's life back at the Manor. Mike's cousins, Teresa and Peter, drove up with their respective spouses, and what we all felt was a combination of sadness and also relief that Jeanne was now at rest.

***

It was something of a surprise that same week to receive a phone call from the estate agent who had undertaken the sale of Quorn House. He had been approached by a successful local businessman, who had been the other party interested in buying Quorn House before it had been bought by Lafarge Tarmac. Now he was very interested in buying the Manor! The only problem was that we didn't want to sell it. It wasn't on the market and we didn't need to sell it thanks to the sale of Quorn House. While we would have to pay tax on any funds we took out of our pension fund, which had owned Quorn House, there was enough to enable us to stay at the Manor for a few years yet.

This wasn't the first time the businessman had shown an interest in the Manor. Six months before, at the time when Quorn House was sold, he had asked the estate agent where we lived. But we weren't interested in selling, added to which was the fact that Jeanne was living with us; she was in such a frail state that the idea of moving her was out of the question. It was good for us to talk about it, though. In the end, we decided definitely to stay where we were for a few more years, and we went on to plant new trees and shrubs, decorate the gardener's cottage and do various other odd jobs to keep the whole place in good order.

We loved the Manor and the village of Ashby Folville, but this second approach made us think. Jeanne was no longer with us and, after Mike and I chatted it through, Mike agreed that we would allow the prospective buyer to come over for another visit but that I would see him on my own. Mike really didn't want to move, which was quite ironic because, before, it had been Mike who had wanted to sell and I had fought hard to keep it. I had always said that the day we left the Manor it would break my heart because I loved it so much.

25

Heartache and a house move
2016–18

The prospective buyer arrived at the Manor on his own, and he and I walked over the land and all around the house. Then the conversations began. A week later, he made us an offer we couldn't sensibly refuse, plus he offered us a very significant deposit and afforded us nine months in which to find a new house. He had been looking at many beautiful houses in the locality ever since he had first seen the Manor six months before; but, just as we had discovered 20 years previously, he realised that Ashby Folville Manor was a unique gem. Yes, it was large, but not unmanageable. It was well designed for family living, majestic in appearance and tucked discreetly away in the centre of a very beautiful village. It was an exceptional property and he recognised that.

Having agreed the sale, Mike and I set about finding a new place to live. The fifth house we found was perfect. It was a large farmhouse and it even had a fountain at the front and a huge live-in kitchen with a garden room within it and a gardener's cottage. These were three things we loved at the Manor and here they were again. The gardens were magnificent and surrounded the house, which was nestled in the centre of its own beautiful, undulating farmland. We knew immediately it was the right house for us. Of course, it was smaller than the Manor and completely different in character. The Manor was very grand, whereas our new home-to-be had ceiling beams but was still very spacious. Above all, it had more land and the views were magnificent. It was perfect.

Over the next few months, we set about sorting through the mountain of stuff we had accumulated over our lifetime and particularly the last two decades at the Manor.

***

While all this was happening, Dawn continued to visit her dad every day; only she and Trish, his wife, were allowed to visit because he was so vulnerable to infection. Sadly, his first course of chemotherapy hadn't worked, but the next course did, and we were all so thrilled to hear that his leukaemia had gone into remission. He was even allowed home for his 70th birthday weekend at the end of October and I was able to call round with his present. It was really good to see him, though of course he looked very different. He had lost so much weight and all of his hair. Phil had always had such a wonderful head of hair, which in recent years had gone slightly grey and looked very distinguished, but now it was gone and he hated being without it.

The next day, Phil went back into hospital for a bone marrow transplant. We knew this was a major step, but the doctors and nurses at Leicester Royal Infirmary Haematology Unit were outstanding and we had every faith that things would go well. Very sadly, after just a few days, there were complications and he became very poorly. Two weeks after his birthday, while Dawn was with him, Phil lost his brave battle. Dawn rang me immediately to pray for a miracle, but that was not to be. It was heartbreakingly sad.

We were all in shock. It was devastating for all of us but especially for Dawn and for his wife of 25 years, Trish.

Phil and I had stayed the best of friends ever since we had split up, exchanging birthday presents and popping in to see each other once or twice a year. But it was while he was ill that the hugs we exchanged became stronger and lasted longer. It made me realise how much we still cared for each other, despite the fact that our marriage hadn't worked.

As Dawn had sat by Phil's bedside over the previous five months, the two of them had had the chance to chat about everything under the sun. She also set up a closed Facebook group so that she could post a daily update of Phil's progress and condition. She asked everyone to check on this rather than ringing her because, with a three-year-old whom she hadn't seen for most of the day, she really couldn't cope with lots of phone calls in the evening. This was such a sensible idea and everyone appreciated being kept informed. It worked really well on many levels, as Dawn could chat about the various postings with Phil the next day.

They also discussed what Phil wanted should the worst happen. So, when the time came to organise Phil's funeral and memorial service, Dawn knew exactly what to do.

I was so pleased that Dawn stayed with us the night before the funeral. The service was very moving, with just family and closest friends attending. Later, there was a memorial service which Dawn decided to hold at our church, Meadows Community Church in Wigston, where over 300 people attended. Phil would have been amazed at how many people loved and respected him, and some turned up from areas of his life Dawn didn't even know. For instance, none of us had any idea that when he said he was going off to coach some youngsters on a Saturday morning, he was in fact coaching a Paralympic team in Leicester.

Amazingly, Dawn managed to hold it together as she gave a wonderful tribute to her dad. I don't think there was a dry eye in the church. There was a common sense of grief that we had lost someone who was very special, and it was particularly sad that, after putting up such a courageous fight, he had finally succumbed to this cruel disease. It was a shock to everyone, but there was a realisation that, for each one of us, our life was richer for having known Phil.

As December approached, it was sad to realise that this year Christmas would be very different and I think it really affected me. I went down with a very nasty chest infection that turned into whooping cough and it took weeks before I felt really well again. And just when we thought it couldn't get any worse, Laurie's mum, Dawn's mother-in-law (also named Dawn), became critically ill and was in intensive care over the Christmas period. Having lost Jeanne and Phil, the possibility that we could lose Dawn Sr was unbearable. Thankfully, she survived after spending many weeks in hospital.

Ever since we decided to move house, I had spent about four hours a day sorting through the monumental amount of 'stuff' that we had accumulated in and around the Manor. It was a marathon task but such a worthwhile one. The charity shops and a friend who supplied 'car boot' dealers did well out of it all, and a few items went to auction. As far as our new house was concerned, the furniture that was there suited it so well that we asked if we could buy the house with most of the contents, and the vendors agreed.

Our purchaser had asked for the furniture in some rooms in the Manor to be included in the sale so, in the end, we decided to leave a lot of items behind. Having sold the contents at Quorn House at auction for next to nothing, we weren't prepared to do that again. We had lots of furniture that had been refurbished to fit in with the curtains and colourings of the Manor and it seemed a shame to move it. In the end, we realised we would rather give it to the delightful family who would be moving in, and leave them to decide what to do with it.

We took possession of the new house a month before we left the Manor, which was really helpful. It meant that Peter could set up the office and be there for the tradespeople who were coming in daily to redecorate and make a few alterations and additions. With each daily trip I made, I loaded up my car, taking clothes and kitchen items, pictures and pottery. It worked brilliantly and was very exciting.

Our friend, Gwen, worked around every room in the Manor to check that each drawer and cupboard had been emptied and, together with our housekeeper, Gill, thoroughly cleaned it. It was one of those methodical processes that we just had to work our way through.

On the final day, our buyer came round to the Manor for the keys. He brought us champagne and we gave him a framed copy of a beautiful watercolour picture we had been given by the grandson of the original owners of the Manor. As I drove away, I said goodbye to this magnificent house and thanked it for 20 fabulous years.

When the new family moved in, they not only took possession of a substantially furnished home; there were also five beds made up and ready for them to sleep in. We were all happy at how everything had worked out and, amazingly, I wasn't sad. Leaving Ashby Folville was the end of a great chapter, and new adventures would now begin.

Having had the new house for a month had meant that on moving day we were well on the way to being settled. Within days we were straight. Once we were in and sorted, Mike admitted that he had fallen in love with the new house and had no regrets.

But what happened over the following few weeks was the most unexpected surprise of all. We had viewed the house in October, exchanged contracts in November, taken possession on 1 February, and Mike and I moved in on 1 March. Over the next few weeks, the garden transformed its already beautiful form into something extraordinary. Trees of so many varieties came into leaf in all kinds of shapes and colours. Shrubs and plants suddenly emerged out of the soil with an array of bright and beautiful colours. Then, to top it all, the sun shone on the house all day long as it moved around the four sides of the property. We could not believe what we were witnessing. It was the most beautiful garden and plot of land we had ever seen, let alone owned.

Some time later, I asked David and Jo, the previous owners, for the name of the person they had employed to landscape the grounds. Apparently, when they bought the property 15 years previously, it hardly had a proper garden at all, but their gardener had designed it himself and created a masterpiece along the way. We were so thrilled to be here and we knew we had made the right decision to move. We felt blessed that we now had a perfect new home for us to enjoy for the rest of our days.

The Rosemary Conley Online team of Directors were very good in covering for me during this hectic transitional period and it was lovely to welcome them to our new abode for the next Board meeting. They all *loved* their new 'B&B'!

Unfortunately, having spent so much time on my feet over the last few months as I cleared two large houses, I discovered an unexpected health problem. I had developed an acute pain in one of my feet – as though I had a small ball inside my instep – so I consulted my GP. Dr Gareth Childlow is brilliant and he had been wonderful with Jeanne; in fact she had said she was in love with him, which always made me smile! When I showed him my feet he remarked, 'Blimey! They've done a few miles!' And indeed they had. I had taught over 10,000 aerobics classes and squeezed my toes into stilettos for the last 50 years. Now I was paying for it, as he thought it was osteoarthritis and suggested I see a specialist. An MRI scan revealed acute arthritis, and I proceeded to have steroid injections to help with the pain. Before long, the other foot was affected too.

***

At the end of the year, I celebrated my 70th birthday. On the Saturday before the actual day, Peter and his partner, Paul, had invited Mike and me to lunch on a steam train on the Great Central Railway. The route starts from Loughborough and travels along the line past Quorn,

Mountsorrel and Birstall. This is a somewhat remarkable coincidence because our offices used to be in Quorn, where we could regularly hear the train's whistle as it passed by; we had lived at the Old Parsonage in Mountsorrel; and now I hold my weekly classes at Birstall Golf Club, right next to the steam railway station!

Peter has been a volunteer on this heritage railway since he was a lad, and now is a qualified driver of its vintage diesel trains, but today we were dining on the steam train with all its luxury of bygone years. When we returned to Loughborough station, some two hours later, who should be there to greet us but Dawn, Laurie and our grandson, Isaac! They then escorted us into the waiting room, where I was bowled over to see a wonderful group of very special people. There were our dear friends Ian and Ruth Coffey, Angie and her husband Simon Higgins (Angie had worked with Mike and me for 25 years), Joan and Peter Stephens (Joan is my journalist friend who was there when I found out I was pregnant over 40 years ago and has been a close friend ever since), John and Alex Montague (John is Chairman of our Trustees at Steps and is a close friend) and Sarah Skelton (ex-franchisee and now my friend and Co-Director at Rosemary Conley Online). I was astonished that these special friends had travelled from far and wide to be there for my birthday.

Apparently, Dawn and Peter had cooked up this great idea of hiring a *private* steam train, no less, and had arranged for a birthday cake and champagne to be served to the special guests as we were taken along the whole railway track again. But the great bonus, now, was that all the men could go on the footplate and be part of the process of driving the train. Our four-year-old grandson Isaac was in his element, of course, and Mike loved it! All the male guests took their turn and had a whale of a time. It was such a special day for me – and everyone – and yet again, Dawn had come up with a wonderful surprise for my special birthday. She was aided and abetted by Peter, who knew how to arrange such a privileged special event. It was truly memorable.

***

We had a wonderful Christmas but, as I was dismantling all the trimmings, I had an accident. Wearing my varifocals, I missed my footing on the staircase, fell down just two stairs and landed with my right foot twisted under me, straining all my ligaments. After lots of physiotherapy I was still in great pain, so I asked my foot specialist to X-ray it. When he looked at the results, he could see that two of my toes had in fact been dislocated, and now had relocated themselves. No wonder I was in such pain! He told me that he would have to operate to break these two toes and screw them back into the correct place.

The operation was a success, but sadly my feet were still in agony. Walking around the food hall doing my weekly shopping or indeed walking *any* distance made me feel sick with the pain. What I found surprising was how tiring being in constant pain can be. I have never, ever, been someone to close my eyes and doze off on the sofa watching TV at the weekend, but suddenly I found I needed to. Dealing with constant pain is exhausting, and I decided to do everything I could to try to resolve it. I was determined not to give up.

I tried acupuncture, physiotherapy, orthotics, everything I could think of – when I suddenly found an old TENS machine. 'TENS' stands for 'transcutaneous electrical nerve stimulation' and is a non-invasive, drug-free method of controlling pain. TENS uses tiny electrical impulses which are sent through small pads placed on the skin to the nerves to modify your pain perception. TENS does not cure any physiological problem, but it can help control the pain.

On the basis that I couldn't have any more steroid injections and, in any event, they had had a really bad effect on my skin, making it paper thin, I thought I would give TENS a try. Remarkably, it did help, so I decided to use two TENS machines, one for each foot. By applying four pads to each foot every evening for 45 minutes, I was able to dramatically ease the pain. I did this for a year, and then we happened to visit Murray Watts, the acclaimed writer and director, who was helping me with this book. We stayed in his wonderful part-renovated castle in the far north of Scotland. Mike and I had flown up to Scotland and on to Freswick, which is three miles (about five km) from John o' Groats, so that Murray and I could go through the manuscript together. Extraordinarily, my feet felt much better, so for the duration of our stay I didn't use my TENS. Upon returning, and apart from a couple of really heavy days when I was on my feet all the time, I haven't used them since. It would seem that the electric current from the machine has programmed my brain to get used to the pain. The great news is that I now have significantly less pain and can walk relatively normally, often pain-free, in my cushioned trainers. My feet hurt if I wear high heels, but I keep those occasions to a minimum.

***

Meanwhile, in the middle of 2017, a few changes were happening within our online business. Tom, our IT whizz-kid Chief Technical Officer, decided he wanted to become a chef and sold some of his shares to enable him to live while he climbed the chef-ladder. Then Simon, our CEO, who was approaching his 60th birthday, wanted to retire, so it was decided that Sarah would take over responsibilities and become CEO. Sarah is an extraordinarily capable businesswoman and very hard-working, and naturally relishes challenges and initiatives. I was always around to discuss ideas and forward planning, but I knew that Sarah was totally capable of running the company on a day-to-day basis. I still recorded my daily 'Motivational Minutes', so there was fresh content on the site every day. I did press and PR and the photoshoots for our slimmers, but it soon became obvious that Sarah was enjoying being in control and, while I was Chairman, I was more of a sounding board than a controller.

At the end of 2017 I was approached by the European distributor of the anti-ageing facial exerciser called Facial-Flex® that I had been using for almost 20 years. We had started selling Facial-Flex® within our mail-order business with our Clubs, and we continued to sell it through our Rosemary Conley Online shop.

In January 2017 I had been interviewed by *The Times* and later by the *Mail on Sunday*'s *You* magazine with some positive comments being made about my appearance. If my face looked a little younger than the 70 years I now was, it was totally due to Facial-Flex®. As a result of this positive publicity, the European distributor called me to ask if I would like to take over personally the distributorship of Facial-Flex® for the UK. I immediately asked Mike for his opinion and he was all for it, as was Peter.

So, with Mike's blessing, Peter and I began a new adventure. It was fun to be creating a business of our own again and we worked hard to create a new website, marketing and supporting literature to promote and sell the product. It was just like old times when we used to sell my audio cassettes from the Old Parsonage over 30 years ago. Even our former Clubs Director, Angie, came back to help us with our accounts.

***

In 2018 Waise, my beloved lurcher, was showing signs of ageing, which was not surprising now that she was in her 13th year. The vet had recommended that she have a couple of teeth out but, when a blood test was done, he discovered that her kidney function wasn't good enough to put her under an anaesthetic. She was also diagnosed with a weakness in the base of her spine. However, I decided that no matter what her problems, for the moment, she was cheerful and lively and loved trotting with me into the wood each morning with our two other dogs, black Labs BB and Sky, and then spending the rest of her day sleeping. Waise looked very healthy for her age but, most of all, she was happy – provided she could sit with us on the sofa.

In the summer, we decided to relive one of our past pleasures and take a canal boating holiday with the dogs. We fondly remembered our first canal boating experience from 30 years ago and thought it would be fun. With a life jacket for Waise and great excitement all round, we boarded the narrowboat a few miles from where we live. BB, Sky and Waise were very excited, and it was even more exciting when Dawn and Isaac joined us on that first evening as we sailed up the river. So far, so good.

After we ate together, Dawn and Isaac left for home and Mike and I settled down for the night with the dogs in their respective dog beds. Then, the heavens opened and it began to blow a gale! As we lay in bed, the boat was rocking and Sky was shaking from head to toe. Waise kept pacing up and down the length of the boat and neither Mike nor I could sleep in the narrow double bed. Tempers became frayed, resulting in a virtually sleepless night for everyone – except for BB who seemed cool with everything.

I decided to take the dogs for a walk along the towpath at 5.30 am and was grateful for the peace after such a disturbed night. We both felt shattered; so when I returned to the boat, Mike and I took an executive decision. We would call Peter, my PA, and ask him to collect us, drive us all home and then return to fetch the boat! Having been a boat-owner himself, Peter was very happy to take the opportunity to sail a narrowboat again. Over the following couple of evenings, Peter and his partner Paul took great delight in sailing the vessel back to base with gin and tonic in hand, relaxing in the peaceful pleasure of river-boating that had sadly eluded us.

***

It was in the spring of 2019 that Waise suddenly lost her back-end strength and couldn't climb on to the sofa. I helped her up, but I knew there was something wrong. Over the next two days she went from bad to worse – to the point where she couldn't even climb up a 4-inch (10-cm) step from the garden into the kitchen. We tried a ramp, but it didn't help. Then we had to take that horrible, heartbreaking decision.

The vet and a nurse came to the house and I said goodbye to my beloved, faithful friend, while she lay in my arms. I had never loved a dog as much as I loved Waise.

Mike's cousin, Peter Saunders, who had shared a sofa with Waise when he and his wife Belinda stayed with us after supporting our A Question of Brains event, texted me when he heard the sad news. He said Waise had so much personality he was sure she was 50% dog and 50% human! That summed her up. She was such a character and had us all wrapped around her elegant paw.

26

Fresh opportunities and new beginnings

2019–20

Losing Waise left a gaping hole in my life. I really loved that dog as she was such a character and a real friend. We created a beautiful space where she could be buried, under a pretty little tree that I call our 'Bethlehem tree'. This tree is very old and has a striking outline, with rocks all around it, making it look almost biblical. It grows randomly, all alone, in the middle of one of the fields at the back of our house. I enjoy visiting the grave and chatting to her as I pass by on my walks.

Despite the sadness of losing my lovely Waise, the year developed into a very exciting transitional period of my life.

As I have already mentioned, I loved working on my own magazine for the 18 years that we published it, so you can imagine my delight when I was asked to become Editor-in-Chief of an in-house magazine entitled *Life & Style* for FirstPort, a residential development management company. FirstPort forms part of the group of companies that included Appello, the firm that bought Rosemary Conley Online in 2014. From my point of view, knowing the drastic decline in sales of printed media, it was a joy to be asked to oversee a publication with a guaranteed distribution of around 100,000 copies, because it is given to all residents of the retirement developments managed by FirstPort across the country. *Life & Style* was to be given a major revamp and the company wanted me to oversee its transformation.

I was thrilled to take on the role, particularly as the magazine is only published twice a year, which meant that I could fit it in around all my other activities. The first issue was published in the autumn of 2019 and looked impressive as it was printed on high-quality paper with high production values.

***

My keen interest in ice skating continued, and I suggested to Mark Hanretty that perhaps he could teach me a brand-new routine, similar to how we had skated together on *Dancing on Ice*. So Mark set about choreographing a skating programme that would be within my capability but would hopefully show that I had progressed since I last appeared on *DOI* in 2012. So, in 2018, we started practising this new routine and it was fabulous to be working together on a new 'skating project'. To help me keep my strength and posture during those six months when Mark was unavailable (as he was back preparing for the 2019 series of *Dancing on Ice*), I started having ballet lessons with a dancing professional, Rosie McSwiney, who came to the house each week. I was also keen to learn to be more elegant with my hands (a big ask for my knobbly arthritic hands – but hey, it was worth a try!) and also to have more elegant arms for when I skated. I really looked forward to my ballet sessions and I still do today. Rosie was committed to helping me look my best when, ultimately, I performed the new skating routine.

Once back from *DOI* in April, Mark started to work with me in earnest to perfect the routine that he had choreographed the year before, with a view to recording it. My arthritic feet were a major handicap, but I was determined not to give in. I always need a goal and this was a personal one. I was now 72 and I wanted to prove to myself that I could still perform an ice-dance routine and, hopefully, one that I could be proud of.

Mark and I skated every week, and in June I booked the whole ice rink at Nottingham Motorpoint Arena so that we could film on our own. Make-up artist Jane Tyler, and a film crew made up of Susannah and another camera operator, completed the team. It was really exciting and, with Mark's help, I skated for all I was worth. It was so exhilarating, even magical.

We were pleased with the way it went and looked forward to the end result once Susannah had edited the shots from both cameras. However, as I stepped off the ice at the end, I could hardly walk. It's amazing how adrenalin can anaesthetise your pain! I didn't feel a thing while I was skating, but once I stepped off the ice I was in agony.

I had already seen an orthopaedic foot surgeon and was awaiting my operation at the end of July, and this was part of my motivation to complete the filming. While I had managed my arthritis reasonably well, I had been suffering because my right foot now had partly collapsed after my accident 18 months earlier when I fell down those two pesky stairs. I knew I would be out of action for several months – and then Mark would be off again to do *DOI* – so it was a now-or-never opportunity.

Within a week, Susannah had edited the film and I showed it to Mike. He was really surprised and kept saying, 'Show me again.' In fact, he watched it three times in a row. Rosie, my ballet teacher, was also keen to watch it as she had a vested interest in my performance. She too was amazed and thrilled to see the finished video.

(For anyone interested, the video can be seen at <www.rosemaryconley. com> in the Rosemary's World – Ice Skating section.)

Some time later, I visited my chest specialist, Professor Ian Pavord, and I knew he was very interested in my ice-skating activities. I showed him the 90-second video on my iPad and he was astonished – not at my skating skills of course, but at the fact that this elderly person who had such limited lung capacity could complete such an activity at all! He asked if I would send him a recording of the routine 'so that I can show it at one of my Conferences – you are an inspiration!' Apparently, on paper, I should not have been physically able to do it, and he was really proud of the fact that I had.

Because of my chest issues and because I was feeling the effects of being over 70, I had been attending a local gym, run by physiotherapists, for personal training sessions. Within a few weeks, I could see the fitness benefits, which were printed out in technicolour after every session. The results are based on your performance determined by the heart monitor you wear for the duration of your session. To be able to see my calorie burn, as well as the increase in my stamina and endurance, was immensely encouraging. So much so that after six weeks I showed it to Mike. The next day he said, 'Book me in! I could do with some of that!'

As soon as I knew my date for my foot operation, I was determined to strengthen my legs so that I would be as strong as possible before I went into surgery. Hopefully, it could help me to recover faster. I had never previously looked forward to surgery, but I was really looking forward to this one. I had been in agony for months and I was optimistic that things were about to change for the better.

My surgeon, Mr Maneesh Bhatia, had told me that it would probably be 18 months before I would be back to full fitness again and he asked if I was prepared for that. I was determined that it would not take that long but, if it did, so be it.

I had the surgery with a 'spinal block' because my asthma specialist wasn't keen on my having a general anaesthetic, and everything went well. Judith, my physio/trainer, gave me some post-operative exercises, explaining that while I was having an operation on my foot, it was not affecting my knee or my hip so I could still exercise the leg as a whole. From day 3, I started Judith's simple rehab exercises while lying on the sofa, and I did them several times every day. Keeping my leg moving not only proved unbelievably effective in retaining leg strength and mobility; it also reduced my risk of deep vein thrombosis, particularly as I couldn't wear compression socks due to the plaster on my foot.

During those three months, and while I was wheeling myself around in a wheelchair or hopping about with the help of a zimmer frame, Peter and I organised that year's A Question of Brains dinner for the charity Steps. I was due to be signed off after my op the following week, but on the actual night of the event I was still wearing a surgical shoe. However, because I was so agile, I am not sure anyone noticed it under my long evening dress.

The following week, I saw Mr Bhatia. He was amazed and delighted with my progress and I was signed off. I could walk perfectly well and everything was almost back to normal. I was even back ice skating (in a fashion) after four months. To be out of constant pain was liberating. I felt like a new woman. Such swift progress was due to the skills of a superb surgeon, combined with dedicated physiotherapy that I could practise myself and personal training at Bridge4, the physio gym that had helped me. It was life-changing.

This experience was part of the motivation behind my creation of a video-based resource website in 2021, but more on that later.

Ironically, my foot operation also created something of a minor miracle totally unassociated with my feet. For the previous five or so years I had been struggling with my voice, which permanently sounded as though I had a cold and was croaking. This was particularly embarrassing when I was doing radio interviews, and I had no idea how I could resolve it. Extraordinarily, after the operation on my foot, my voice was completely normal again. I didn't have a general anaesthetic, so there was no pipe put down my throat that could have dislodged something. Whether it was the special antibiotics I have no idea. But, whatever it was, my voice is now totally back to normal – thank goodness!

***

In the December of 2019 I had a big, but very welcome, surprise. Sarah Skelton, who was now CEO of Rosemary Conley Online (RCO), called me for a chat. I was the largest shareholder of the company Digital Wellbeing Ltd, the parent company that owned the online weight-loss Club, and she was wondering if I would like to trade in some of my shares in exchange for getting my name back. I couldn't quite believe it! *Wow!* I was so excited.

One of the hardest things for me when our company went into administration in 2014 was the fact that someone else could use my name. I had never asked to get my name back, but I had hoped, even prayed, that one day I would. I was *so* grateful to Sarah for thinking of me and of course I said 'Yes, please!' She explained there would be a transitional period of 13 months while the company phased out the use of my name and introduced new branding.

By now I had very little to do with the online business anyway, apart from attending Board meetings and recording 'Motivational Minutes', so I was more than happy to step down as Chairman and as a Director; basically I walked away. Financially, it made no difference to me as I had decided not to take a salary over the last few years. Also, since then, two of the other Directors had left – Simon had retired and 'tech-whizz-kid' Tom had left to train as a chef. So now, in 2019, Sarah was very much running the business as CEO, supported by a Non-Executive Board of Directors, and she was doing it brilliantly.

I had always had a great deal of respect for Sarah from the days when she had her highly successful Rosemary Conley franchise. She was the only franchisee who had been appointed by our company as a Consultant.

Sarah is one of the most capable, hard-working, prepared-to-learn-anything people I have ever met. I had no hesitation in walking away from Rosemary Conley Online, feeling totally confident that the company could go from strength to strength under her leadership.

I had no particular plans to use my name going forward other than for writing books and possibly creating a website for older people, but at least I knew that after 1 February 2021 no-one else could trade or use my name. That was personally not only a relief but also exciting.

***

I continue to be inspired by what visionary individuals can achieve when they set their mind to it. One such example is a visitor attraction that has been created in Leicestershire, not far from where we live. As a Deputy Lieutenant of Leicestershire, I was asked to assess an application for a Queen's Award for Voluntary Service, which had been made on its behalf.

In 2007, Steve Cramp had been walking with his wife and children when he looked down over a bridge at an abandoned railway track. At that moment, a seed was sown in his mind to transform this jungle of undergrowth and restore a length of what used to be the Mountsorrel Railway. Through Steve's vision, and with the dedicated support of his wife and children, the Mountsorrel and Rothley Community Heritage Centre was born, benefiting the local area in a multitude of ways, from encouraging community cohesion between volunteers, to offering a local attraction that is free to visitors and that embraces history, wildlife, a museum, construction initiatives and a cafe. In 2019, and before the Covid-19 pandemic, it attracted 138,000 visitors in a year!

It was 18 months later that I had the privilege of supporting Leicestershire's Lord Lieutenant, Mike Kapur OBE, in June 2021, as he officially presented the centre with the Queen's Award for Voluntary Service, and witnessing the pure joy and drive experienced by the scores of volunteers who had created such a positive environment for the benefit of the community. It was a memorable day and one that I felt immensely privileged to share.

I am learning more and more to value each day and the experiences that come along. The older we are, inevitably the more aware we become of the fragility of life and the preciousness of every single day. This feeling is never more poignant than when a close friend succumbs to a life-threatening disease. In 2019, three close friends fell victim to cancer and it was heart-wrenching to witness.

***

Claudia Stevens was one of our earliest franchisees, and she was one of those really special people who always thought of others before herself. Whenever she saw me featured in the press, and always on my birthday, Claudia would write a lovely card full of words of encouragement. One year, she joined Mary and me for our Austrian activity holiday and I had the opportunity to get to know her even more. Then one day, Claudia called me to tell me that she had cancer and that her time was limited. It was devastating news and I felt so helpless. Thankfully, she had a wonderful family around her and a loving husband, John, to support her, but for those of us further away there is that feeling of helplessness; all we can do is to write letters and cards, send flowers and pray.

One lesson I learned a few years ago was to write to those we love before they are gone to express how much they have meant to us in our lifetime, detailing the way they have enhanced our lives and putting into words how special they really are. I wrote such a letter to Claudia. When she received it, she called me and asked if I would read it at her funeral.

Claudia lost her battle on Christmas Day, 2019, and in the following January I had the privilege of reading out my 'letter to Claudia' to a packed church where Claudia had been an active member. Over our heads on the big screens was a picture of Claudia looking like a film star, utterly defying her 64 years. It was a sad but beautiful occasion.

***

Marion Vaughan first joined my classes at the Holiday Inn as a member, but it didn't take me long to see her energy and talent. So I invited her to work out facing the group and exercising at a high-impact level for those who wanted to work out more energetically. She had supported me in my classes for 30 years. Recently, she had survived breast cancer surgery and, throughout her extensive treatment, the whole class was incredibly supportive. We all signed a get-well card every week that she was unable to be with us, and she came through her radiotherapy and chemotherapy with great bravery and fortitude. Marion was back with us and all was well – until she found herself experiencing severe pain in her hip. As the months passed and the pain persisted, it was discovered that Marion had developed bone cancer. We were all in shock. Marion had always been there, always cheerful, always supportive and always fit. We couldn't believe this was happening.

Sadly, after Christmas, Marion's condition worsened and I visited her in hospital. Three days later her husband, Roger, called me to say he had been told that Marion was unlikely to last the night; would I like to go and see her to say goodbye?

It was heart-wrenching to see her so very poorly. We had so many happy memories and it was unbelievable that this was happening to superfit Marion. She died in the early hours of the following morning, aged 61.

I hired a minibus for all the class to attend Marion's funeral. Everyone was devastated that we had lost such a good friend but felt privileged that we had enjoyed her company over so many years. The fact that 30 class members attended the funeral said it all. We loved Marion.

***

Joan Stephens had been a close friend ever since I first started my business in 1972. She was a journalist and had always been encouraging and a strong advocate of my work. We had shared the ups and downs that each of us had experienced in our lives, and our friendship had deepened over the years. I never knew Joan's age and it didn't matter. We would meet up once or twice a year for a catch-up lunch and put the world to rights. We were genuinely fond of each other and respectful of each other's careers.

When I received a phone call from Joan in 2019 to say she was in hospital not far from where we live, I immediately visited. Joan was always bright and sparky and I loved her. She was very bright, had her opinions and knew everyone around Leicestershire, having worked for decades on our local newspaper and, before that, on Radio Leicester where I first met her. She was something of a celebrity in her own right, having interviewed such notable names as Omar Sharif and Margaret Thatcher! But now she had been diagnosed with cancer.

'I don't want any fuss and I don't want it to be public knowledge,' she said to me. 'I don't want people to feel sorry for me.'

We would chat about old times and always had a chuckle when I visited her, whether in hospital or later at home. I decided to write one of my 'Thank you for being you' letters to Joan, because she had been such a great friend for almost 50 years and I wanted her to know how much she meant to me. Then I received a phone call to say that Joan was back in hospital, along with her husband Peter, who had suffered a fall. Joan passed away peacefully aged 89, and it was only a short while later that Peter passed away too. It was so, so sad.

***

Having lost three such special friends, I was shaken. Life suddenly became even more precious with the realisation that none of us knows when a health disaster is likely to strike. And one thing is for sure: none of us could have anticipated what was about to sweep across the planet. The world as we knew it was about to change for ever.

27

A changing world and boosting immunity

2020–1

As we celebrated the dawning of a new decade, I welcomed the year with great anticipation. Mike and I were looking forward to our family skiing trip with Dawn, Laurie, Isaac and Harriet. We would stay at our favourite hotel, Der Berghof, in Lech, Austria, at the February half-term and I was excited to be thinking I would be back there four months later, as the bookings for our Austrian activity holiday in June were flowing in.

Just as we were packing for our skiing trip, there were rumours and rumblings of a new virus that was now causing concern among the medical profession, not just in the UK but in other countries too. As I walked about in the city of Leicester, I could see some people wearing masks and it all seemed a bit strange.

When we returned from our relaxing holiday in Austria, everything began to change. The virus was given a name, Covid-19, and around the world more and more people were dying from it. In the UK there was talk of drastic measures – even a national 'lockdown' – coming into force soon. So, for the first time in almost 50 years, I decided to suspend my Monday evening classes – for what I thought would be just a few weeks. We created a closed WhatsApp group, which went on to provide an invaluable means of connection between us all over the coming difficult months. Through that app, we celebrated birthdays together, supported one another through life's trials and tribulations, and became a really tight circle of friends. Early each morning two members, Jennie and Michelle, posted beautiful pictures and wise words to greet us, and every day I put together a fitness challenge to try to keep everyone active. It was a rewarding enterprise and kept the spirit of the class alive throughout the lockdown.

I was due to have surgery on my hand (I had several snapped ligaments) and was booked into hospital for Monday, 23 March 2020, but with all the news of an imminent lockdown I was understandably anxious on many levels. The surgeon called me to say he was prepared to proceed if *I* was. Without hesitation I agreed. I knew that if I didn't have the surgery, I was in danger of more ligaments snapping, causing my hand to be unable to even pick up a pen!

Thankfully, the operation went to plan and I was home that evening just as the announcement was made that the country was going into lockdown and everyone was to stay at home.

None of us realised how momentous this change was for the whole nation. We were all told to 'work from home', so Peter, my brilliant PA (and Manager of our Facial Flex® business), took immediate action. He rushed to the office and whisked away everything he needed to be able to work from his home five miles (8 km) away. We also suggested that our home help should stay at home too.

Then I had a call from my GP, Dr Gareth Chidlow, explaining that because of my lung conditions (asthma and bronchiectasis), I was considered 'clinically extremely vulnerable', so it was imperative that I should now self-isolate and not go out at all. As this new coronavirus, Covid-19, was causing life-threatening breathing issues, Dr Gareth knew that the implications for me would be extremely serious if I were to contract it. Mike and Dawn were really worried.

With my hand and arm in a half-plaster and bandaged up to the elbow, I wasn't going anywhere anyway, but I hadn't quite anticipated how helpless I would become following the operation. Thankfully, Mike, as well as looking after me, took over every task in the house: cooking, cleaning, laundry, bed making, dog feeding – everything!

Ahead of the op, I had been practising with my left hand in an attempt to learn to write, clean my teeth and apply make-up, but the one thing I could not do with one hand was curl my hair. Mike scored double gold stars for effort as he tried to be my hairstylist too! I so appreciated all his efforts.

It soon became obvious that the coronavirus was causing havoc everywhere, but I think it was when the Prime Minister was hospitalised that we all realised how serious this situation had become. So many people were dying in hospital and the daily tally of diagnosed cases was increasing exponentially. It also became apparent that the individuals at greatest risk were those who were older and/or overweight or obese. Mike and I would sit down every evening at 5 pm to watch the Downing Street briefing to learn of the latest statistics and get an update on matters such as the supply of personal protective equipment (PPE), the need for more ventilators and the rising numbers of deaths. I felt for the government ministers and the experts standing alongside them who, in the absence of the Prime Minister, had suddenly been placed in the firing line of the press and members of the public and expected to answer unanswerable questions. It was a dreadful situation and it is not surprising that sometimes there was a look of panic in their eyes.

Everyone's heartfelt sympathy was going out to the NHS staff who were working so hard and selflessly to save lives. In desperate circumstances they were trying to get on top of this invisible enemy that was waging war on the world. It must have been harrowing for them. The word 'unprecedented' was being used so many times in news bulletins. It was truly frightening and the effect of the virus was heartbreaking.

With no-one coming into the house, we felt I was protected. Mike and I found ourselves settling into a pace of life that was very different from what we were used to. Dawn immediately volunteered to do our shopping and also cooked some delicious meals for us, which were such a treat, but she refused to step inside the house.

It seemed as though normal life had paused and, thankfully, because of where we live in the countryside, it was no hardship to be isolated; but we were very mindful of those who would find themselves on their own with no family to support them. It must have been unbearably tough, and our hearts particularly went out to those families who lived in tower blocks with children, unable to go outside. I kept wondering what I could do to help in any possible way, but at this early point I was forced to recognise my own helplessness.

Mike was amazing in doing all that he did, and he also became my nurse – carefully following directions from the hand-physio, via video chat, when it was time to change my dressings. Before long, I was able to do a little more with my recovering hand and arm, and the physio visited me at home to remove the stitches and supervise my physio sessions. Soon I was out of plaster and could type, sort out my hair and also help with the housework.

Despite all the heart-wrenching devastation that Covid-19 had created, there were some truly positive stories too to lift our hearts. Perhaps the most famous example was that of Captain Tom Moore, who set himself the challenge to walk 100 lengths of his garden every day until his 100th birthday in order to raise funds for NHS Charities Together. As Mike and I sat up in bed each morning to watch BBC Breakfast TV, it came as no surprise that Captain Tom, with his wit and wisdom, had captured the hearts of the nation. On the day of his birthday, 21 days after he started, he had raised an astonishing £30 million. Captain Tom's words of wisdom inspired us through this dark time. As a Second World War veteran who had seen active service in Burma (now Myanmar), he had the experience and authority to assure everyone that 'tomorrow will be a good day'. He even recorded a song, 'You'll Never Walk Alone', with Michael Ball that went to No.1 in the singles chart. In the end he raised almost £34 million and, with Gift Aid, the sum approached £40 million for NHS Charities Together!

A few months later, we watched Captain Tom become Captain *Sir* Tom Moore on the lawn at Windsor Castle when the Queen gave him a knighthood. This was the sort of tonic we all needed, and Captain Tom's example inspired us all and kept us going on the darkest days. There is no doubt that he sowed a seed of hope in my own heart.

First of all, Mike and I began to benefit from a different rhythm of life. We appreciated that we had a spacious house and garden and could go out for walks in the countryside around us. We enjoyed each other's company and even embraced being away from the hustle and bustle of normal everyday life. It was good for us as a couple as life took on a different pace, and we enjoyed it.

After taking a couple of weeks off to recover after the surgery on my hand, I felt the urge to be creative. I realised that I had the golden opportunity of 'having time', which was too good to miss, so I put my thinking cap on and made a plan. I began to think about the future for others and to consider how 'tomorrow could be a good day', despite the challenges. I thought some more about the possibility of creating a video-based website to help the over-50s live longer, healthier and happier lives. In a little under a year's time, on 1 February 2021, I would have my name back and I could create a website with the domain name <www. rosemaryconley.com>. This was an opportunity to reconnect with those people who had been fans of our Clubs, magazine, books and videos/ DVDs in the 1990s and 2000s and beyond – people who were probably around my age now but who still wanted to stay fit and healthy. I started putting out a few feelers to experts, hoping to interview them for the site, and I received nothing but enthusiastic encouragement and engagement. It was really exciting.

It soon became clear that the country would be in lockdown for quite a while, so I also found myself with the urge to write – to do something! I called my Literary Agent, Luigi Bonomi, with an idea for a new book and he said, 'What the publishers are really looking for is a book based on boosting immunity, but it needs to be done super-quickly, within six weeks, so it can be published as an e-book while the coronavirus is still topical.'

Looking back, we had no idea that Covid-19 would still be topical more than a year later!

I love a challenge, so I thought I would call my friend and fitness-expert-colleague Mary Morris to put the idea to her. Mary was really up for it and we both agreed that, inspired by Captain Tom, we would give the royalties for the e-book to NHS Charities Together.

Between the two of us, Mary is the academic, so she directed me to various academic papers and books on the subject of 'how to boost immunity'. It made fascinating reading and I set about putting the information into understandable language that would hopefully educate those, like me, who were learning about it for the first time. Then I put together a 28-day eating plan and recipes that incorporated immunity-boosting foods.

Mary set about creating an immunity-boosting workout which was inspiring. She designed it so that folks would be able to increase the intensity of their workout over the four weeks. We both worked full-on to create our little e-book of around 25,000 words, and within five weeks *The 28-Day Immunity Plan* was finished and sent off to Luigi, ready for him to engage with publishers to see if anyone was interested. Penguin jumped at the opportunity, and by the beginning of August 2020 the e-book was published. The *Daily Express* and *The Mirror* bought serialisation rights, which meant that headline banners and centre double-page spreads, offering extensive coverage, launched the media publicity campaign.

Penguin asked if I had any contacts with national radio. I had met Michael Ball on a few occasions and was a big fan of his, so I hoped I might be able to get on his Sunday morning Radio 2 show. On my 'bucket list' was the wish to meet Chris Evans. I knew he had moved to Virgin Radio, so I wrote to the programme's celebrity-booker explaining that I was a huge fan and that I knew Chris followed a plant-based diet so I had specifically included plant-based options for each meal within the eating plan and *please* could I be interviewed by Chris?

When I heard from Penguin that both Chris Evans and Michael Ball were happy to invite me on, I was thrilled! I knew that appearing on their shows would make a massive difference to the success of the e-book and, if the e-book was sufficiently successful, the publishers had said they would consider publishing it in paperback for January – which is what Mary and I really wanted.

On the Sunday after the e-book publication, I woke up early like an excited child at Christmas. I was so thrilled at the prospect of chatting to Michael Ball. He is such a kind and generous, lovable guy and I had seen him in concert and chatted with him on *This Morning* several times back in the day.

The interview was a joy and Michael was fabulous. I love that man. My class members were so excited that I was on BBC Radio 2 because they too love Michael. In fact, who doesn't?

The following Wednesday, I was to appear on Chris Evan's *Breakfast Show*. I had been a huge fan of Chris ever since he took over from Sir Terry Wogan on BBC Radio 2, and we had followed him when he moved to Virgin Radio. There is something magical about Chris Evans. He is a force for good and someone who transforms your space in the early mornings as you prepare for the day ahead, to the point where you forget the time and become embraced and engrossed in his enthusiasm for life, which exudes from his every pore.

As I prepared to speak to Chris I was as nervous as a kitten. Over the years, I have observed that Chris has one of the fastest brains I know and he is famous for not asking the obvious questions, which of course makes him a brilliant interviewer. Realising this, Mike was pacing up and down the kitchen in nervous anticipation. I was in Mike's study, where we have built a radio studio cubicle. I regularly do interviews from there, usually without any nerves – but this was different. I found out later that Dawn was pacing up and down in her house too!

Moments later, Chris came on through my headphones and we chatted happily. He thought it was funny that I was nervous. By now, the e-book had become a bestseller in its category, so he waxed lyrical with encouragement and congratulations as he always does with his guests. We talked for about 10 minutes and it was electrifying. At the end of the interview, I said my goodbyes to Chris and the producer and went back into the kitchen, where Mike was waiting with very supportive comments and a big hug, which I felt I desperately needed. In fact, I felt as though I needed to lie down in a darkened room! I was exhausted and elated all at the same time. Of course, I would have loved to have been with Chris in person, but that wasn't possible due to the Covid restrictions – so actually meeting Chris Evans in person is still on my bucket list!

A few weeks later, we heard the great news that Penguin was happy to publish *The 28-Day Immunity Plan* as a paperback, but to do so we needed to double the content. Mary and I quickly stepped into action, fired up with encouragement from knowing that the e-book had done so well. We were also receiving some wonderful feedback on how good it was making people feel, and how much weight they had lost.

I had always been optimistic that Penguin would take the book to paperback so, once the manuscript for the e-book had been sent off, I decided to run a 'diet trial'. Historically, I had done many diet trials to test the effectiveness of my diet books, but *The 28-Day Immunity Plan* was a different kind of eating plan from any I had written before. It was not a calorie-counted eating regime. It was a new approach. You could eat as many vegetables and salad as you wanted, but snacks were forbidden. This was an eating plan that asked you to commit for 28 days and, if you did, hopefully you would feel much healthier at the end of it.

By running a diet trial, I would get an idea of what the average weight loss might be after 28 days. I also knew that people's experiences and comments, results and responses would provide useful extra words and be a valuable endorsement of the plan for the paperback if it happened.

I decided to ask my class members, via my WhatsApp group, if any of them would like to participate in the trial. When eight of them volunteered immediately, I set about creating the necessary questionnaires and, on 1 June, Brigitte, Lesley, Michelle, Mike, Jennie and her son Kevin and sisters Helen and Dawn commenced the trial.

I phoned them every Monday evening for a catch-up and to see how they were progressing. It soon became clear what wonderful results were emerging.

'I can't believe how well I'm sleeping!'

'My get-up-and-go has come back – I have so much energy!'

'I just feel so well!'

'I can't believe how much weight I've lost!'

The results were incredibly encouraging. Over 28 days, all eight of them had lost an average of 10 lb (4.5 kg). I couldn't have been more thrilled! But what followed next was a real surprise.

At the end of the trial they all said: 'Please can we carry on? I feel so fit and healthy I just want to lose the rest of my lockdown weight and to carry on feeling this good!'

And carry on they did.

By October most of them had reached their goal weight and I decided to organise a photoshoot. There was a break in the lockdown in the autumn of 2020 and so the photoshoot was planned for 3 November. I bought in a variety of clothes, booked the room at the golf club where I normally hold my classes, as it was a large airy space, and asked my photographer of many years, Alan Olley, if he would be prepared to come and photograph my trial team. I even booked a local make-up artist. We were all set. But there was a problem.

We knew the Prime Minister was about to announce another lockdown as the cases of the coronavirus were rocketing and the daily death toll was alarming. The photoshoot was planned for the Tuesday. The announcement was to be on the Saturday evening before, and we were all on tenterhooks. When Prime Minister Boris Johnson announced that the lockdown was going to begin on the following Thursday, we all let out a massive sigh of relief. I called all the volunteers and asked if they were still happy to come, and everyone said an emphatic 'Yes'. The photoshoot was definitely *on*!

On the day, there was a buzz in the air. We had our film crew there too, and everyone was so happy to be meeting up again, albeit with face masks, sanitiser, social distancing and chair covers. My daughter Dawn came along as the 'Covid police' to make extra sure that we all adhered to the restrictions. We had the most special time together. I knew beforehand that two of the volunteers were unable to join us because of work commitments, but the remaining six certainly had a day to remember. They all looked amazing having lost their weight – they were the slimmest I had ever seen them – and now they were professionally made up, with their hair styled, and fashionably dressed, each with two stylish outfits. Photographer Alan did a fabulous job putting them at ease and catching them at their perfect angle. The men looked so handsome in their smart suits, and the women looked beautiful in their dresses or separates.

It was great to see everyone thoroughly enjoying the shoot – and how we had longed for such a precious experience of togetherness! After each volunteer had been photographed and filmed, I said they could go if they wished, but none of them did. They all sat chatting and soaking up the sheer pleasure of being back together again, albeit socially distanced, and feeling fabulous right up to the last minute! We all agreed it was the 'highlight day of the year' because it felt *almost normal*, even though it was anything but.

Because of the success of my trialists at the end of June, Mary suggested she do a trial with some members of her local community but this time focusing on their fitness rather than their weight. She decided that she would specifically select volunteers from the older age group through her local media. Mary recruited 10 volunteers and put them through their paces each week in her garden. The aim was to see if they could show evidence of physical improvement in strength and stamina within the 28-day trial period.

Mary is a great motivator and her volunteers tried really hard to fulfil the tasks she had set them. The end results were impressive. Some had advanced from 'below average' at the beginning to 'excellent' after four weeks. The improvement was remarkable.

All of these results were collated and provided a highly motivational chapter within the book.

Soon the manuscript for the paperback was completed, with extra recipes, a fitness test and an advanced-strength workout from Mary to complete the programme. We managed to almost double the word count, and my Book Editor, Ione Walder, commissioned 24 photographs of the finished dishes made from the recipes. We even managed to squeeze in some 'before and after' pictures of each of my trialists at the back of the book the day before it went to print!

Mary and I both felt an enormous sense of relief when the book finally was emailed across. After all the proof-reading was completed and it had gone to the printers, we could relax – but not for long.

***

As soon as the book was sorted, I turned my attention to my new website. This was going to be a website that was very different. It was a fascinating challenge trying to create something I had never tried before. Unlike most websites, this one would consist entirely of videos – friendly and informative recordings to help the over-50s live longer, healthier, happier lives. However, it needed funding, so I asked Mike if he minded if I spent a chunk of our money to produce a website that would be unprofitable but would, I believed, help a lot of people. It was something I was passionate about and something I felt I would enjoy doing. Thankfully, he agreed, and I so appreciated his support.

Like all our new projects, this one began with Peter and me standing in front of a whiteboard with a marker pen. We soon managed to come up with a plan for the website. The aim was to include the following categories: boosting immunity, ageing well, health, exercise, food and nutrition, and motivation; plus, of course, there had to be an online shop. This resource would be free to the user, it had to be simple to navigate, and we wanted it to have a friendly but informative feel.

As soon as we had an idea of how the site was going to look, I created a very long list of subjects and topics I was aiming to cover and then I started recording with my Producer/Director Susannah Goodwin, who was full of great ideas and valuable guidance. Susannah is a superstar!

After I discussed the site with Mary, she was very enthusiastic and keen to help, particularly with the exercises. Then I wanted to bring in advice from physiotherapists. Fortunately, at the gym that Mike and I attend, the owner/physiotherapist and one of her neuro-physios were both eager to offer their support. I then asked my consultant orthopaedic surgeon, who had operated on my foot in 2019, if he would be happy to help, and he was also delighted to be asked. All we needed now was someone to build the site and, while that was being done, I needed to get recording.

Thankfully, we were introduced to a great web builder, Scott from Fuse4, who completely understood our needs and said he could do the job within the tight timescale.

***

As Christmas approached, everyone was looking forward to a break in lockdown and being able to meet up with families. Dawn had not stepped into our house for nine months, only delivering food and shopping to our doorstep, though of course we chatted on the phone several times a week. Seeing her on the photoshoot day was a special bonus.

Despite some let-up in restrictions during the year, we were being told that anyone with underlying health issues should remain at home. Dawn had lost her dad five years previously, and now she was being super-protective of her mum. As a family, we decided that we would not visit one another over Christmas no matter what was or wasn't allowed, and that included our lovely annual family tradition of meeting up with my brother and his family. It was sad not to see them, but it was sensible.

Mike set up a special portal that enabled us to connect to Dawn and Laurie's TV on Christmas Day so we could 'feel' we were all together as we opened our presents. This worked remarkably well and we still had a lovely day, albeit at a distance.

As another new year arrived, everyone was hopeful that Covid-19 would fizzle out, but sadly infections were showing no signs of abating.

Thankfully and miraculously, however, a vaccine had been developed and had been approved as safe. Soon we would be able to be protected from this evil virus, and life would return to something like normal. Or would it?

28

Exciting times

2021

The new year got off to an exciting start with the publication of the paperback edition of *The 28-Day Immunity Plan* and with it a double-page spread in the *Sunday Telegraph*. It was great to see the paperback with its colour photographs of the food shots. Mary and I were really proud of it, and my team of trialists were so excited to see themselves included.

It is always difficult to achieve the same level of publicity for a publication when it has been published five months before as an e-book, but I enjoyed lots of interviews on BBC stations around the UK and the paperback sold well. The book also gave us an opportunity to promote the new website when it launched in February.

Meanwhile, my GP called me to say that I would be high on the list to be vaccinated because of my 'clinically extremely vulnerable' status. Two weeks into January, on Mike's birthday, I received my first jab. The atmosphere in the sports hall in Melton Mowbray was so warm and welcoming. It almost felt like a party. It was buzzing! Everyone seemed so glad to be there – from the volunteers from the local Rotary Club who were supervising the car parking, to the doctors and nurses delivering the jabs. Mike said my getting the jab was the best birthday present he could have had, and we both felt hugely relieved that I was on the way to being protected. I continued to isolate and three months later I was given my second vaccination. The sense of relief I felt was huge. I knew I now had 90% protection and I was so grateful for that.

Also in January, I had a surprise phone call from Leicestershire Police. I was contacted by the Nutrition and Well-Being Team to help them enhance the fitness and well-being of their staff. Of course, I said I would be delighted and suggested they run a 'diet and well-being' trial for 20 people based on *The 28-Day Immunity Plan*. I also suggested that Mary might be happy to help too.

In fact, within hours of the memo being sent out, 40 volunteers had put their name forward and, on 1 March, the trial was officially launched, with each participant being given a *28-Day Immunity Plan* book, a set of my Portion Pots® and one of my 'Magic Measures' (another useful item I had created) to help them track their inch losses.

Mary and I joined the volunteers, led by their Healthy Living and Fitness Coach, Sally, on a Zoom call, and it was clear that everyone was up for the challenge. Mary and I joined them again after two weeks and then a week after the finish. The results were impressive. There were 37 trialists who had completed the course and their average weight loss was 10½ lb (4.76 kg)! While that was remarkable, the real surprise came from their wellness score. As well as a whole raft of questions the volunteers had been asked at the beginning of the trial, they were asked to give themselves a score out of 10 describing how they 'felt'. At the start, the average score was 4/10, but after the four weeks their average score had risen to 9/10! Mary and I could not have been more excited, nor could the team at Leicestershire Police. Because we knew the benefit of continuing to support the volunteers, Mary and I offered to keep in touch on a monthly basis via Zoom, and some of the volunteers went on to lose significant amounts of weight. Their success led to another trial in September 2021 and more in 2022.

***

As 1 February 2021 finally arrived – the date when I would get my name back – understandably I was very excited. This was a very important day and we celebrated with champagne. It had been a long time coming and it seemed like a new beginning. I felt as if I was attending my own christening party!

We were even more relieved and delighted that the new website, <www.rosemaryconley.com>, was up and running. Scott at Fuse4 had delivered it on time and on budget, and he had been very helpful in guiding us on the journey, right up to the launch and beyond. This was so valuable to us. We didn't publicise the site immediately as we found ourselves 'growing' into it. Also, my PA Peter was going to be operating the site going forward, so it was critical to give him time so that he could completely get to grips with it – which he did amazingly quickly. I was really impressed by how he embraced and ran with it. With Scott, Susannah and Peter, I felt we had created an 'A' team! It was so much fun working together.

While the website attracted significant traffic during February even without any publicity, when we officially launched it on 1 March with a day of radio interviews on BBC stations around the UK, we enjoyed a fantastic response.

We were very excited, but how were we going to encourage people to continue to engage with the site? We then came up with the idea of creating a newsletter which would offer readers recipes, useful weekly information, and links to appropriate videos so all they had to do was click. Mary offered to help by creating a weekly fitness challenge, which made writing the newsletter so much easier for me.

We were surprised how many people had already subscribed when the first edition was ready to go, and it has proved increasingly popular with each week that goes by. The feedback we received was so encouraging and we could not be more pleased with the way people are embracing the site and enjoying and benefiting from the videos. We are now able to offer medical advice from specialists such as my orthopaedic surgeon, physios and a neuro-physio, as well as my demonstrations of how to cook my recipes. We have even extended our repertoire to cover a wide range of exercises from Mary, as well as subjects such as how to dress to flatter your figure shape and how to apply make-up. Every week I receive emails from subscribers, thanking us for our site and telling us how much they look forward to the 'very informative newsletter when it arrives each Friday afternoon' and that they feel like part of a family. They also say it is making a real difference to their health and well-being. Most of all, it is such fun to put together and we love working as a team.

***

As the lockdown eased and the country opened up to some degree later in 2021, I visited my chest specialist Professor Pavord for one of my regular check-ups. He had asked me to have a full blood-test prior to my visit to see if my levels of 'eosinophils' would qualify me to try a new and approved treatment now available for patients with a certain kind of asthma.

Professor Ian Pavord was part of the team at Oxford University Hospitals that had created this treatment, funded by the NHS, which was effectively helping patients with asthma to breathe more easily. It works by opening up their airways so that they can take in more oxygen. I was delighted when he decided I qualified, so in January 2022 I was invited to visit the hospital in Oxford to receive training and my first treatment, which comes in the form of a self-administered injection into your skin around the abdominal area.

The effect was almost immediate. When I walked the dogs the next day, I could go further, and get up the hill without struggling with my breathing. The medication, known by the brand name Nucala (generic name: mepolizumab), is not available on a prescription at your local chemist as it has to be kept refrigerated. Once you are recommended for the treatment and have gone through all the relevant training procedures, your 'kit' is delivered to your home in a refrigerated van for you to place immediately in your own fridge until your next jab is due. It is administered on a four-weekly cycle and, while I still need my inhalers morning and evening, just as before, there is no doubt that it gives me more energy – and it is measurable. When I go to our physio gym, we wear heart-rate monitors; so I can see with my own eyes that I am performing at a 25% higher level than I was before the treatment, and the printout that I receive afterwards proves it in black and white. I honestly believe it has added extra years to my life.

29
The greatest thing

I started writing my autobiography in 2016 and it has been there in the background, ready for me to dip in and out as I felt the urge. It has been a total joy to write.

As I come to the end of my story, I thought I would reflect on various aspects of my life. A life that I am living to the full *and* for six and a half decades longer than was anticipated when it was predicted that I wouldn't reach my 10th birthday.

I feel immensely privileged to be enjoying such an exciting career. I have learned more than I could ever have believed possible and I feel utterly fulfilled. I have no yearnings to run a significant company again or to be in charge of a large team of staff. I have no burning desire to be on this or that television show. I have turned down invitations to participate in programmes such as *I'm a Celebrity*, *The Real Marigold Hotel* in India and *The Chase* – even though it would have been lovely to see Bradley Walsh again.

Peter, my PA, and I have fun running the UK distributorship Facial Toning Solutions Ltd, selling Facial Flex® – these amazingly effective gadgets to help people hold back the tell-tale lines and sagging of ageing. We supply Amazon and eBay, as well as selling directly to our own customers. And long may I continue to sit at my desk, five days a week, finding plenty to keep me busy – and writing a weekly newsletter!

Another side of my business life which I particularly relish is doing radio interviews from the ISDN (broadcast-quality telephone line) machine that we have in my little radio cubicle in Mike's study. Friend and colleague Dan Baker arranges regular opportunities for me to speak on various BBC radio stations around the country. In fact, I *love* doing that. And I also enjoy doing the occasional TV programme when I am asked for my opinion or contribution.

I love recording for our website and working with Mary. I enjoy posting a two-minute 'Daily Fitness Challenge' each evening at 8 pm on Twitter (my personal Twitter account is @rosemaryconley).

Steps Conductive Education Centre is an exceptional charity and I am proud to be Patron of an organisation that supports and develops young children with very special and complex needs. My role in trying to raise funds and organise an annual fundraiser is a privilege and a joy because I can see so clearly how the children and their families desperately need our help and benefit enormously from the service given to them by the staff. It is because of my passion for Steps that all of the royalties from this book will go towards paying for the outstanding teachers (specially trained 'conductors') who change the lives of the children within this exceptional nursery charity. If you would like to support Steps or find out more about the charity, please look at the end of this book.

As President of Young Enterprise, Leicestershire, I consider it a privilege to be involved in such a great initiative. I never cease to be amazed by the remarkable young people who learn so much from the whole experience (with the help of a Lead Teacher and a volunteer Business Adviser from the business sector). They learn how to create a business, form a company, appoint a Board of Directors, develop a product or service and, at the end of the year, how to close the company down. This is all done on top of their normal schoolwork and in their own time. Along that journey they learn so much about themselves – their strengths and their weaknesses. Their natural skills and talents are allowed to shine through, giving them a unique opportunity to discover which career path they might like to follow in the future. They are utterly inspiring and I love to support them in any way I can.

As a Deputy Lieutenant for over 20 years, I enjoy attending all kinds of events, representing the Lord Lieutenant of Leicestershire, Mike Kapur OBE, who, in turn, represents HM The Queen in Leicestershire. The greatest of these privileges for me is officiating at citizenship ceremonies and witnessing the pride of individuals from all over the world who have chosen, and been accepted, to become British citizens. Another thrill is assisting the Lord Lieutenant when he presents the British Empire Medal (BEM) to very worthy recipients in recognition of their outstanding contributions to the local community. Perhaps my most exciting privilege in 2021 was being asked by the Lord Lieutenant if I would deputise for him by hosting a visit of HRH The Duke of Gloucester on his visit to Leicestershire in September 2021.

Another very exciting opportunity arose during 2022 when the Lord Lieutenant asked me, together with a fellow Deputy Lieutenant, Dave Andrews, if we could organise an event to celebrate HM The Queen's Platinum Jubilee in the city of Leicester. Our specification was that we should promote physical activity while incorporating our remarkably diverse population, and so the idea of 'Dance for the Queen' was born.

The event was created around the realisation that the seven decades of Her Majesty's remarkable reign – from 1952 to 2022 – could be seen on a 24-hour clock as 19.52–20.22. Motivated by this fact, we created a spectacular dance event to run for the 30 minutes between 19.52 and 20.22 on the eve of the Platinum Jubilee bank holiday weekend (in early June) in the centre of Leicester in the appropriately named Jubilee Square!

With the help of an outstanding team, we put together a dance extravaganza featuring some of the best local performers Leicestershire had to offer. We approached seven dance schools and groups to ask each of them to choreograph a dance routine to a medley of iconic music tracks from the seven decades of the Queen's reign. This performance took place against a backdrop of royal pictures from the last 70 years – including many of Her Majesty's highly popular visits to Leicester, stretching from her first in 1954 to her most recent in 2018. The dance finale was an explosion of movement and sound right across Jubilee Square to the music of the event's 'anthem', Abba's 'Dancing Queen', believed to be one of Her Majesty's favourite songs.

The 19.52–20.22 dance extravaganza was preceded by a 90-minute variety show featuring a diverse mixture of musical talent drawn from Leicester's wonderful mix of ethnic cultures. Choirs, brass bands, singers and dancers came forward in large numbers keen to be involved, making it a very special community occasion. BBC Radio Leicester broadcast the event live so that people could 'Dance for the Queen' in their homes or in the street simultaneously to the seven decades of musical chart-toppers. It was an incredible occasion and the cooperation between all the local agencies we approached was extraordinary.

Once it was all over, Dave Andrews and I felt honoured to have been given the task of organising such an iconic event and, while there were some hairy moments, it was enormous fun and the huge crowd that came along loved it! Of course, such events are only possible with a tremendous team, which was nothing short of outstanding.

***

When I first started my classes in 1972, little did I know that 50 years on they would still be going strong. I cannot ever imagine *not* doing my diet and fitness classes on a Monday evening. Many of the members who have been loyally attending every week for over 40 years I consider to be my friends. We have cared for and supported one another through decades of disasters and dramas, life-threatening illnesses and joyous recoveries, and celebrated many a special birthday with Prosecco and cake! Here's to the next however-many years!

I still love meeting up with my *Dancing on Ice* professional partner, Mark Hanretty. His patience and encouragement, his friendship and dedication are priceless and have helped me become the best skater I could be. I always look forward to meeting him for a cuppa. Now, sadly, my skating lessons have had to cease due to the enforced break created by lockdown and because I'm now in my mid-70s. Between us, we have developed a very special friendship that I am sure will last the rest of my lifetime. I continue to marvel at his skill and passion, not only as an ice dancer but also as a choreographer and as a commentator on the Eurosport TV network. Through his skill and kindness, Mark gave me the confidence and encouragement to fulfil a childhood dream of being able to skate. And for *that* I will be eternally grateful.

Thankfully, I manage to keep my weight fairly constant, but this is not without effort. I book myself in for two weekly hour-long personal training sessions with physiotherapists Judith and JD. They push me beyond what I would ever do for myself, but because of it I have stronger lungs, and a stronger and trimmer body, and so I truly appreciate their efforts, despite my moaning! I also enjoy a weekly ballet lesson with Rosie which helps me develop a sense of balance, posture and muscle strength – hopefully! Despite my arthritic feet, I manage to always exceed 10,000 steps a day.

What do I eat? I haven't calorie-counted for over 30 years, but I know how much is enough and how much is too much. If I overeat on a special occasion, I just naturally cut back a little the next day and exercise a bit more. I eat low-fat and healthily most of the time: muesli for breakfast, a snack for lunch and a single-course meal in the evening. I then have a small portion of live, plain natural yogurt with a little honey at bedtime. I watch my portion size and, most importantly, I don't snack between meals. I do, however, enjoy a couple of glasses of wine, but I always have three dry days each week. And I take sugar in my tea. Despite that, I manage to maintain my weight at just under 8 st. (51 kg), which is healthy for my height of 5 ft ½ in. (1.53 m). At the end of the day, I want to be slim more than I want that cream cake, and that is where my willpower comes from. I loathed being overweight and I enjoy being slim, and I know Mike is glad I'm slim too, which provides extra encouragement and motivation.

I thoroughly enjoy going around the UK to speak at a variety of engagements, whether it be talking about business, staying fit and healthy, or telling my story of how I found a true faith in God. I love doing these talks, and Steps benefits from any fees I am paid. Long may I continue to be invited to do them.

While I have no particular career or business ambitions, I do have a few things on my bucket list. One of those was to present my own radio show. I am delighted that has now been done when I presented my *Food & Fitness Show* on ExPat Radio, which is heard by listeners in over 113 countries. I did a series of six shows on a Tuesday morning over six weeks at certain times of the year. I have, however, come to realise that presenting a show on radio is not as easy as it sounds!

There have been so many wonderful people I have had the privilege to call my friends. People who have stood by me through thick and thin. Always loyal, always kind and always patient. People such as Peter, my PA, who is consistently there for me, not just as a colleague but also as a friend. And Mary Morris, who has taught me so much and inspired and encouraged me over so many years – and made me laugh!

As well as personal friends, there are special people I have loved working with and who have helped me reach heights I could never have dreamed of. I want to thank you all from the bottom of my heart. You know who you are.

I have no regrets. I hope I have learned from my mistakes and that every one of them has taught me to do things differently next time.

I have been blessed with the most amazing family. I am only too aware of how families can struggle to stay united for a variety of reasons but, thankfully, the relationship I have with Dawn and her family is remarkable and the bond we have between us is truly wonderful. I could not have a more supportive, thoughtful or devoted daughter, and for that I am truly grateful.

I am immensely proud of everything Dawn has achieved in her own life and the beautiful family that she and her husband Laurie have brought into our lives. They are so very precious and we deeply love and treasure them.

Mike and I are incredibly fortunate to enjoy the unconditional love that we have for each other and the desire that we have to naturally care and protect each other. After almost 40 years the relationship we have is golden, and that has only been achieved through patience, understanding and tolerance on both sides. Yes, we hit a bad patch, but through God's grace and our perseverance, love reigns supreme and I consider that to be priceless. I could not have achieved the extraordinary heights of my career without the unquestionable support of Mike. He really has been my rock and I am so grateful that we can grow old together. I feel unbelievably fulfilled in my life. Weekends are precious, and I love nothing better than sitting on the sofa with Mike on a Saturday afternoon, holding hands as we binge-watch a series on TV!

I remember the words from the film *Moulin Rouge*: 'The greatest thing you will ever learn is to love and be loved in return.' Praise God for that!

And finally, 'thank you' to everyone who has followed one of my diets, worked out to one of my fitness videos, attended one of our classes or bought this book. If my eating plans or exercises have helped you to be healthier, slimmer and fitter today, then I am truly glad.

When the following note was included with a Christmas card last year from one of my followers, I asked if she minded if I included it in this book. When I read it, I felt a real sense of pride that maybe we *had* made a difference:

Dear Rosemary,

Another year gone by and I am hoping all is going well with you.

I am still, at 79, getting so many compliments about my level of fitness and size! After being on your programme since 1989 – what else?!

Once again, let me thank you from the bottom of my heart for your input in my life and for the influence that has had such an effect on so many others.

I send you much love and all good wishes.

Ann Vodden x

I absolutely love my life – my marriage, my family, my career. I feel unbelievably blessed – and long may it continue. Thank *you* for being part of it.

Acknowledgments

Writing my autobiography has been a wonderful adventure for me – very different from writing a diet book – but one that I have truly enjoyed. Delving through my huge archive of material, which fortunately I had retained over my 50-year career and from my childhood, was not only helpful in jogging my memory and enabling me to get my facts straight; it also set me on a joyful journey of reliving many of my exciting experiences.

As always, the story of one's life is complicated. How do you decide which bits are important and which bits are not? For this reason, I will be eternally grateful for the help and advice that has been given to me by some very special people.

I could not have written my story without the blessing of my husband Mike. Our depth of love for each other has enabled us to survive some challenging times over the last 39 years, enabling us to come out the other side even closer and more devoted to each other than ever. Mike, thank you for your love and wisdom and for being you. I love you more than you know.

A huge thank-you to Dawn – the best daughter in the world! Your love, encouragement and enthusiasm, your attention to detail and remarkable wisdom helped me so much on the journey of writing this book. You are an exceptional human being and I love you beyond words.

Thanks must also go to my PA, Peter Legg. Thank you, Peter, for all your help across the whole of my work life over the last 10 years and for helping me throughout the journey of writing this book, as well as for supporting me in everyday life as a friend and as my PA.

I also wish to thank our special friends, Revd Ian and Ruth Coffey, and Geoff and Jo Baker, for your guidance and encouragement over the many years we have been privileged to know you. This story would be very different if it were not for your love, friendship and support. Thank you so much.

As I started writing my story, the thought of going through the boxes and boxes of archive material was daunting; then I thought of Angie. Angie Higgins has worked with us for almost 30 years, so who better to ask to sift through it? Thank you, Angie, for taking on such a mammoth task and fulfilling it wonderfully and also for everything you have done for us over the years – and continue to do.

A big thank-you also to friends and colleagues Susannah Goodwin and Dan Baker. Thank you, Susannah, for suggesting the title *Through Thick and Thin* and to Dan for your wisdom and guidance on my journey of completing it.

When my Literary Agent, Hannah Schofield from Luigi Bonomi Associates, told me that SPCK wanted to publish my book, I could not have been more delighted. Thank you, Hannah, for doing such a wonderful job in finding me such a special publishing house. I have really enjoyed working with SPCK's Publishing Director Philip Law, who has made the whole process fun and exciting – and fast! Thank you, Philip, for being a dream to work with.

There is one person I particularly wish to thank and that is Murray Watts. Murray has been my Editorial Consultant and mentor on the journey of writing my memoir – a story that will hopefully touch your heart, encourage you to keep the faith when the going gets tough and inspire you to follow your dreams. Most of all, I hope you will under-stand how utterly wonderful life can be despite some inevitable bumps in the road. It was always with great excitement that I looked forward to our editing sessions, occasions when I learned so much from Murray as I made progress with the book.

Murray, thank you from the bottom of my heart for your remarkable wisdom, gentle guidance, unfailing encouragement and unfaltering belief that my story was worth telling, and thank you for becoming such a special friend to Mike and to me.

Finally, thank you to my gracious God who has blessed me with such an exciting and wonderful life, way beyond the limited years anticipated by my doctors when I was a little girl. Praise God for that!

Appendix 1
Books by Rosemary Conley

Eat Yourself Slim (Hamlyn, 1983)

Eat and Stay Slim (Arrow, 1985)

Positive Living (Arrow, 1987)

Rosemary Conley's Hip and Thigh Diet (Arrow, 1988)

Rosemary Conley's Complete Hip and Thigh Diet (Arrow, 1989)

Guide to Fat in Food (Grafton, 1989)

Looking Good, Feeling Great (Marshall Pickering, 1989)

Rosemary Conley's Hip and Thigh Diet Cookbook with Patricia Bourne
(Ebury Press, 1989)

Rosemary Conley's Inch Loss Plan (Arrow, 1990)

Rosemary Conley's Metabolism Booster Diet (Arrow, 1991)

Rosemary Conley's Whole Body Programme (Arrow and BBC, 1992)

Shape Up for Summer (Arrow, 1993)

Rosemary Conley's New Hip and Thigh Diet Cookbook with Patricia
Bourne (Arrow, 1993)

Rosemary Conley's Flat Stomach Plan (Arrow, 1994)

Rosemary Conley's Beach Body Plan (Arrow, 1994)

Be Slim, Be Fit (Arrow, 1995)

Rosemary Conley's Complete Flat Stomach Plan (Arrow, 1996)

Rosemary Conley's New Body Plan (Arrow, 1997)

Rosemary Conley's New Inch Loss Plan (Arrow, 1998)

Rosemary Conley's Low Fat Cookbook (Century, 1999)

Rosemary Conley's Low Fat Cookbook 2 (Century, 2000)

Rosemary Conley's Red Wine Diet (Arrow, 2000)

Eat Yourself Slim (diet and cookbook) (Century, 2001)

Rosemary Conley's Step by Step Low Fat Cookbook with Dean Simpole-
Clarke (Century, 2005)

Rosemary Conley's Gi Jeans Diet (Arrow, 2006)

Rosemary Conley's Ultimate Gi Jeans Diet (Arrow, 2007)

Rosemary Conley's Gi Hip & Thigh Diet (Arrow, 2008)

Rosemary Conley's Slim to Win: Diet and cookbook (Century, 2008)

4-in-1 Recipe Collection (RC Enterprises, 2009)

Rosemary Conley's Amazing Inch Loss Plan (large-format exercise plan) (Arrow, 2010)

Rosemary Conley's Amazing Inch Loss Plan (diet) (Arrow, 2011)

100 Great Low-Fat Recipes, My Kitchen Table series (Ebury Press, 2011)

The Secrets of Staying Young (Century, 2011)

The FAB Diet (Arrow, 2013)

The 3-2-1 Diet (Arrow, 2015)

The 28-Day Immunity Plan with Mary Morris (Penguin, 2020)

Appendix 2
Videos and DVDs by Rosemary Conley

Rosemary Conley's Hip and Thigh Diet and Exercise (Video Gems, 1989)

Rosemary Conley's Inch Loss Plan (Video Gems, 1990)

Hip and Thigh Cookbook (Video Gems, 1990)

Rosemary Conley's Whole Body Programme (BBC, 1991)

Rosemary Conley's 7 Day Workout (BBC, 1991)

The Pregnancy and Postnatal Exercise Video (BBC, 1991)

Rosemary Conley's Whole Body Programme 2 (BBC, 1992)

Rosemary Conley's Top to Toe Collection: For a better bust (BBC, 1992)

Rosemary Conley's Top to Toe Collection: For your hips and thighs (BBC, 1992)

Rosemary Conley's Top to Toe Collection: For a flatter tummy (BBC, 1992)

Rosemary Conley's Top to Toe Collection: To stretch out (BBC, 1992)

Rosemary Conley's Whole Body Programme 3 (BBC, 1993)

Rosemary Conley's Flat Stomach Plan (The Video Collection, 1994)

Kellogg's Special K Health and Fitness (Kellogg's, 1993)

Rosemary Conley's New You Plan (The Video Collection, 1994)

All New Hip and Thigh Workout (VCI, 1995)

M&S Food and Fitness Programme (VCI, 1996)

Rosemary Conley's New Body by Design (VCI, 1996)

Ultimate Fat Burner (VCI, 1997)

Rosemary Conley's Complete Flat Stomach Plan (VCI, 1997)

The Best Rosemary Conley Workout in the World . . . Ever! (VCI, 1998)

Rosemary Conley's Fat Attack (VCI, 1999)

Five Day Fat Burner (VCI, 2000)

Ultimate Whole-Body Workout (VCI, 2001)

7 Day Slim Down (VCI, 2002)
Slim and Salsasise (VCI, 2004)
Shape Up and Salsasise (VCI, 2005)
Gi Jeans Weight-Loss Workout (Universal, 2006)
Brand New You Workout with Coleen Nolan (Universal, 2007)
Real Results Workout (Universal, 2009)

Abbreviations

ASO	Association for the Study of Obesity
BEM	British Empire Medal
BFA	British Franchise Association
CBE	Commander of the Order of the British Empire
CEO	Chief Executive Officer
DL	Deputy Lieutenant
DOI	*Dancing on Ice*
DVLA	Driver and Vehicle Licensing Agency
Gi	Glycaemic index
GP	General Practitioner
HM	Her Majesty
HRH	His Royal Highness
HRT	hormone replacement therapy
ICI	Imperial Chemical Industries
ISA	individual savings account
ISDN	Integrated Services Digital Network
IT	information technology
JP	Justice of the Peace
MD	Managing Director
MOT	Ministry of Transport
MRI	magnetic resonance imaging
NHS	National Health Service
PA	Personal Assistant / Production Assistant
PCC	Parochial Church Council
PPE	personal protective equipment
PR	public relations
RADA	Royal Academy of Dramatic Art
RCO	Rosemary Conley Online

RFU   Rugby Football Union
RSA   Royal Society of Arts
RSPCA   Royal Society for the Prevention of Cruelty to Animals
TB   tuberculosis
TENS   transcutaneous electrical nerve stimulation
UCB   United Christian Broadcasters
VCI   Video Collection International

Units of measurement

ft   feet
g   grams
ha   hectares
in.   inch(es)
kg   kilograms
km   kilometres
l   litres
lb   pounds
m   metres
oz   ounces
sq. ft   square feet
sq. m   square metres
st.   stone (= 14 lb)

All author's royalties from the sale of **Through Thick and Thin** will be donated to **Steps Conductive Education Centre**, a charity based in Leicestershire.

Steps provides Conductive Education and support to children with cerebral palsy, Down syndrome and other motor disorders and delays, and their families.

Each year **Steps** needs to raise £250,000 to run the **Steps Conductive Education Centre** and pay for the outstanding staff who work so hard face-to-face and online to transform the lives of the very special little children they help.

If you would like to support **Steps Conductive Education Centre**, or find further information about the charity, please go to www.stepscentre.org.uk

If you wish to contact Steps, email info@stepscentre.org.uk or call 01509 506878

If you would like a **FREE COPY** of the book **POWER FOR LIVING**, please send a stamped (£2.05* postage), self-addressed envelope (16cm x 22.5cm) to the following address:

Rosemary Conley Enterprises, PO Box 10470, Markfield, Leicestershire, LE67 9XP

NB: UK only. *Please check current postal rates for '200g large letter' at time of posting.